ALIEN SPACE GODS OF ANCIENT GREECE AND ROME -
REVELATIONS OF THE ORACLE OF DELPHI

"RETURN OF THE ANCIENT SPACE GODS - IN THE TRADITION OF ERICH VON DANIKEN."
Tim Swartz - Conspiracyjournal.com

By W.R. Drake
With Timothy Green Beckley
And Sean Casteel

Global Communications

Alien Space Gods of Ancient Greece and Rome
Revelations of the Oracle of Delphi

By W. R. Drake, Sean Casteel, & Timothy Green Beckley

This revised edition and new cover art
Copyright © 2011
Timothy Green Beckley
DBA Global Communications, All Rights Reserved

EAN: 978-1-60611-097-3
ISBN: 1-60611-097-7

No part of this book may be reproduced, stored in retrieval system or transmitted in any form or by any means, electronic, mechanical, photocopying, recording, without express permission of the publisher.

Timothy Green Beckley: Editorial Director
Carol Rodriguez: Publisher's Assistant
Sean Casteel: Associate Editor
Cover Art: Tim Swartz

Printed in the United States of America
For free catalog write:
Global Communications
P.O. Box 753
New Brunswick, NJ 08903

Free Subscription to Conspiracy Journal E-Mail Newsletter
www.conspiracyjournal.com

ORACLE OF DELPHI
Inspirational Portrait by The Hon John Collier

Alien Space Gods of Ancient Greece and Rome

Contents

TIMOTHY GREEN BECKLEY UFO & Paranormal Pioneer v

REVELATIONS OF THE ORACLE OF DELPHI ix

    When The Gods Mingled With Humans xiv

    Mystical Moments xviii

    Vapors At Delphi xxii

    A Twist of Fate xxvi

    Critics Be Damned xxvii

Sean Casteel xxxi

WILL THE GODS OF OLD BE RETURNING IN FULL FORCE SOON? ... xxxiii

    The Perfect Humans xxxvii

    Humanoids In Greece xl

    An Earlier Visit From The Unknown xliv

    What The Firemen Saw xlvi

    UFOs In Ancient Rome xlix

    The Story of Bruno Facchini lii

    Fetus Of The Gods? lvi

    The 1978 Italian UFO Wave lix

Alien Space Gods of Ancient Greece and Rome

W. RAYMOND DRAKE lxiii

GODS AND SPACEMEN IN GREECE AND ROME 3

    Chapter One Invaders From Space 7

    Chapter Two Space Gods of Ancient Greece 11

    Chapter Three The Golden Age 24

    Chapter Four Ancient Athens 45

    Chapter Five Spacemen in Ancient Greece 62

    Chapter Six Helen of Troy 84

    Chapter Eight Spacemen in Ancient Italy 120

    Chapter Nine Spacemen in Ancient Rome 143

    Chapter Ten Space Chronicles of Ancient Rome 168

    Chapter Eleven Space Gods of Scandinavia 203

    Chapter Twelve The Cross 228

    Bibliography 239

Alien Space Gods of Ancient Greece and Rome

TIMOTHY GREEN BECKLEY
UFO & Paranormal Pioneer

Timothy Green Beckley has been described as the Hunter Thompson of UFOlogy.

Since an early age his life has more or less revolved around the paranormal. His grandfather saw the apparition of a headless horseman. His life was saved by invisible beings around the age of three. The house

Alien Space Gods of Ancient Greece and Rome

he was raised in was thought to be haunted. Beckley also underwent out of body experiences at age six.

He saw his first of three UFOs when he was but ten, and has had two more sightings since – one of which included an attempt to communicate with one of these objects.

Tim grew up listening to the only all night talk show in the country that revolved around the strange and unexplained. Long John Nebel's guests included the early UFO contactees who claimed to have visited other planets and built time machines in the desert. Tim was fascinated by everything that went bump in the night – or even in the daylight for that matter. Years later, Tim was to appear on Long John's show numerous times and over the years has been a frequent guest on hundreds of programs which have come and gone just like ghosts in the night.

Tim started his career as a writer early on – at age 14 he purchased a mimeograph machine and began publishing a small UFO newsletter. Over the years he has written over 25 books on everything from rock music to the secret MJ-12 papers. He has been a stringer for the national tabloids such as the Enquirer and editor of over 30 different magazines, most of which never lasted more than a couple of issues. His longest running effort was the newsstand publication

Alien Space Gods of Ancient Greece and Rome

UFO UNIVERSE, which lasted for 11 years. Today he is the president of Inner Light/Global Communications and editor of the Conspiracy Journal and Bizarre Bazaar.

He is one of the few Americans ever to be invited to speak before closed door meetings on UFOs presided over by the late Earl of Clancarty at the House of Lords in England. He visited Loch Ness in Scotland while in the UK and went home with the belief that Nessie was somehow connected with the dragons of mythology as well as strange discs engraved on cathedrals and ghostly phenomenon.

The Inner Light Publications and Global Communications' catalog of books and video titles now number over 200, including the works of Tim Swartz, Sean Casteel, T. Lobsang Rampa, Commander X, Brad Steiger, John Keel, Tracy Twyman, Wendelle Stevens and a host of many other authors. His own bestsellers include Our Alien Planet, Strange Saga, Subterranean Worlds Inside Earth, John Lennon – We Knew You

As the horror movie host Mr. Creepo Beckley has made numerous films, including Skin Eating Jungle Vampires and Blood Sucking Vampire Freaks.

MRUFO8@hotmail.com www.ConspiracyJournal.com

Alien Space Gods of Ancient Greece and Rome

Alien Space Gods of Ancient Greece and Rome

REVELATIONS OF THE ORACLE OF DELPHI

By Timothy Green Beckley

Before setting out on my long voyage across a good expanse of the world, I had heard that the Delphian oracle back in her day had undergone some incredible visions and that politicians, generals, and the upper echelon of Grecian society often journeyed over the roughest terrain, from all over the region, on a sort of pilgrimage or vision quest to have her prophesize for them specifically. I guess just like those celebrities who seek out a specific psychic today, her upper crust clients wanted to know what direction life would take for them. Would they wed a wealthy Greek? Would they live a long life with many children? Would they be favored by the gods? Would they be successful in battle and survive without battle scars? You must understand that, apart from the Oracle Of Delphi, all other prophets in the territory were men. But the Oracle was special for she was a vessel by which the gods could speak directly to mere mortals. She wasn't one of those who read the entrails of animals or tossed bones to see the future. Pythia, the prophet's actual name, had been hand picked by none other than the great god of thunder and lightning, Apollo himself, to lift the veil between this world and the next.

Pythia was herself considered somewhat of a sub-goddess because of her official relationship with the heavenly fold – she was, in short, their official channel on Earth. Nowadays, you have your space channelers who claim to cross paths with Venusians as well as your channels who speak with ten thousand year old Tibetan monks, but the Oracle was the real thing, not your average UFO contactee speaking in tongues in a dugout room beneath Giant Rock in the Mojave Desert. This was true advice from on high (and speaking of "high," as we shall see Pythia might have, in fact, been taking a "hit" of more than just "fresh air" while going through her channeling routine.)

Most channelers who ply their trade in what are understood to be sacred or holy places like Sedona, Arizona – the Delphi of our day – boast a pseudo eminence in society, in that they are often thought of as being priestly and spiritually superior to the average person because of their ability to communicate with a "higher authority." Likewise, the Oracle was essentially the highest authority both civilly and religiously in male-dominated ancient Greece. She responded to the

Alien Space Gods of Ancient Greece and Rome

questions of citizens, foreigners, kings, and philosophers on issues of political impact, war, duty, crime, laws. . . and, of course, personal issues. Nevertheless there was a catch. The Pythia, when about to deliver, would chew leaves from Apollo's sacred laurel tree and would then sit on her holy tripod, seated in the innermost sanctum, over a crack on the rock from where noxious volcanic fumes emanated. Dazed and disoriented, she would then be "possessed by the voice of Apollo" and utter inarticulate sounds before fainting. Only the priests were present there, and they had the task of "translating" her utterances in plain speech. The priests were extremely well versed on the various matters of state, as part of their work was to debrief pilgrims about all that they knew. In addition, no question to the god was ever dealt with immediately. After the query was submitted, several days of prescribed ceremonial protocols had to be observed before Apollo was sufficiently satisfied as to speak through his priestess.

But trust me, we get ahead of our story. I found myself taking the same trek as those who ventured to speak with the Oracle first hand back in the day when the gods walked across the face of the Earth as if they owned it – need I say more?

Alien Space Gods of Ancient Greece and Rome

Alexander the Great visited the Delphic Oracle wishing to hear a prophecy that he would soon conquer the entire ancient world. To his surprise the oracle refused a direct comment and asked him to come later. Furious, Alexander the Great dragged Pythia by the hair out of the chamber until she screamed "Let go of me; you're unbeatable". The moment hearing this words he dropped her, saying "Now I have my answer"

Alien Space Gods of Ancient Greece and Rome

Stopping to catch our breath from time to time as we trudged up the ancient steep cobblestones that lead to the temple where the Oracle of Delphi prophesied, it was almost as if we had disembarked from a time machine. The scene before us hearkened back to the magnificent era of Greek gods and goddesses. Stone pillars reached toward the heavens, while a large, outdoor amphitheater seemed to come alive with the specters of the past, ghosts who had congregated to reveal secrets hidden from a modern, materialistic world less concerned with the spiritual nature of the cosmos.

We were 100 miles from the traffic-snarled, smog-drenched capital of Athens, and had soon come to realize that those who live in the Greek highlands to the northeast are more accustomed to the simpler life, as they have lived for thousands of years. They rise at dawn to feed the livestock and labor over olive and lemon groves that provide them with a stable income. Their homemade cheeses are as legendary as Apollo and Zeus – to that we can personally testify.

As a student of ancient mysteries, I have long wanted to visit Delphi to search out the truth about the mysteries of the female oracle who is said to have forecast the future and is probably more famous than even Nostradamus, thought the oracle's accuracy rate and method of scrying are in wide dispute.

Recently, an opportunity presented itself, and so I packed and was off and hiking in Greece.

I was fortunate to be accompanied on this mind-opening excursion by a psychic friend who happens to be of partial Greek origin. Penny Melis is a gifted seeress who is enchanted by the mystical nature of her ancestral homeland and thinks she might possibly be psychically linked to the Oracle.

Before arriving in Greece, Penny spent hours drilling me about what we were going to see. She explained that Delphi was actually the original shrine built for the god Apollo and that it rests on the side of Mount Parnassus. In the valley directly below there are many groves, caves and ravines sacred to the gods of antiquity.

When The Gods Mingled With Humans

This was hallowed ground indeed, reserved for both Apollo and the nine daughters of Zeus. This is where they came down from the sky and took on physical form. Yet the chief mountain place of worship was the

Alien Space Gods of Ancient Greece and Rome

Delphic shrine. It was here that the most famous oracle of ancient times presided and prophesied.

It is here at the Temple of Apollo that the nine daughters of Zeus are said to have come down from the sky and taken physical form while the Oracle went into a trance nearby and began to delivery prophecies for individuals who would wait in line for hours for a personal reading.

Alien Space Gods of Ancient Greece and Rome

To Penny, whose father is Greek, the stories told to her as a child seemed more real than mythological fantasies. She explained that to many living in this part of Greece, the gods are not imaginary beings, but survive on a higher plane of reality, still accessible to those who acknowledge their awesome powers.

"Greek mythology speaks to a time when the gods came down and defeated the elders of the earth," Penny explained as we stood overlooking the Temple of Delphi. So busy was I videotaping the surroundings for a forthcoming motion picture that it was all that my companion could do to gain my undivided attention. With a hint of irritation, Penny continued with the lineal history of the gods, revealing that, while Apollo was still a baby, he seized control of Parnassus by slaying Python, the dragon-snake that had ruled the territory. Following this conquest, Apollo shape-shifted into the form of a dolphin that swam out to sea where he captured a group of sailors who became the first priests at Delphi.

In this same area, near the ruins of Delphi, around the Corycian Cave, was a place held sacred by Pan. It is said that each November pagan rituals were conducted there that attracted many who indulged in drinking and sexual rites.

Alien Space Gods of Ancient Greece and Rome

It is said that the gods felt much closer to earth at that time, establishing themselves not only atop Mount Olympus but at other sacred sites as well.

Alien Space Gods of Ancient Greece and Rome

"Pan is depicted in art as a being who is half-man, half-woodland creature who has horns," Penny said. "This image was adopted by the early Christians, who tried to portray him as their devil. A pretty deceptive ploy, I would say!"

Later, as we continued our strenuous hike up the toward the place where the oracle prophesied, we stood in the amphitheater at Delphi, located directly above the Temple of Apollo. Looking all around, we couldn't help but become emotionally charged by the historical significance of the treasured place. The theater was constructed in the second century B.C.E., and rebuilt several times. Consisting of 35 rows of seats and holding about 5,000 spectators, the amphitheater was used for recitals in honor of Apollo and Dionysus.

Mystical Moments

Finally, we reached the main temple, known as the *temenos*, or "sacred space." Here we rested before forging ahead in our vision quest. Penny seized the moment to fill me in on her childhood realization that she was somehow different from her playmates. At age seven, she began to experience strange forms of knowing, such as who would be on the other end of the line before the phone rang. More recently, she revealed, something was happening that was disturbing – she had begun to see friends who had passed away, and they were even speaking to her and making predictions that were eerily coming true. In light of the many strange psychic experiences she was continually having, she had come to think of herself as a witch.

Before arriving at Delphi, we had visited Pompeii, where the victims of the Vesuvius volcanic eruption on August 24, A.D. 79, had been frozen instantly, their bodies encased in hardening lava when the mountain exploded and spewed a hurricane of ash far and wide. Penny told me that she had experienced some of the pain and utter shock of the residents of Pompeii, who had also suffered an earthquake as well as the death by molten lava and ash that had rained down from the sky.

"At Pompeii," Penny told me, "there are man homeless dogs that wander the grounds, attaching themselves to the tourists who visit there. One dog followed me around. I had the feeling that it was trying to lead me to the different areas of importance. Perhaps these strays contained the souls of those who had perished there eons back."

Strange as this might seem, this phenomenon was not just that of a psychic "bubbling over," as the dogs were indeed all over the place. Furthermore, in Delphi, we were followed by cats that have made the ruins their home. Penny thinks these felines may have been attracted to the spot because of its high spiritual energies.

Penny noted that this was not the only time she had visited Delphi.

"On the first occasion, I came with my mother and brother, and it wasn't as powerful an experience then. But now that I have been drawn back as an adult, I can almost see people carrying out the religious rituals that they practiced here."

Penny says there were many violent practices associated with the time – even human sacrifices, though this has been downplayed and even denied. Most of the offerings were in the nature of precious gold and silver, and as many as 3,000 beasts were given up to the gods at one festival alone. No one can dispute that there was an official of the temple known as the "sacred executioner," who wielded a deadly sharp sword as he saw fit, taking the lives of some willing and certainly some unwilling victims as the gods had instructed him.

At one point, Penny looked down at her feet, as though she were trying to force the sadistic ghostly figures from her thoughts.

Alien Space Gods of Ancient Greece and Rome

The remains of marvelous Greek and Roman architecture still exists throughout the region serving as a reminder that the greatest sculptures' lived thousands of years ago influencing art for a millennial.

"I'm feeling a strong pain in my head," she said, rubbing her brow. "I feel like someone is inside me here. I can feel the energies that were once here. At times, it's actually a good feeling. There's more of a religious well-being that was here, as opposed to Pompeii, where there was a lot of pain and anguish."

Vapors At Delphi

Historians agree that there was actually more than one prophetess at Delphi who acted like a medium or channel would. Actually, the oracle did not predict the future herself, but passed on the information she received while in a trance to one of the high priests who presided over the gathering, which attracted the high and the mighty of Greek society as well as lower class members. To most, the oracle seemed to be speaking in indecipherable rhythms. She usually began her discourse with utterings such as: "I know the number of the sand; I know the measure of the sea."

And then she would improvise from there, often speaking in unknown tongues that only her priestly handlers could comprehend. Crowds would gather to ask questions, and they were most likely to receive a Yes or No answer.

Alien Space Gods of Ancient Greece and Rome

Spiritual channeler and clairvoyant Penny Melis says she can say with certainty that Delphi remains highly charged with psychic vibrations from the past.

Alien Space Gods of Ancient Greece and Rome

Frequently associated with the oracle's ability to see foresee events was a mysterious vapor, which critics say rose from the cracks in the floor of the cubicle where the visionary would be seated on a tripod-like brass stool. The Christians propagated the idea that the prophetess was intoxicated by the fumes in order to step across the border into the void of the next world. They saw the oracle as a tool of the devil, much as fundamentalists today believe spirits are all Satan's conjurations used to fool people into believing there is life beyond the pale.

A Christian writer, Adamantius Origines, wrote about his pagan foes who were still foretelling future events at the time. He came up with the following condemnation: "It is said of the Pythian priestess, whose oracle seems to have been the most celebrated, that when she sat down at the mouth of the Castilian cave, the prophetic spirit of Apollo entered her private parts. She sat with parted thighs on the tripod of Apollo, and the evil spirit entered her from below, passing through her genital organs, and plunged her into a state of frenzy, so that she began with loosened hair to foam and rage like a drunkard."

Alien Space Gods of Ancient Greece and Rome

The greatest thinkers of all time were in the region. Is it possible they were channeling their philosophy from a "higher source?"

A Twist of Fate

Unlike Jeanne Dixon or John Edwards, neither the oracle nor her priestly guides wrote books or even kept a ledger. (If they did, they have long since turned to dust.) So the tales of old come to us through second-hand verbal recollections handed down to the present.

Leaders of the ancient world who paid homage to the oracle included Alexander the Great, who wanted to know about the outcome of his military skirmishes.

And if someone was not satisfied with a particular reading or didn't link the prediction that was made for him, he could ask the oracle for extra time – that is, if another donation of gold was made. The rule of thumb seems to have been caveat emptor: let the buyer beware. To paraphrase Heraclitus, the Greek philosopher, "The oracle neither conceals nor reveals the truth . . . only hints at it."

For the common person not embroiled in the machinations of war and politics, the oracle was available to answer personal questions. "How do I cure my son of lovesickness?" would receive a therapeutic, albeit vague, response of, "Treat him gently."

Critics Be Damned

Obviously, there were cynics and skeptics afoot even in those ancient of days. On the positive side, the lines for readings were said to extend as far as the eye could see along the route to the temple. Furthermore, some of those who mingled with the crowds were powerful members of the elite who would not normally be caught dead mixing with those of lesser distinction.

In some regards, consulting the oracle was like visiting a psychic retreat today. Upon arriving at the temple, those wishing a reading would register and pay a fee. Before seeing the oracle, they would purify themselves in the nearby healing waters Castilian Spring, where the bathing troughs can still be seen. Like pilgrims to any other spiritual event, they would form a line and proceed along the Sacred Way. The route was adorned with waving flags so the pilgrims would not wander from the prescribed path to the temple.

We can certify that it was a strenuous journey of a mile or more, but along the way one could marvel at the great statues and sculptures of the period, some of which are preserved in the Delphi museum, which we later visited.

Alien Space Gods of Ancient Greece and Rome

Some of those who traveled to the site did so on a regular basis. Perhaps it's the same today. When you find a good psychic, it's best to stay with that person.

I asked Penny what she thought of the idea of the aforementioned vapors being responsible for mesmerizing the oracle.

"I do sense a strange smell around here," she said. "The vapors may still exist underground, but I don't see any association with demons. Given the right conditions, I do believe this place could still be used to touch the other side – to see into other dimensions."

As she stood in front of the Temple of Delphi, Penny clutched her head.

"I got the distinct impression," she said, "that I was in another location. Not in modern times. I was in an older time. I could even smell that time."

Explaining further, Penny told me that she had received a vision of one of the ancient oracles. The vision was of an older woman in a white robe who appeared to be blind.

"It was like her eyes were clouded over. They were cloudy eyes. She appeared to me in my head and I was able to communicate with her. She gave me a message. It's very cryptic, so I have to figure it out for myself.

Alien Space Gods of Ancient Greece and Rome

"I wanted to know where my life is going, and what I should do, and her answer was more or less, 'You can make yourself happy through your next steps.'

"So what steps do I take? She said, 'You have to make your own path and find your own happiness.' I mean, it's very cryptic."

I asked Penny again what she thought it all meant.

"I can see that I'm not on the right path now," she replied. "I might need further guidance or further reaching out, because I don't see it yet. Maybe it's supposed to be coming, and I just don't know it yet. They basically want me to be happy.

"I think what I've done is lost my way a little bit, and that's what they're trying to lead me back to – to get back to my roots and to being what I used to be. Up until recently, I was a devoted witch. But in the last few years, I haven't been. I'm trying to get back to being what I remembered. That's the path I need to be walking now, instead of worrying too much about materialistic things here."

So Penny had sought the Oracle of Delphi and had been rewarded by the same ambiguous warnings as the ancients who went before her. Can she make use of her dreams and visions there in Greece to help build a more happy life for herself? Did she journey those

Alien Space Gods of Ancient Greece and Rome

thousands of miles with me in order to find only what was within her all along? Whether we're dealing with a "Wizard of Oz" type of banality or fortune cookie wisdom is not really possible to know at the moment. What is real is the memory of that rainy afternoon in Greece, when Penny and I touched the fabric of time and it reached out and touched us back.

It was an odyssey I will never forget and it lead me to further accept that the mystery of the ancient space gods, which Britisher W. Raymond Drake delves into throughout the bulk of this book, were as real as you and I. Apollo and Zeus and all the others such as Artemis, Hestia, Hermes, Athena, Heda, once occupied the picturesque Mount Olympus and played footsie with us mortals, and spoke through the Oracle of Delphi acting as their cosmic conduit for prophetic messages from the stars.

We await their return as surely they must be coming back soon.

Alien Space Gods of Ancient Greece and Rome

Sean Casteel

Sean Casteel is a journalist who has been writing about UFOs, alien abduction and other paranormal topics since 1989. He has worked for "UFO Magazine," "FATE Magazine," and "The Conspiracy Journal." His articles have also been published in the U.K, Italy and Romania.

He is the author of several books for Inner Light Publications and Global Communications, to include "UFOs, Prophecy and the End of Time," "Signs and Symbols of the Second Coming," and "The Excluded Books of the Bible." Casteel coauthored the book "Round Trip To Hell In A Flying Saucer" with Tim Beckley. Casteel has been a guest on the radio talk show program "Coast To Coast AM" with George Noory as well as on Kerrang Radio out of Birmingham, England.

He has a website at www.seancasteel.com

Alien Space Gods of Ancient Greece and Rome

WILL THE GODS OF OLD BE RETURNING IN FULL FORCE SOON?

By Sean Casteel

- ❖ Why do the ancient myths of Greece and Rome still "speak" to us today? Are the old gods really the immortals they claimed to be, still capable of communing with modern man?

- ❖ Greece and Italy both have a rich history of UFO, alien and other paranormal encounters. Read the stories here of Greek and Italian UFO witnesses and alien abductees as they participate in the universal cosmic dance that dates from the times of antiquity when the gods ruled more openly.

- ❖ Are the ancient gods like Zeus and Apollo biding their time before making a triumphal return in full view of the entire world? Or is it that they have never left their Mediterranean homelands at all?

Alien Space Gods of Ancient Greece and Rome

* * * * *

The school of thought categorized as "Ancient Astronauts" has been a longtime staple of UFO research and lore, most often attributed to Erich von Daniken, whose "Chariots of the Gods?" sold millions of copies worldwide and made it to the top of the bestseller list when it was first published in 1968. It presents a case for, in general, the firm belief that ancient man and his various civilizations were created and guided by creatures from outer space or from some as yet unknown dimension. The theory most often focuses on the stories from the Bible or the records of the earlier Sumerian and Babylonia societies, giving short shrift to the equally compelling stories from Greek and Roman mythology.

In this study you are now reading, the late Britisher W.R. Drake impressively offers up almost inarguable evidence that the so-called Gods of Antiquity were not just illusionary but were instead real flesh and blood beings who emerged from the sky and made themselves right at home as if this was their world to begin with. Perhaps it is, and we are but pawns in some unknown chess game being played out as part of the grand design. As an extension of Drake's understanding of primordial cosmology, we must state

Alien Space Gods of Ancient Greece and Rome

our unwavering belief that the Space Gods continue to keep a watchful eye on the Mediterranean region and haven't forgotten their past interaction with the people of the area, some of whom still hold a high degree of reverence for the deities their ancestors encountered and held forth with and conceivably even copulated with. The old stories from Greece and Rome continue to resonate today, and are given new life by the UFO mythos that began to take hold on the public mindset in the 1940s.

For example, there are the stories surrounding the Greek god Hermes, born the son of Zeus, who was considered by the Greeks to be the father of gods and men, the ruler and preserver of the world. Hermes plays many roles and appears in many different ways in the Greek pantheon.

Writes author Keith Thompson in his book "Angels and Aliens," "Hermes is the swift-footed messenger of the gods between heaven and earth, from which he derives his character as a god of oracles. As a messenger or herald, Hermes has access as well to the underworld, guiding the souls of the departed to rest across the threshold of life and death."

Hermes also serves as the mediator between conscious and unconscious, surface and depths. He is the god of "persuasive speech," or oratory, as well as a patron saint of liars and thieves.

A story is told about Hermes that took place when he was barely a day old. He stole a herd of cattle belonging to his half brother Apollo, covering his tracks as best he could. When the theft was reported to Apollo by a local mortal named Battos, Apollo dragged Hermes off the couch where he pretended to sleep and delivered him to Zeus, who would surely punish Hermes for his cattle rustling. Without a hint of shame, Hermes denied the accusation and then took up a lyre and began to make music for Zeus and Apollo, much to their delight. They did not believe Hermes' protestations of innocence, but they were irresistibly charmed in any case.

When Hermes further ingratiated himself to Apollo by giving him the lyre he had been playing, Apollo made a present to Hermes of a divining rod and along with it the power of prophecy, which Hermes must communicate not by words, which was Apollo's domain, but by signs and occurrences.

All of which added to the complex nature of Hermes' communications and revelations.

"Whereas Apollo insists on single meanings, clear and straight like an arrow," Thompson writes, "communications under the sign of Hermes borrow from twisted pathways, shortcuts and parallel routes. It makes many round trips and ends up sometimes in meaningful dead ends. The paths of Hermes are multiple."

Yet if Hermes were merely a liar, Thompson observes, then no one would listen to his stories.

"This is a crucial point for the UFO phenomenon as well," he writes, drawing a comparison to our fascination with the wonders from the heavens we have come to call the flying saucer mystery and the gods of the sky. "If each and every sighting invited a definitive explanation, there would be no controversy about 'meanings.' UFOlogists (pro and con), like Apollo, are interested in 'proving' things. Hermes (like UFOs themselves?) wants to win over the audience and get applause, even if it means twisting the truth."

The Perfect Humans

Admittedly, we know very little about the true nature of the Greek religion beyond the myths and legends that have survived into our present time. What we do know is that about 1200 B.C.E., the residents of what we would call Greece and Asia Minor shared a common, undisputed belief in a group of deities from the heavens that came to be known as the Olympians.

Alien Space Gods of Ancient Greece and Rome

The world famous Erich von Daniken has devoted an entire book to the subject of Greek mythology called "Odyssey of the Gods," in which he suggests that the Greek gods were in fact extraterrestrial beings who arrived on Earth thousands of years ago.

On a website devoted to the Greek/Roman UFO connection as part of the NetScienta posting, an unnamed author writes, "Archeological evidence and the writings of the ancients, including Aristotle, prove these gods interbred with humans, performed genetic experiments, and bred 'mythical' creatures, such as centaurs and Cyclops."

The same author explains, "Greek gods were a way of explaining the unexplainable in a person's life. According to Greek mythology, there once was a time when great events had occurred and the gods had involved themselves in human affairs. These gods were described as 'the perfect humans.'"

Zechariah Sitchin once remarked that people often say the gods of old, with their love affairs and various intrigues and jealousies, are "just like people." But Sitchin said it's the other way around, really, that we as people are just like the gods who made us, imperfect and weak in many ways.

Alien Space Gods of Ancient Greece and Rome

Did a real Cyclopes live amongst us? Were these monstrosities created by space beings? *Polyphemus*, by Johann Heinrich Wilhelm Tischbein, 1802 (Landesmuseum Oldenburg)

The Greeks' creation story goes like this: Prometheus and Epimetheus were spared imprisonment in Tartarus because they had not fought alongside their fellow Titans in the war with the Olympians. Having found favor, they were given the task of creating man. Prometheus shaped man out of mud, and Athena breathed life into his clay figure. This is a method similar to genetic splicing, the author declares, which

Alien Space Gods of Ancient Greece and Rome

makes the story all the more feasible given that we can splice genes ourselves now and there is much evidence that the UFO aliens/gods can do the same. Witness the human/alien hybrid children that are so much a part of the present day alien abduction phenomenon.

Humanoids In Greece

Shifting gears into the modern era, we come to the sightings in Greece of humanoid forms, which include a high number of encounters of the third kind. On the website of our good friend Brian Haughton, Mysterious People.Com, he devotes several pages to the research of Greek UFOlogist Thanassis Vembos, a fulltime journalist, author, translator and researcher whose versatile lifelong interests include the paranormal in all its aspects as well as Astronomy, Astronautics and science fiction.

Vembos makes the important point that UFO sightings and alien encounters have never received the attention they deserve in his nation's press.

"After World War II," he writes, "the only relatively credible medium of information was the newspapers. So the only source of ufological information was the local press, even though it usually distorted the narratives and presented information with no substantive details due to a complete lack of knowledge about UFOs. In fact, the UFO subject was unknown to the greatest part of Greek society until the 1960s."

The heaviest wave of sightings in Greece was in 1954, when all of the European theater was overcome with flying saucer fever. On Vembos' own personal site, which you are invited to visit (at www.Vembos.gr), there are many apparently well-documented reports listed from that fateful year. We found the following incident to be without a doubt the most puzzling and intriguing:

"November 20. A strange report comes from Vovoda village, near Aegion, Peloponnese. At 7:00 A.M., 84-year-old Helias Coromilas was at his field, at Voulomeni, outside Vovoda, when he noticed a small object, resembling a small car, rolling on the road and then entering the field at a distance of about 100 meters (300 feet) from the witness. Coromilas ran to warn the driver of the 'car' that there was a steep cliff in front of him, but when he approached it, suddenly the 'car' took off, making no sound at all and, engulfed in dust, flew away into the sky. Coromilas said later that the 'car' was dark in color, had two wheels and was 1.5 to 2 meters in size and one meter in height. He considered the whole event 'supernatural.'"

Alien Space Gods of Ancient Greece and Rome

In addition to the wave of 1954, other UFO incidents related by Mr. Vembos keep us fascinated, especially the experience related to him firsthand by a Greek university professor identified simply as Mr. G. P., with the name of his home city also withheld in order to protect his privacy.

It was the year 2001, and the professor was at home, in the wee hours of Sunday, June 24, watching a late-night talk show on television. It was approximately 2 A.M. His wife and son were asleep and his daughter was out. The talk show began to bore him intensely, so the professor went to bed. He was walking to the bedroom when he noticed that the kitchen light was on.

"Reaching out to switch it off," Vembos writes, "he felt a sense of coldness, like a cold wind on his back. He turned to see what it was. The thing he saw was like a bolt out of the blue. A strange humanoid was standing right there, before his eyes. It was a slim, tall creature – almost six feet – and seemed to be wearing a tight-fitting light blue 'coverall.'"

The witness would explain later that, "It was like the stockings that burglars put on their head, but it was covering the whole body, from head to toes."

The face of the creature was "coarsely formed." It had only bulges and cavities where the eyes, the nose, the ears and other facial characteristics should be. The witness said the humanoid's whole appearance was like that of a "coarse computer graphic."

"The witness had the impression," Vembos goes on, "that the apparition was masculine. It was moving in 'slow motion' with large strides showing great flexibility, 'like that of a dancer not touching the floor.' It came out of the kitchen and went right to the bathroom (the bathroom door was open). Its movement reminded the witness of a hurdler in action. In spite of his shocked astonishment, the witness was curious enough to run after the creature. But it disappeared into thin air. Before the witness realized what he had just seen, the humanoid appeared for a second time. Now it came out of his daughter's bedroom and ran into the kitchen, where it again disappeared. After that, it made its appearance for a third time, coming out from the bathroom and disappearing again – for good – in the living room. The whole 'chase' had lasted approximately 30 seconds."

It was at that point that the professor felt the sheer magnitude of what had just happened, and he nearly collapsed from the shock. During the incident he had not had time to realize how weird, how out of the ordinary the experience was.

"The high strangeness of the incident," writes Vembos, "was intensified by the complete lack of any sound. He had the impression that the apparition was 'running away from something, trying desperately to avoid contact with something that was chasing it.'"

Could it have been Hermes, on the run from his fellow gods after some new form of godlike mischief? Or was Hermes there to deliver some message to the professor, a message that the gods deemed him worthy of? If that was the case, one must assume the message was lost in a haze of mystery.

An Earlier Visit From The Unknown

The anonymous professor has by no means been a stranger to the unexplainable, offering up another earlier experience to the Greek investigator/author Thanassis Vembos.

"In 1974, the professor was at home, in another Greek city," Vembos writes, "where he was residing with his family. The doorbell rang and he went to open it. There was a woman standing on the doorstep, apparently dressed like a 'nun.' Her face was 'indescribably beautiful,' 'radiating dazzling splendor.' (Maybe it is useful to clarify that the professor is not a religious person.) The 'nun' seemed to be 'self-illuminated,' even though the outdoor light was off. The woman asked him for some money. He turned and reached out to get some from a small box. But when he turned again to the door to give her the money after a few seconds, the woman had vanished.

"He was shocked, realizing that there was not enough time for the woman to vanish. He went out, pressed the elevator button and saw that the elevator was somewhere on the upper floors. He came down the stairs and went into the street but he could not find any trace of her. The experience was not as subjective or illusionary as it seems at first glance, since his family also heard the doorbell ringing."

We wonder if this might have been a materialization of the Oracle of Delphi, disguised in more modern garb. She has often been depicted wearing a head cloth or covering like a religious figure such as a nun. Perhaps she comes back from time to time, and has done so down through the ages, taking on human form in an attempt to provide us with contemporary revelations and prophecies.

The professor also told Vembos about a third experience that took place in 1986 in which he saw an apparition of his mother-in-law as he rode a city bus full of people. His mother-in-law had died six months prior to the bus incident.

"He was so stunned that he could not believe his eyes and could not even try to speak to her," Vembos writes.

Alien Space Gods of Ancient Greece and Rome

Seeing an apparition of a deceased relative is also sometimes part of an abduction experience, according to researcher Dr. David Jacobs. For instance, one may be undergoing a typical bedroom abduction and see one's late grandmother at the foot of the bed. Experiencer Whitley Strieber has frequently commented that the border between the worlds of the living and the dead is something the aliens can cross over like we would cross a street.

What The Firemen Saw

Vembos also learned of another incident there in Greece that took place a couple of months after the professor's visit from the humanoid in his home. The site of the incident was Perati, near Vravona, which is the location of the beautiful ancient temple of Artemis, also called Diana. The temple is still standing and in rather good condition.

"Perati is a hill that John Keel would have classified as a 'window,'" Vembos writes. "Lots of strange happenings, apparitions, UFOs and other unorthodox phenomena are reported there."

The witness to the Perati event was a 45-year old fireman who was doing a nightshift with two other colleagues, watching for forest fires. It was the end of

Alien Space Gods of Ancient Greece and Rome

August 2001. From their vantage point atop a peninsula in the area, which had a panoramic view, there was a deserted heliport – a landing platform about 15 meters in diameter – and a small wooden kiosk. It was a hot but peaceful night and the firemen were talking idly right beside a fire engine.

"It was about 10 P.M. when they noticed a disc-shaped light-colored object flying low and noiselessly above the sea, coming towards them from the northeast. As the UFO was approaching, their mobile phones, the CB and their portable radio ceased to function."

The fireman had a slight impression of hearing a faint noise, "like a small electric motor."

"Astounded, the three men saw the UFO coming down and landing softly on its belly upon the old cement heliport platform. It was just three meters in diameter, seemed like 'two deep plates glued together,' and its color was whitish or gray metal. It did not have any discernible characteristics or features. It was half-hidden from their sight by shrubbery. All three of them were flabbergasted and a little afraid. 'What are we supposed to do now?' they wondered. The fireman felt strange that he was witnessing something that he had read about or watched on TV programs."

Alien Space Gods of Ancient Greece and Rome

After a while, a door seemed to open on the UFO. From inside, a dim light was coming out. Three small humanoids emerged from the open door and came down a stairway, one after the other. It was too dark to see details, but the humanoids seemed to wear tight-fitting, apparently metallic "scuba diver suits." A hood covered their heads but not their faces. The witness could not make out any perceptible complexion or details on the humanoids' limbs or bodies. The three aliens walked in line for six or seven meters and then disappeared into the night but the door on the ship remained open.

The three men, still reeling from the shock of what they were seeing, started to discuss what they should do. One of them started to walk towards the landed UFO, but when he was halfway there he came back, saying that "something" had prevented him from going any further.

A few minutes later, the creatures appeared again, coming up the same path they had earlier disappeared on. Walking in line, they entered the UFO. The door was closed and the UFO took off noiselessly. It flew until it vanished, to the south, behind Perati Hill. After it was gone, the electronic devices began to function again. The witnesses searched the landing area for traces, but found nothing.

Alien Space Gods of Ancient Greece and Rome

They did not report their experience to the authorities for fear of ridicule. A couple of days later, they were doing the same nightshift duties when they saw another UFO, this time a much larger 30 meters in diameter. The ship passed right over their heads at a height of about 100 to 200 meters, had a whitish-metallic color and emitted a sound like "an electrical motor." The UFO vanished into the distance, flying above Perati, and presumably over the nearby temple of Artemis/Diana.

"Detailed research," writes Vembos, "can unearth even stranger tales from the rich lode of Greek Forteana – usually disguised as 'folklore' or 'religious miracles.'"

UFOs In Ancient Rome

Ancient Rome had its share of UFO sightings as well. From the Roman writer Julius Obsequens, who was believed to have lived in the middle of the fourth century C.E., came a great historical work called "Liber de Prodigiis," or "The Book of Prodigies." The book was an account of the wonders and portents that occurred in Rome between 249 and 12 B.C.E.

Obsequens clearly is reporting on a UFO sighting when he writes of an event that took place in 100 B.C.E.:

Alien Space Gods of Ancient Greece and Rome

"When C. Murius and L. Valerius were consuls, in Tarquinia towards sunset, a round object, like a globe or a round circular shield, took its path in the sky from west to east."

Of the year 91 B.C.E., he says that, "At Aenariae, while Livius Troso was promulgating the laws at the beginning of the Italian war, at sunrise, there came a terrific noise in the sky, and a globe of fire appeared, burning in the north. In the territory of Spoletum, a globe of fire, of golden color, fell to the Earth gyrating. It then seemed to increase in size, rose from the Earth and ascended into the sky, where it obscured the sun with its brilliance. It revolved toward the eastern quadrant of the sky."

There is finally a third report from Obsequens, for the year 42 B.C.E., that states, "Something like a sort of weapon, or missile, rose with a great noise from the Earth and soared into the sky."

Since Obsequens was writing in the fourth century C.E., after Rome had converted to Christianity, he makes no reference to the ancient gods of his forefathers. Nevertheless, it was no doubt this sort of observable UFO activity that kept both the Greeks and Romans of the pre-Christian era further enthralled by the legends of their gods from the skies.

Alien Space Gods of Ancient Greece and Rome

Thousands of visitors each year to the Church in Montalcino near Tuscany, Italy, marvel at the strange "sputnick-like" painting commission by the Church in the late 1500's. Could this be a UFO? Many seem to think so, including the caretakers of the church. More remarkable, on a walk through the Vatican courtyard Coast to Coast guest Tim Beckley photographed a giant sphere commissioned by his Holiness which remarkably resembles the "UFO" at Montalcino. Is there a Vatican UFO/alien connection?

Alien Space Gods of Ancient Greece and Rome

The Story of Bruno Facchini

One may recall the mega-hit HBO television series, "The Sopranos," about a crime boss named Tony Soprano and his nuclear, extended and crime families. In one episode, Tony says to his henchmen, all of Italian descent, that as sons of Italy they are also descendants of ancient Rome, born of a kind of superior breeding stock that they should feel proud of.

And so it was that Rome became Italy over the intervening centuries, and the sightings recorded from antiquity became the UFO and alien encounters of the present time.

One such Italian encounter story comes from 1950 and happened in the small town of Varese. According to Billy Booth, writing on the About.com website, "On the 24th day of April, 1950, 42-year-old factory worker Bruno Facchini was working the late shift and stepped outside to get some fresh air on his break. His home city of Varese had just had a severe thunderstorm. The last distant streaks of lightning were still visible as Bruno decided to see if the electrical system had popped a circuit breaker. He was completely taken aback at what he saw not far from the factory doors."

Alien Space Gods of Ancient Greece and Rome

Bruno went to investigate a bright light that he thought was part of a transformer problem and was shocked to see a circular-shaped, glowing object with a ladder descending from its bottom. At the top of the craft was a greenish glow which partly obscured a light-skinned being. The strange being appeared to be welding something on the ship.

"Bruno's first impression of the craft," Booth writes, "was that it was a type of experimental craft from a nearby air base. His impression was quickly altered by the sight of several other small alien creatures which emerged from the craft. In a moment or two, the ladder began to be drawn up into the mysterious craft, and the beings began to reenter the craft through an invisible door of some kind."

The full realization of what he was seeing caused Bruno to simply flee on foot, at which point he began to hear a sound like that of a large beehive.

"One of the remaining creatures," the post continues, "pointed a type of weapon at the scared worker and a beam of force knocked him to the ground. Although in pain, he was able to watch the last activities of the strange aliens as they prepared the craft to take off. The beehive-like sound increased as the object made its way into the skies and vanished from view."

Alien Space Gods of Ancient Greece and Rome

Taken in near Rome in July 1967,
here is ample evidence that UFOs
are returning to the region.

Alien Space Gods of Ancient Greece and Rome

The following day, Bruno filed a full report with the local police. Signs that something really had been there the night before were still visible, such as burned patches on the ground and the indentation marks of an extremely heavy object. The police also found some odd, green pieces of a metal-like substance, which were sent off for analysis.

"The results of this test concluded that the fragments were an 'anti-friction' material," Booth writes, "containing several types of metal along with a lubricant."

Later tests of the same material commissioned by UFO investigators and conducted by a scientific institute specializing in metallurgy found that the debris was 74 percent copper, 19 percent tin, and other trace elements, which does in no way cast doubt on Bruno's story since we cannot know whether those metals are found only on Earth.

"Bruno's story was taken very seriously by all who knew him," Booth says. "He was a respectable man, very well-liked and considered to be reliable and trustworthy. He gained nothing from his tale of the strange object and occupants he described."

Alien Space Gods of Ancient Greece and Rome

Fetus Of The Gods?

In an online posting from the Unexplainable.net website circa 2010, writer Chris Capps relates the story of an Italian woman named simply "Giovanni," who claims to have been taken aboard a UFO for the purpose of creating a hybrid alien/human race. The notion of an ongoing alien genetics program has been considered a central element of the aliens' plan since 1987, when Budd Hopkins' seminal work "Intruders" revealed that abductee Kathie Davis was also used for breeding experiments and even met one of her own half-alien children while onboard a UFO. The fact that there is an Italian woman reporting the same thing should come as no surprise.

In Giovanni's case, there is plenty of supporting evidence, including implants in her brain, a strange phosphorescent material embedded in her skin in strange symbols, and even a fetus which was not detected until complications from her up to that point unknown pregnancy required an examination by a team of doctors.

"The phosphorous material in her skin," Capps writes, "has been analyzed and shown to be a singular glowing material that experts are saying has not been fully identified and is thought to be made only under

Alien Space Gods of Ancient Greece and Rome

extremely specific circumstances, using magnetic fields comparable to those found in the CERN Large Hadron Collider. The material was not only discovered within her skin, but also in her home and in a small patch of burned grass in her yard."

Meanwhile, her doctors don't understand the tiny artificial metallic implants which Giovanni has had in her brain for several years. She claims they were put in her brain by the creatures who had been abducting her since she was four years old. She has no idea what the implants do or what their intended purpose is.

Did a program to create a race of alien hybrids start centuries ago in Greece, and is this program about to come to fruition in our lifetime? Photo of "the man behind the alien mask" from the movie Communion starring Christopher Walken.

Alien Space Gods of Ancient Greece and Rome

The well-known abductee, Whitley Strieber, once had his own brain implants verified by doctors using an MRI machine. The scan proved the objects were indeed there, but were positioned in such a way as to make surgically removing them impossible without causing some degree of brain damage in the process. It is generally believed that implants in the brain simply come with the territory where alien abduction is concerned.

"Finally," Capps writes, "the most grim bit of evidence is the undetected life sign in Giovanni's body that ultimately ended in abortion. After the fetus was removed, doctors claimed it was certainly not what they expected. Though human fetuses can at an early stage resemble what many describe the Grays as looking like, they also said that several developed features were distinctly not normal for a fetus at that stage, and that it was likely that the child was either developmentally mutated, or something else had caused it to exhibit abnormal features."

Of course none of this was any surprise to Giovanni, who already suspected that the child was a hybrid implanted in her by her alien captors. By itself, the fetus could have been an earthly aberration, but, when combined with the other evidence, her claim of an alien abduction becomes all the more believable.

Alien Space Gods of Ancient Greece and Rome

The gods of Greece and Rome would mingle their seed with the occasional mortal woman, breeding creatures half human and half god who would go on to live their own mythical adventures. Was the strangely misshapen fetus found inside Giovanni intended to be just such a hero of prose and poetry?

The 1978 Italian UFO Wave

The February/March 2011 edition of "Open Minds Magazine" (website at openminds.tv) featured on its cover a fascinating account by Umberto Visani of the 1978 wave of UFOs sighted over Italy that was so undeniably real that politicians of the time demanded an investigation.

One such sighting took place on September 16 of that year, in a section of Naples, at 10 P.M.

"Antonio Attansio and Franco Prezioso, two fishermen, were fishing on the dock. All of a sudden, the water in front of them appeared to boil, with huge bubbles seven feet in diameter appearing on the surface. At the same time, the two men could see an underwater beam of light illuminating the boats out at sea. This beam was very long, thin and greenish in color. After a few minutes, the beam moved slowly away, and the fishermen could no longer see it because other boats were hampering their field of vision. As the strange beam disappeared, the water stopped boiling. The two fishermen were astonished and could not think of any possible explanation as to what they had witnessed."

Was it perhaps a visit from Neptune, the Roman god of the sea? While it is true that some modern day "Romans" still believe in the ancient gods, maybe there are those who need reminding that the world is stranger and the gods more powerful than one might be comfortable with.

Another sighting recounted by Visani took place on December 24 of that fateful year of 1978, in a place called Matera, near Mount Gran Sasso, at 7 A.M.

"Benito Franchi, an employee at the power station, had barely started to work that morning when he began to suffer from a strong headache that nearly paralyzed him. Bizarrely, at the same time, he felt as if his hair was crackling. During this time, the controls of the power station went wild, and the generator progressively lost energy for no apparent reason. Then, after seeing a strange flash coming from a window, Franchi went outside and observed a dazzling spherical object flying high in the sky. Franchi called his colleague, Guido di Varano, and informed him about the events. Together, they tried to call the police station, but the telephone did not work. The sighting was corroborated by a local hotel owner and its guests."

This has been a sampling of the cases reported by Visani, whose article was itself a small sampling of the many sightings that took place in 1978. At the time, the Italian military admitted to having collected several reports from prominent and reputable members of the community, and a member of Italy's parliament demanded to know "which measures Parliament wants to take to establish the origin of such phenomena and calm down the population."

* * * * *

There has been an enormous amount written about the idea that the gods of old have manifested themselves in our relatively new technological age as highly- advanced creatures exhibiting a technology still light years ahead of our own. The gods of old and the present day UFO occupants appear in many guises, but their origins and purposes remain mostly unknown and are likely unknowable. But perhaps Zeus is still up there, observing the Earth from a flying saucer and seeking a new mortal woman to impregnate as he savors mischievous Puck's comment, "What fools these mortals be."

Alien Space Gods of Ancient Greece and Rome

Alien Space Gods of Ancient Greece and Rome

W. RAYMOND DRAKE

A British historian (1913-1989), and a disciple of Charles Fort, W.R. Drake is one of the most credible researchers of the "Ancient Astronauts" theory, which maintains that aliens arrived on Earth and interacted with the human race throughout antiquity and in all parts of the globe. Author of a dozen books on the Space Gods phenomenon, Drake's work complements that of "Chariots of the Gods?" author Erich Von Daniken, but Drake's first book appeared in print prior to Von Daniken's international bestseller. In this book about the ancient Mediterranean's strange relationship with the Sky People, Drake utilized over fifty writers of antiquity and scrutinized their main works through a UFO "lens."

Drake spent many years digging through huge archives of material, looking for supposed anomalies that could support his scenarios of space aliens impacting human history. As Drake himself said, "I aspired to collect as many facts as possible from ancient literature to chronicle for the past what Charles Fort has so brilliantly done for the present century."

His published books include: Gods or Spacemen? (1964). Gods and Spacemen in the Ancient East (1968). Mystery of the gods – Are They Coming Back To Earth? (1972). The Ancient Secrets of Mysterious America – Is Our Destiny Upon Us? (1973). Gods and Spacemen in the Ancient West (1974). Gods and Spacemen in the Ancient Past (1975). Gods and Spacemen Throughout History (1975). Gods and Spacemen in Ancient Israel (1976). Cosmic Continents (1986). Several additional manuscripts have been privately circulated and will eventually be published.

SPACE GODS OF ANTIQUITY - AND THE FALL OF MAN

The greatest writers of antiquity agree that once there was a wonderful Golden Age on an earth ruled by 'gods'. But it was destroyed by wars and cataclysm when Man degenerated through the Silver and Bronze Ages to our own Iron Age.

Research into the classics reveals how the deities of Greece helped the valiant city of Athens defeat the invading armies of Atlantis in 10,000 BC. They inspired the Greeks and Trojans to fight for the beauteous Helen, surely a space queen. The literature of ancient Greece, its great plays and sublime philosophies show reverence for the 'gods', who intervened at Marathon and Salamis, sending flying shields to aid Alexander storming the walls of Tyre.

The magic land of Italy still dreams of the Age of Saturn and the mysterious voices and apparitions which were manifestations of higher beings. Near Troy a UFO saved the army of Lucullus from destruction, omens from the sky foretold the murder of Caesar, men in white watched from the heavens as Hannibal ravaged Italy.

Surely these and other supernatural phenomena add up to real evidence that a race with advanced knowledge was at work in the classical world. Here is that evidence, presented so that you can judge.

Gods and Spacemen in Greece and Rome

W. RAYMOND DRAKE

'No man is wise but all men may be lovers of wisdom.'

Copyright © W. Raymond Drake 1976

To my wife, Marjorie

CONTENTS

1	Invaders From Space	7
2	Space Gods of Ancient Greece	11
3	The Golden Age	24
4	Ancient Athens	45
5	Spacemen in Ancient Greece	62
6	Helen of Troy	84
7	Space Literature of Ancient Greece	93
8	Spacemen in Ancient Italy	120
9	Spacemen in Ancient Rome	143
10	Space Chronicles of Ancient Rome	168
11	Space Gods of Scandinavia	203
12	The Cross	228
	Bibliography	239
	Index	248

Acknowledgements

The author would like to express his sincere appreciation for the encouragement of John G. Williams of Abergavenny whose research into Stone Age history so brilliantly supports the theory that the gods achieved an advanced electrical civilisation.

Chapter One
Invaders From Space

Lightning flashed, night roared, Earth shook in sheets of flame spewing mushrooms of smoke to dim the stars. Electric blasts blitzed the mountain-peaks fusing the solid rock, waves of heat fired the forests. The world exploded. Those silver Spaceships winging down from the Moon ceased their destruction, descending warily over this wild scene they sought to land. Suddenly the mountain spat forth beams of light shrivelling the ships like moths; one solitary survivor in frantic turns evaded the heat-ray tracking him and fled swiftly to Space.

Deep within the hillside the besieged Giants did not rejoice, this raid had failed, there would be others with fusion-bombs to blast the bowels of the Earth. For ten savage years the planet had suffered assault from the skies waged with terrible nuclear weapons, mountain piled on mountain, continents quivered and crumbled to the ocean depths. Earth quaked in devastation, the fair lands of the West lay desolate. Invaders from the stars had overthrown the glorious civilisation of the Sun aided by treacherous wizards from their workshops underground. Earth's last defender stood at bay in the lofty Caucasus defying attacks from the skies, the hope of the world.

In his cavernous operations-room the Leader scanned the telescreen flashing scenes from the battle-fronts. The Giant's eyes sorrowed as he saw the once-proud Empire die in defeat; the towers of Atlantis toppled to the sea, the Pacific fleet burned in the harbour of Tiahuanaco; in Italy the Imperial capital smoked in ruins, its aged Emperor imprisoned on the island of Britain. From the blazing North-West hordes of refugees trudged towards the Middle Sea. The Leader's ascetic features frowned. Why did God permit such suffering? Must the innocent always ... ?

Computers clicked, symbols glowing on the wall spelled grievous news. An atom-bomb in the last raid had wrecked the energy-plant charging the laser-light defences. The Leader sighed, then spoke into a microphone spurring his men to speed repairs. Time! He needed time. In subterranean laboratories his scientists were striving to control that primordial force which motivated the stars; soon he would free beloved Earth and carry the war to the planets to conquer Space.

The Leader stood on a rock outside and watched the sun gild the mountain-tops in glory. He filled his lungs with the sweet dawn air and prayed to the Creator, who destined the affairs of men. The stars faded from sight, night fled before the wondrous splendour of a fresh day, from the sun-dappled valleys far below murmured the sounds and scents of awakened Earth reborn to new life.

Such blessed tranquillity recalled those last days of peace. The Leader's gentle face smiled in reminiscence as he recalled that daring mission to Jupiter which had provoked this war; when rebelling against Space Overlords he with his two brothers landed on that giant planet and stole the secret of solar fire to benefit mankind, that escape by Spaceship through the planetary patrols still thrilled his adventurous soul. The outraged Jovians and their Allies promptly invaded Earth, assisted by rebels from the old regime who lived underground, their fantastic sidereal weapons blitzed the world. The peace-loving Emperor soon suffered defeat; his forces routed by Supermen from the stars. In that last battle both the Leader's brothers were captured; the youngest still defiant was imprisoned on a mountain in Africa; the other collaborated with the Jovian King and married a beautiful physicist, who as dowry brought a nuclear-reactor, this exploded catastrophically, its deadly radiation decimating the world.

Sirens howled. From the clouds swung a sinister Spaceship.

The Leader swore as the enemy approached, the laser-rays were out of action, the fortress sprawled defenceless. Was this the end of Man on Earth? Must the planet yield to Aliens from Space? He gazed across yon sunlit hills, this radiant world he loved like a woman. Compassion for all humanity surged through his soul; for Earth he lived, for Her he died. The invader circled lower for final assault. From out of the Sun swooped a Scoutship, its blazing ray-guns ringed the assailant in flames and hurled it down to the valley exploding its nuclear-bombs.

Before this hero landed the Leader recognised that swashbuckling Giant whose exploits in battle and boudoir were the scandal of the Universe. His mediation brought honourable truce; the Jovians appointed the Leader Governor of Earth to rebuild civilisation. For many years he taught men all the arts of peace until the long-prophesied comet from Sirius menaced the world. As the fiery dragon approached, the Jovian King massed the planetary fleets to launch sidereal rockets to shatter the comet's head. Earth was spared total destruction but storms of fiery stones scourged the planet. Mankind degenerated to wickedness, the waters rose in mighty flood. The Giant rescued a man and a woman to start humanity again.

Science-fiction? Fantasy of the future?

This story forms the earliest history of our Earth told with tragic brilliance by Hesiod,[1] Aeschylus,[2] Ovid[3] and all the classic writers of Greece and Rome.

Greek legends relate how Cronus (Saturn) ruled Italy in a Golden Age; his rebellious son, Zeus (Jupiter), was reared by the Cyclops, who under Vulcan were said to have great factories underground. Zeus revolted against his father and aided by the Cyclops overthrew him. The Titans refused to submit to Zeus; the leader, Prometheus, with his brothers, Atlas and Epimetheus, stole fire from heaven in a hollow tube. Finally Zeus chained Prometheus to a rock in Caucasus where during the day an eagle devoured his liver, magically renewed by night. Hercules killed the eagle and freed Prometheus. Atlas was condemned to bear the sky on his shoulders; to Epimetheus was given Pandora created by Vulcan, who brought with her a box containing every human affliction; on opening it all the evils escaped to plague the world but left therein was Hope. Later Zeus fought a sky-monster called Typhon, then he sent a great flood to destroy degenerate mankind. Prometheus made a huge box and saved his son, Deucalion, also his niece, Pyrrha, Pandora's daughter, to carry on the human race.[4]

Memories of Prometheus's heroic defiance of the Gods, appear to be world-wide. In India the Rig Veda mentions a race of priests called Bhrigus to whom Matarishvan brought the secret fire stolen from heaven.[5] The Chinese extol the hero, Kun, who stole from the 'Lord' a 'swelling mold', magical soil which expanded and filled the dykes to hold back the floods. The 'Lord' angered at the theft had Kun executed at Feather Mountain, a darksome place in the Far North.[6]

Plutarch wrote that Cronus, Ruler of the Golden Age, was deposed by Jupiter and imprisoned in Britain; Diodorus Siculus[7] described the 'Arrow of Apollo', which destroyed the Hyperboreans in their Land of the Blest. Celtic bards and Norse scalds sang of the same war in the skies with titanic blasts and the weary Gods retreating to the stars leaving the shattered Earth for Man to build again.

The peoples of Antiquity marvelled at these brilliant civilisations illuminating the past, yet their souls with wondrous inspiration sought mystic communion in that transcendent secret wisdom of the Gods, the glorious Spacemen, whose plaintive echoes still haunted those silent, shrouded, ancient Lands of the West.

Chapter Two
Space Gods of Ancient Greece

'Sky was the first, who ruled over the whole world.'[8]

The Greeks gloried in the patronage of the Gods, immortal Spacemen, disporting beyond the clouds on Mount Olympus, whence they would oft descend in mortal disguise for amorous adventures inspiring all the Poets of Antiquity. Athenians, proud of their democracy, disdained all lesser humanity as barbarians and fought to the death against those great Kings of Persia, who sought to enslave free men in oriental despotism, yet those same Democrats cherished an affection for their Celestial family like absent friends. People rarely associated the Gods with religion, their barnyard morality brought blushes even to Greeks still savouring sensual delights; such virility aroused the envy of Ovid, whose erotic 'Art of Love' scandalised Augustan Rome. In national crises Deities winged down to aid the hard-pressed patriots at Marathon[9] and Salamis;[10] should one linger to seduce some willing wench no father complained. Who could lock up his daughters against the lust of the Gods? Were not the greatest heroes of old heaven-born, the sons of virgins, the noblest men in the land? What pleased the Greeks most perhaps was that the Gods showed such good sense; unlike Jehovah, Who dominated the daily lives of the Jews, Father Zeus during the last few centuries was content to leave the Athenians alone to work out their own democracy, the wonder of the world. He need not interfere. Certainly no Greek grudged Zeus retirement. The old tales were much confused, even learned philosophers disputed these legends of ancient times, no one was sure who lived in the stars, though all believed the first Kings of Earth came down from the sky. Zeus had toiled and suffered to save mankind in titanic wars and cataclysms; His power still preserved the free peoples of

Greece.

The virile Gods and vivacious Goddesses of Greece in warm humanity inspired poets and artists to enchant the world. Surely those marvellous tales were more than allegories with hidden meaning, symbols for sacred truths or personifications of natural forces theorised by our mythologists, who ignorant of Visitants from Space are confined to conventional thought-patterns of Earth. Myth is not imagination, aery fiction from long-forgotten yesterdays, but oral tradition, dim memory of events in far Antiquity with immense impression on people's minds; each muted testament bequeathed down so many generations far transcends stone monuments preserving living proof of memorable happenings in the history of Man. The epics of Semitic minstrels down dusty millennia were copied by Moses in 'Genesis' to teach the Children of Israel, their story of Jehovah's manifestation to men inspired our religions of the West; if the early Books of the Bible are to be believed for Palestine, should we not accept similar stories of Ancient Greece only a few hundred miles away? Theologians allay modern doubts by asserting that the Scriptures were never meant to record actual history being figurative revelations of the Will of God to His Chosen People, the Jews; the great tragedians of Athens swore the old legends told of the Will of Zeus for His Children, the Greeks. We today with our new knowledge of the inhabited Universe, Extraterrestrials ruling Earth in Ages past, world-wide traditions of Sky Gods, wonder whether Jehovah and Zeus were Spacemen.

The history of our twentieth century seems sadly confused, few people could agree on a common account; in fifty thousand years' time what traditions will our remote descendants cherish of events today? We know almost nothing of our own ancestors, the Ancient Britons, not very long ago, yet the Greeks preserved legends from far prehistory, garbled through the chasm of time. Considered anew by our Space Science these delightful tales suddenly resolve in wondrous illumination giving a tremendous, exciting revelation of Earth's Golden Age with Celestials from the stars.

In his book 'Spacemen in the Ancient East' the present writer reviewed the mythologies and chronicles of India, Tibet, China, Japan and Egypt in the light of our latest knowledge and found a clear, consistent story confirming a world-wide culture millennia ago inspired by Space Kings. The relative legends from most countries agreed so precisely that prior to studying the Space Gods of Babylon it was quite apparent that

'Before even considering Babylonian religion and myths we can confidently expect to find a primeval God, Who created the Universe, Earth and Man from Chaos, Gods of the Sun, Moon and Planets, a fertility-Goddess, who would descend to the Underworld, a God who would be slain to rise again; old Gods dethroned by virile young Gods. Celestials ruling Earth in a Golden Age followed by War between Gods and Men waged by aerial ships speeding like light with annihilating-bombs, fights with Sky Dragons, cataclysms ravaging Earth, change of climate, collapse of civilisation, a Wagnerian Götterdämmerung, a Twilight of the Gods abandoning our planet to be worshipped by men at whose urgent prayers a God would land in secret to give aid or cosmic instruction to Initiates. We have heard all this before, over and over again, as yet we may not know the names which hardly matter. Were cuneiform never deciphered, we could still predict with accuracy the Gods and myths of Babylon from the universality of the Spacemen.'[11]

Detailed study showed that the mythology of Babylon basically agreed with the common legends of other Eastern countries.

Myth becomes science, the old fables subject to empirical proof. As a chemist can predict the properties of an element he has yet to isolate, so from our knowledge of the Ancient East and modern Space lore we can guess the earliest legends of Greece confident its mythology must agree.

The story of Creation told by the Ancient Greeks reveals a cosmic wisdom surprising from an allegedly unsophisticated people. Hesiod states that Chaos 'came into being', it had not existed eternally,[12] implying therefore some Supreme Power had evoked a gaping Void into existence with the purpose of creating the Universe. The Hindus teach that Brahm thinks a finite Universe into existence for a predetermined period, at its dissolution while He sleeps, the new Universe exists only in a state of potentiality conditioned by the Karma or accumulated experience of its predecessor, then Brahm dreams, His thoughts manifest into energy materialising into suns, worlds and all the sentient Beings in Creation from archangel to insect. Our cosmologists theorise that the Universe expanded from a primeval atom, Hesiod in his 'Work and Days' like the 'Rig Veda' suggests a state existing even earlier. Whence did Hesiod, a humble peasant living on a lonely farm in the Greece of the eighth century BC learn this Secret Wisdom distilled by the most subtle minds? Was such recondite knowledge inherited from some ancient civilisation or taught by Spacemen?

Creation legends in homely imagery explained that Chaos and Nyx, Goddess of Night, produced Erebus (Darkness), who mated with his Mother until dethroned by their two beautiful children, Aether (Light) and Hemera (Day); these Deities aided by their own child, Eros (Love) then created Ouranos (Sky), Pontus (Sea) and Ge (Earth). Some versions differ slightly. One legend stated that Erebus and Nyx produced a gigantic Egg from which Eros emerged to create the Earth.[13] Creation of the Universe from a Cosmic Egg has great occult significance and was taught in the 'Rig Veda', the Chinese 'Panku' myth[14] and the Japanese 'Kojiki' suggesting the cosmologies propounded by modern astronomers.

Later Greece, according to Ovid, believed that a God, 'a natural force of a higher kind', appeared suddenly amid Chaos, who separated the Earth from Heaven, and the waters from the Earth, and set the clear air apart from the cloudy atmosphere. This unknown God, sometimes called Phanes, then created countries, rivers, mountains, forests; He made stars and Divine Forms occupy the Heavens, then gave life to fishes, wild beasts and birds. Lastly the Creator made Man from divine seed in the Image of the all-governing Gods to stand erect, bidding him look up to Heaven, and lift his head to the stars. Had Darwin told the Athenians they descended from monkeys the outraged Greeks would have tossed him into the Piraeus; their classic ideal of beauty conceived men like Gods. This myth resembles the Japanese legend of Izanagi and Izanami creating Earth from chaotic brine, also the Gilgamesh Epic, where the Babylonian Goddess, Arwin, made the first man, Eabani, from a piece of clay.

'And God said Let there be light, and there was light.'[15]
'And God said Let us make man in our own image.'[16]

The Greek account of Creation, more poetical perhaps than the terse story in 'Genesis', is similar to Creation legends from many countries, suggesting a common origin; most ancient peoples agreed that Man was fashioned by God in His own Image, thus associating Man with the Gods or Spacemen.

Ovid wrote that God shaped Earth into a great ball, the Poet probably quoted the teachings of Pythagoras regarding the sphericity of the Earth. The Ancient Greeks generally believed Earth to be like a disc with their own country in the middle; in the exact centre stood Mount Olympus, abode of the Gods. The Earth was divided into two equal parts by the sea, all around the flat circular Earth flowed the great river Oceanus from which the sea and all the rivers received their water. The Northern portion of Earth was supposed to be inhabited by the Hyperboreans living in eternal Spring, free from disease, old age and death; their land was inaccessible by land or sea but was frequently visited by the Gods. South of Greece lived the Ethiopians, a happy people whom the Gods loved to visit. Far away in the West lay the beautiful Isles of the Blest called the Elysian Fields,[17] whither mortals favoured by the Gods were transported without tasting Death to enjoy immortality. Beneath the Earth loomed Hades, the Underworld, Kingdom of the Dead.

The Greek myths recall the earliest civilisations on Earth in terms still baffling to our scientific minds; events spanning vast ages are condensed to confused incidents sung by bards down thousands of years until Hesiod and the romantic Poets set down their own interpretations as literature. We in Britain should scarcely criticise; no British myth mentions the beginnings of mankind, although the Britons were contemporaries of the Ancient Greeks. Those unsophisticated tribes of remote Antiquity preserved their cherished traditions in symbolism they understood; such thought-patterns are alien to ours: it is exceedingly doubtful many millennia hence whether our distant descendants will comprehend the few fables from our twentieth century. The fascinating primeval myths were race-memories of peoples living long before the Greeks of history, superficially the story they tell seems naive making little sense; now in our context of Spacemen ruling Earth in ages past, those same tales assume pregnant importance.

Uranus (Heaven) married Ge (Earth) and fathered twelve gigantic children, the Titans, also three rebellious sons, the one-eyed Cyclops; greatly fearing their powers, he hurled them down to the dark chasm of Tartarus, a gloomy underworld, so far distant from Earth that it would take a falling anvil nine days to reach its bottom;[18] there they set up smithies and fashioned wondrous weapons for the Gods. Sorely distressed at the tyranny of her husband, Ge implored the Titans to take revenge and wrest the kingship from him. All except the youngest, Cronus (Saturn), feared their redoubtable father. Ge, understandably perhaps considering all the progeny she had to bear, decided on the first and most effective birth-control expedient in all history; she armed young Cronus with a flint sickle; grasping his father's genitals in his left hand as he slept, Cronus castrated Uranus and flung the severed penis far into the sea; from the fertilised foam sprang Aphrodite, Goddess of Beauty, a fair exchange. Drops of blood spurting the Earth gave birth to the Furies, Giants and Nymphs. Uranus[19] cursed his son and prophesied that one day Cronus too would be usurped by his own children.

Cronus married his sister, Rhea, and ruled the world in a Golden Age, extolled by all the Poets of Antiquity. Men lived like Gods in blest content, free from toil and grief in sweet innocence for sorrow and sin had not yet afflicted their souls. Miserable old age did not sadden humanity nor did they suffer sickness, men prospered in perfect physical and spiritual health beyond all evil, making merry with feasting; when at last they had to die it was as though their eyes were overcome with sleep. In this idyllic bliss men needed no laws or punishments since wrongdoing was unknown; untroubled by wars, all peoples enjoyed peaceful leisure, their cities undefended by soldiers or swords. The sun shone with beneficence giving pleasant climate, the rich soil of its own accord brought forth fruits and berries without cultivation, warm zephyrs caressed the flowers and fields of golden corn, flocks of sheep and cattle pastured in the verdant meadows, lands flowed with rivers of milk or nectar and golden honey dripped down from the green oak. Men communed with the Gods in wondrous peace, for the Poets all agreed that in this Age of Perfection Man was not yet distracted by Woman.

While his subjects rejoiced, Cronus, tortured by conscience, was mindful of the warning of Uranus. To avert dethronement by his own sons, Cronus every year swallowed the children Rhea bore to him; first Hestia, then Demeter, Hera, Hades and Poseidon. Before the birth of their youngest son, Zeus, the enraged Mother sought advice from her parents, who sent her to the island of Crete, where Zeus was born and hidden in a cave on Mount Ida. Rhea substituted a stone in swaddling clothes and dutifully handed it to Cronus which he surprisingly swallowed. The young Zeus was protected by the Priests of Crete, and on growing to manhood challenged Cronus, whom Rhea with an emetic had forced to disgorge all the children he had devoured. The stone too was disgorged by Cronus and was set up at Delphi. Ages later the great traveller, Pausanias, saw[20] it about AD 180 and commented 'A stone of no great size, which the Priests of Delphi anoint every day with oil.' Such trickery rivalled their notorious double-tongued Oracle.

For ten long years war raged between Cronus aided by the Titans against Zeus armed with magic weapons from the Cyclops whom he freed. The conflict raged throughout Earth, sea and sky, waged with all the cosmic forces of the Gods. Mother Earth promised victory to Zeus, who finally subdued the Titans with lightnings and thunderbolts then bound them in chains in darksome Tartarus. Cronus was imprisoned on the mysterious island of Britain, guarded by Briareus, a monster with a hundred hands; another tradition declared he fled to Hesperia (Italy) where he repented of his former cruelties and as Saturn ruled a wonderful civilisation building fair Saturnia, the future Rome.

Zeus from his abode beyond Mount Olympus hated mankind and deprived them of fire. The hero, Prometheus, stole fire from heaven. Zeus swore vengeance, the Giants rebelled and piled mountain on mountain to storm Heaven. After titanic war convulsing Heaven and Earth, Zeus prevailed; to punish Man he created Woman, Pandora, whose notorious box released afflictions to plague humanity. Zeus chained Prometheus to a peak in lofty Caucasus, where by day an eagle tore his liver magically renewed at night; later he was released by Hercules, pardoned, and devoted his genius to teaching Man the arts of civilisation. When Zeus decided to destroy the degenerate race of Men, Prometheus counselled his son, Deucalion, to build a boat; in the great floods only he and his wife, Pyrrha, were saved. The ship rested on Mount Parnassus. As they prayed for guidance in a slimy, moss-grown temple they heard a voice from the skies exhort them to throw behind them the bones of their Mother. After some reflection they cast over their heads the stones of Mother Earth; the stones thrown by Deucalion changed into men, those by Pyrrha became women.

The troubles of Zeus were still not finished. A fearsome sky-monster, Typhaeus, drove the terrified Gods from Mount Olympus to Egypt, stressing most ancient links between these two countries. Zeus finally slew it with a thunderbolt.

Hesiod believed that Men of the Golden Age still dwelled on Earth as pure Spirits clothed in mist and kept watch on judgements and evil deeds and gave rewards and wealth, invisible Guardians of mankind.

The Wars between Heaven and Earth fought with titanic weapons had changed the world's climate from eternal springtime when Nature bloomed in blessed fruitfulness to a cycle of four seasons, in summer the air became parched, lands glowed with heat, in winter the blast of winds chilled over the ice. Men no longer lived in fair cities basking in peace and beauty, the people of this Silver Age sought refuge in caves or rude huts, ignorant of the culture of their wise ancestors, they committed sins, quarrelled and forgot the immortal Gods.

Zeus outraged at such neglect destroyed them all and created a third generation in an Age of Bronze. This brazen race, terrible and strong, ate flesh; adamant and unconquerable, these warriors wore armour of bronze, wielded weapons of bronze and built great houses of bronze. Their fierce souls exulted in warfare plunging mankind to barbarism. All were destroyed by plagues like the Black Death.

In atonement perhaps, Zeus created a fourth race of godlike heroes, men of renown and glorious adventure, who fought with the Seven against Thebes, sailed with Jason's Argonauts searching for the Golden Fleece, or stormed those topless towers of Troy. Some of these righteous sages were rewarded by Zeus and translated to the Islands of the Blessed, possibly Britain, along the shore of a deep-smiling ocean, for whom grain-giving Earth bore honey and sweet fruits thrice a year, ruled by Cronus.[21]

Last of all Zeus in his questionable wisdom created the Age of Iron, which still afflicts the world. Treachery and crime, deceit and violence, influenced mankind; Earth, which had been common to all, became divided into contending countries, war appeared in all its horror, gold became more desirable than iron, families and friends quarrelled in strife, with the last of the Immortals justice fled.

Today a recital of Greek myths provokes students to exasperation and sad disappointment. Is this nonsense the only evidence for Spacemen long ago? In our scientific Age can any sane man really believe such crazy tales compounded by cavemen, written down by romantic poets? Does all this drivel about a Golden Age, Wars of the Gods, Zeus destroying mankind four or five times, represent Celestials from the stars? These legends happen to be the earliest history of our Earth; admittedly not penned in the lucid logic of our own professors; paradoxically this confusion proves their authenticity suggesting oral transmission through vast periods of time, had all been false they would surely have long been forgotten. Some of us cannot quite recall what happened yesterday, we marvel at the memories of these age-old Greeks. Critics reluctantly concede that the story of Theseus and the Minotaur inspired Sir Arthur Evans to excavate the brilliant civilisation of Knossos, the 'Iliad' prompted Heinrich Schliemann to unearth the necklace of naughty Helen under those much-quoted Towers of Troy, even today fables of El Dorado lead to lost cities of the Incas; such exceptions cannot possibly prove that all myths must be true. Scepticism should be encouraged, traditions must be questioned; mankind has suffered too much from doubtful religious dogmas; in its brief history science has made many wrong guesses but it constantly seeks new facts to modify its truths.

If we ridicule the Greek myths, it must be because these curious tales conflict with the conventional thought-patterns of today; the Ancients believed in the Gods, today our minds are conditioned by contemporary culture, we cannot attune to the mental climate, the spirit of ages past. Translated to the walls of Troy, we would feel as alien as Achilles lost in the traffic of London.

What is our general opinion on those legends of Greece? That alleged fountain of commonsense, the Man-in-the-street, associates the names of the Gods with the losing racehorses he backs and confuses Zeus with television's 'Superman'. Politicians may envy Zeus as a smart Prime Minister; instead of changing the Government every few years, why not change the people instead and create completely new voters to whom they could tell the same old tales?

Theologians argue that the Bible makes no mention of the Gods of Greece, the Christian Fathers cursed pagan deities as devils. Moses, alleged Author of 'Genesis', was educated as an Egyptian Prince, versed in the Secret Wisdom he probably knew of Lemuria, Atlantis and civilisations of the East. The 'Talmud' asserts he became a famous General in Ethiopia, a shepherd in Midian, then was chosen by the 'Lord' to lead the Israelites from bondage to the borders of Canaan, an enterprise demanding divine inspiration. No Egyptologist confirms the existence of Moses, the Jews make him contemporary with Rameses II at the zenith of the Egyptian Empire in the thirteenth century BC, that glorious age of Minoan Crete, golden Mycenae and the Siege of Troy. Moses, steeped in all the traditions of his tremendous times, must surely have known the legends of Greece, it is difficult to believe that his great mind could have reduced Creation to that garbled account in 'Genesis' when he could have written an epic about the Space Kings.

Who are our experts? Archaeologists cannot comment on the Greek myths, they have dug through the back streets of Athens down to 6000 BC and found no one lived there. Had Howard Carter stopped digging a week earlier he would never have discovered the wonderful tomb of Tutankhamun, much of our knowledge of Ancient Egypt would never have been learned. Historians hesitate at Homer then come to a stop; palaeontologists finger the skull of Prometheus ('Alas, poor Yorick! I knew him well, Horatio!') and conclude he could not have the brains to rub two sticks together to make a fire, anthropologists laugh that in those prehistoric days Zeus would be swinging in the tree-tops like Tarzan of the Apes. Classical scholars remain somewhat cautious awaiting new texts, intriguing descriptions are found in Crete in Linear 'A' but no one can read them.

Most of our Makers of modern thought regard the Greek Myths as irrelevant, irrational intrusions like the Sphinx, alien to our scientific world. By a startling paradox it is Science which now supports these old legends. The latest discoveries in astronomy and biology agree there must be millions of inhabited worlds in our own galaxy. The illustrious Joseph Shklovsky[22] of the Moscow Observatory suggests that Supreme Intelligences can modify the stars. M. Agrest,[23] the Armenian Physicist, claims that Spaceships once landed in the Libyan Desert. The world-wide sightings of UFOs make the Greek Myths shine more wondrous than ever with glorious meaning.

Evaluation of myth becomes a problem in semantics of prime importance to the proof of Spacemen visiting Earth in ages past. People promptly construe the word 'Myth' as meaning a philosophical allegory, a sentimental fable, romance or melodrama, elevating or entertaining, but pure fiction describing incidents which never happened, therefore quite irrelevant indeed irrational to any serious, scientific study such as Extraterrestrials in Antiquity. To the Greeks themselves 'Mythos' originally denoted a tradition of actual events in the far past, so tremendous that the facts, garbled perhaps during transmission were handed down orally before the use of writing from generation to generation; centuries later the classical Poets elaborated 'pseudo-Myths' from local legends alleging the love-life of Gods and mortals. Pythagoras and Initiates of the Eleusinian Mysteries distrusted the written text and sternly refused to put their teachings in writing; Socrates, whose logic still influences the West, never left a single word. The most ancient Myths were accepted by the Greeks as Gospel truth and became the basis of their religion. Thucydides,[24] whom Macaulay regarded as 'the greatest historian who ever lived', still honoured by scholars for his judgement and insight, clearly accepted the old traditions as historical material. Introducing his own great history, Thucydides wrote

>'Minos is the earliest ruler we know, who possessed a fleet and controlled most of what are now Greek waters.'

Thucydides was quoting a myth, which he and his fellow-Greeks accepted as true; our sceptical modern minds scoffed at this claim unsupported by corroborative texts and accused him of swallowing the legend of Theseus and the Minotaur. Belief in the legend inspired Sir Arthur Evans to unearth the wonderful civilisation of Minoan Crete. Latest revelations of the Bronze Age confirm the basic truth of many of the old legends from Antiquity.

We stress yet again that the fundamental impediment beclouding dispassionate consideration of Spacemen in ancient times is our prejudiced thought-pattern. Few people know the precise meaning of the words they use or the exact connotation of words used by someone else. Failure of communication confuses Society today; world events prove we hardly understand each other. How can we understand the minds of Greeks millennia a go? Instead of dismissing all the Greek Myths as nonsense, thereby learning nothing, we should recognise our limitations and in humility try to elucidate what those people in ages past were trying to tell us.

Chapter Three
The Golden Age

Since the Greek word 'Ouranos' meant 'Sky' Uranus could generalise Spacemen from anywhere in the heavens, although it might still refer to the planet, Uranus, known to the Ancients. Uranus does not appear to have been worshipped by the Greeks at any time, nor was the God associated with any cult or art, suggesting he symbolised a most ancient race of Spacemen ruling Earth vast ages beyond Greek cognisance. The Titans or Uranidae, sons and daughters of Uranus, originally dwelled in heaven, they were very ancient figures little worshipped in Greece[25] and belonged to a most remote past quite alien to those mythmakers of Greece; it was vaguely believed that they were giant Nature Powers, magicians with wondrous arts controlling Nature. 'Ouranos' was probably identical to Varuna, the powerful primeval God from pre-Indian mythology mentioned in the Vedas, who was associated with heavenly bodies; he controlled the Moon and the stars, the name 'Varuna' meant 'the encompassed sky', clearly indicative of Spacemen. The Titans equate with the giant Asuras of India; later Varuna became Chief of the Adityas and a kind of Neptune riding on the Leviathan, possibly a Spaceship plunging into the sea.

    The Uranids may represent some Galactic race from an advanced planet circling a star near the centre of the Milky Way, who exploring our Solar System installed a transit-station on Earth millions of years ago. The one-eyed Cyclops, sons of Uranus, who rebelled against their father and were cast down to deep Tartarus below the Earth may conceivably have been Visitants from another star, who chanced to land here and fought cataclysmic wars with the original colonists; admittedly such a theory smacks of Science-Fiction yet it seems quite logical, even likely. Our Earth cooled down more than three thousand million years ago, there were probably several Galactic Empires, on the cosmic scale in the most remote past Invaders from rival stars could have battled for domination of Earth just as the British and French fought for Canada. The Titans are said to have ridden the starways, they are believed to have been the first builders on Earth being the Immortals of our legends, the God Race or the Elder Race that preceded 'hu-man' beings. Hesiod in his 'Theogony' wrote

'The poet of the "War of the Titans" whether Eumelus of Corinth or Arctinus writes thus in his second book "Upon the shield were dumb fish afloat, with golden faces, swimming and sporting through the heavenly water."

Theolytus says that he (Heracles) sailed across the sea in a cauldron, but the first to give this story is the author of the "War of the Titans".

First of all the deathless Gods, who dwell on Olympus made a golden race of mortals who lived in the time of Cronos when he was reigning in heaven.'

The 'shield' with fishes having golden faces sporting through the heavenly water and Heracles sailing across the sea in a cauldron may be some garbled reference to Celestials in Spaceships.

The Cyclops may be identified with the Els,[26] a stellar race of non-human physique, who built the labyrinthine cities underground utilising cosmic energies, still associated with the subterranean civilisation of Agharta alleged to exist today. The castration of Uranus is difficult to resolve; this dramatic mutilation by his son, Cronus, must have immense significance. It may possibly be some primitive explanation for the race of Uranids coming to an end, the first civilisation of Ouranus (Sky) being supplanted by the Golden Age of Cronus (Saturn); the severance of Uranus's penis and the birth of Giants and Nymphs from drops of his blood suggest later overtones of the Dionysian fertility-cults.

In ancient times all the planets were identified with Gods, Celestials in human form who descended to Earth to teach Mankind. Mythologists allege that the Gods were merely anthropomorphic symbols of natural forces or human emotions, it was natural for primitive man to create the Gods in his own image. Were our Earth the only inhabited world in the universe as mythologists believed, their theory might be plausible. Even so, the conception of an abstract force as a Superman requires a lofty, philosophical reasoning unlikely for an illiterate tribe and probably beyond most people today. If an ignorant peasant describes in picturesque detail some wondrous Personage alighting from a sky-ship, whom he subsequently worships, it is surely because he himself or someone, whose word he believes, actually did see such a Being descend from the heavens not just once but many times. Hoaxes do delude the superstitious, but frauds seldom deceive for long. Most Christians worship Jesus because the Gospels describe Him as a real Man; for two thousand years His gentle Image has been impressed upon human consciousness by inspired paintings, His Life and Death have been extolled in books and sermons by countless disciples. Without this haunting Image could ordinary men and women for twenty centuries have worshipped an unpersonified Ideal of Love? Buddha, Jesus, Mahomet, were Men, admittedly overshadowed by Higher Powers, but in popular consciousness they were human like our Truth-seeking Selves today. Uranus, Cronus, Zeus, Apollo, were real Beings, perhaps each may have been a generic term for Celestials from a specific planet; in ages to come Martians may worship a God called Jack generalising cosmonauts who once descended to them from Earth.

Why did peoples of Antiquity all over the Earth almost always give to planets the names of the chief Gods? When our astronomers discover a new star they classify it by a code-number in the Cambridge Stellar Catalogue or call it after its finder. Xenocrates,[27] a pupil of Plato, greatly esteemed by Aristotle and Cicero, wrote a lost work on the nature of the Gods in which he dealt with the eight Gods of the heavenly bodies and called them the Olympian Deities. Pluto was so-called merely to harmonise with all the other planets named after Gods. The claim by astrologers that people born under the various planets have distinctive physical and mental characteristics may possibly be a race-memory of the salient appearance and temperament of the average visitor from each of those planets long ago, embellished perhaps by lyrical poetic licence.

Esoteric traditions teach that all the planets around our Sun are surveilled by Cosmic Intelligences on Sirius who in the Miocene Period sent Migrants to colonise Earth. In ancient times people all over the world held mystic reverence for Sirius, the Dog Star, such a Celestial might have been revered as 'Ouranos', a Being from the Sky.

The Babylonians identified Uranus with Anu, who was believed to dwell in the Constellation of the Great Bear like the 'Seven Shining Ones' in Egyptian Mythology; significantly the direction from which the space-ships today approach Earth through the polar-vents in the Van Allen Belts.

The planet Uranus was known to the Magi of Persia and to the Hindus, although they excluded it from our Sun's Seven Sons of Light, associating its baleful influence with evil. The vast distance of Uranus roughly 1,700 million miles from Earth made its observation in northern skies difficult, the planet's existence became therefore forgotten until rediscovery by Sir William Herschel on 13th March 1781. The Shilluk[28] tribe in South Africa have always called Uranus 'Three Stars', a planet with two moons; it is difficult to believe that Uranus was actually visible to them, certainly not its satellites, which require the largest telescopes. Whence did the Shilluks derive this knowledge before Western astronomers knew of the existence of Uranus? Were those South African natives taught by Spacemen?

Official astronomy insists that this giant planet, 31,000 miles in diameter, rotating in 34 years around the Sun, shudders in temperatures minus 100 degrees Centigrade under clouds of methane and ammonia possibly with hydrogen and helium; a warming process is believed to occur through the absorption of solar ultra-violet radiation. Astronomers interpret the universe strictly according to the facts evaluated by their own scientific methods, we must respect their judgement and integrity. Science however is just one technique of examining the universe, we must surely give consideration to other revelations since Science alone holds no monopoly for absolute Truth. If Uranus depended on radiation from the Sun, life there would be improbable, though latest theories suggest that the planet does have a source of internal heat, the amount of thermal energy emitted is not known. Space Intelligences are said to insist that chemical light is exuded from vegetation and ionisation of gases in the atmosphere, analogous to our own Earth-shine, though much more intense; this is perhaps confirmed by the fluctuations of brightness observed in recent years suggesting surface disasters. The astronomers, mesmerised by their spectroscopes and transient theories, who swear that Uranus simply cannot be inhabited, might care to reflect that thousands of photographs taken of our own Earth by the satellite Nimbus 1, a mere 400 miles away, show not the slightest sign of life here. The inhabitants of Uranus are said to be tall and muscular with large eyes and over-developed heads having blood and organs different from our own.[29] Were the Uranids those Androgynes whom Plato believed to have been the first inhabitants of Earth?[30]

Adepts of the Cosmic Hierarchy[31] inspiring the evolution of our Solar System state that the Uranids are on a higher plane of existence and are more advanced spiritually than men on Earth. Dr. George Hunt Williamson, who was present when George Adamski met Orthon from Venus on 20th November 1952 in the Californian Desert, claims to have had radio-contact with Solar Intelligences including benevolent Beings, all concerned about the tribulations of Earth.[32] Such revelations are ridiculed by scientists yet even the most bigoted astronomer must in honesty admit that no one can possibly know what does exist on Uranus until Man lands there. If Sensitives today are telling the truth and the Uranids are interested in our Earth now, is it too improbable to suggest that their ancestors ages ago actually did land here and created a great world-wide civilisation, dimly recalled in race-memory as the reign of Uranus and the Titans? It is even possible that 'Ouranos' symbolised Extra-terrestrials from beyond our Solar System, who originally used Earth as a Space-station during their exploration of our Galaxy.

Cronus, known to the Romans as Saturn was regarded as a Son of Uranus: this could have been a convenient representation for a new generation, a completely different race of Spacemen ruling Earth. Plausible theories are advanced to prove that Cronus symbolised vast ages swallowed by Time; a philosophical conception too abstract perhaps for deification by a primitive people. His name might not have originated from the Greek 'Kronos' – 'Time' but from 'Kraino' meaning 'Completer' or 'Ripener'. Today he is wrongly depicted as old Father Time with a scythe; originally the Ancients simply thought of his venerable figure as a 'harvester'. Cronus was probably a pre-Greek God little worshipped with only one festival, the Kronia at Athens, Rhodes and Thebes, where he was known as the Barley God, Saluzius, annually cut down in the cornfield and bewailed like Osiris. This association of 'Cronus' with corn is paralleled by Varro, who declared that the Roman 'Saturn' was derived from 'satus' meaning 'sowing'.[33] It is significant that occult traditions teach that barley and wheat are not indigenous to Earth but were brought here by Celestials from the stars. Was Cronus (Saturn) so-called because he was remembered as the Bringer of Wheat, the planet whence he came becoming known as Saturn? The innocent, perfect paradise provided by Cronus seems contrary to the myth that Cronus was a monster who devoured his own children. Homer does not mention this; Hyginus, a Roman scholar and writer of immense versatility, Librarian of the Palatine Library of Augustus, disagreed with Hesiod, and wrote in 'Hyginus Fabulae' 139-1 that Cronus did not swallow his children. Perhaps Hesiod's version relates in some garbled fashion to subsequent conflict between the Saturnians and their usurpers from Jupiter?

In the 'Secret Doctrine' Cronus is identified with the 'Ancient of Days', a mysterious Being also mentioned in the Egyptian 'The Book of the Dead' associated with 'Spirits of Light', 'Sons of Darkness' and 'Deities in the Divine Eye', which perhaps referred to Space Gods descending to Earth long ago. Acknowledgement of Cronus appears to have been world-wide; outside Greece he was apparently known as the British Bel or Alan, the Semitic El, the early Hebrew Yahweh, the Hittite Kumarbi, the Egyptian Set and the Indian Indra. Manetho mentioned Cronus as a Divine King of Egypt. It may be significant that in Babylon Cronus was paralleled by En-lil meaning 'Chief Demon', a Sky God, 'Lord of the Storm', possibly a Spaceman. Berossus, a Priest of Bel at Babylon, who lived about 250 BC at Athens and wrote in Greek 'Babyloniaca', a history based on Chaldean records, believed that ten Kings (Divine Dynastics) reigned 432,000 years, then the God Cronus (Spaceman?) foretold the Flood to Sisithrus, who built an Ark, sent out three birds and landed in the mountains of Armenia. Cronus also advised Sisithrus to write a history from the Beginning and to bury the account in the City of the Sun at Sippara; unfortunately for posterity most records from the remote past were destroyed by the megalomaniac King Nabonasir about 730 BC. Sanchoniathon, the Phoenician historian, fragments of whose manuscript were preserved by Eusebius, described the War between Ouranos and his son, Cronus, who conquered his father and also his own brother, Atlas, explaining in some confusion

'The God Tautus (Thoth) contrived also for Cronus the ensign of his royal power having four eyes in the parts before and in the parts behind two of them closing as in sleep and upon the shoulders four wings two in the act of flying and two reposing as at rest. And the symbol was that Cronus whilst he slept was watching and reposed, while he was awake. And in the manner with respect to his wings, that while he rested he was flying yet rested while he flew. But to the other Gods there were two wings only to each upon his shoulders to intimate that they flew under the control of Cronus, he had also two wings upon his head, the one for the most governing part the mind, and one for the sense."[34]

Surely no writer would invent such a chaotic description as this! This garbled tale must be true; in just such bewilderment would an ignorant peasant describe a Spaceship; indeed Ezekiel's famous sighting by the River Chebar reads little better. The Gods with wings on each shoulder evoke television's 'Superman' or even the American Army commandos equipped with rockets on their bodies for short flights. This account by its very incomprehension does seem a genuine description of war in the skies by someone utterly baffled. Even so could Shakespeare ignorant of modern Space-science have described the ship much better?

'The Old Egyptian Chronicles' preserved by Syncellus state that Cronus and the other twelve Divinities ruled Egypt for 3984 years. Manetho in his 'Aegyptica' records that Cronus preceded Osiris as King of Egypt; a fragment of the lost 'Chronicles of Mabolas' quotes Manetho as referring to the planet Cronos (Saturn) called the 'Shining Star'.

It is most important to realise that although our main source regarding Cronus (Saturn) is to be found in the confused myths of Greece, independent references to him are scattered in the scanty literature left to us from Ancient Egypt and Babylon in addition to parallel Deities as far distant as Britain, Palestine and India. Such world-wide confirmation of the God's influence and his association with the planet, Saturn, seems to suggest that Cronus was no figment of imagination but an actual Spaceman, well-known all over the Earth.

Astronomers deny the possibility of life on Saturn, diameter 75,000 miles, rotating in 29 Earth-years around the Sun 886 million miles distant; its atmosphere with deep clouds appears to be mainly hydrogen with some methane, ammonia, and a complex of ethane, ethylene and acetylene; surface temperatures are said to be minus 80 degrees Centigrade; it is now suggested that radiation is warming the atmosphere and that the planet has internal heat. Scientists, if any, on Saturn, would probably make a similar assessment of our own Earth. The characteristic three flat rings girdling Saturn may have been the debris of a Moon demolished by a Comet, although conventional theory suggests they consist of tiny particles of ice. A noble race of Beings in astral bodies are said to inhabit two of the ten moons, Titan larger than Mercury holds biological interest and might support some form of life. Dino Kraspedon somewhat doubtfully alleges that a Space Intelligence told him Saturn has no atmosphere and is not inhabited; Adamski[35] however writes a vivid report of a trip he made to Saturn in a Spaceship in only nine hours; he describes a world of breath-taking beauty with spacious cities enchanted by divine music and living colours; there Adamski had an inspired interview with an Illumined Master who pitied the plight of Earthlings. Howard Menger,[36] who claims to be a reincarnated Saturnian, gives a somewhat controversial description of an etherean Saturn and lyricises over a Saturnian whom he met in 1956 in an old cabin in the American backwoods; this Wonderman taught him to play the piano in only one lesson, a feat which surprised Menger nearly as much as it surprises us. Both Adamski and Williamson infer that Saturn is the Seat of Justice for all our Solar System. An inspired discipline for ascension to cosmic consciousness was revealed to the Reverend Doctor George King, Founder of the Aetherius Society, an international Metaphysical Order, by Cosmic Intelligences who disclosed that Beings on Saturn have formed themselves into an Advisory Council to which those accepted into the Interplanetary Council of Worlds, send their most highly Evolved Masters, so that they may receive advice, guidance and help from the Saturnians, who give this freely. Dr. George King states that Jesus, the Master from Venus, was delivered to Earth in a Space Satellite, which came from Saturn. Dr George Hunt Williamson[37] records that a Knight of the Solar Cross surveying our Earth in a Spaceship revealed that Saturn was the ancient God of Seed Sowing; as a Man sows, so he reaps; the Saturnians actually did descend to Earth long ago and sowed the seeds of civilisation.

People all over the ancient world held mystic reverence for Saturn; astrologers associated the planet with wisdom inspiring men born under its influence, occultists held Saturnians in great respect suspecting their alleged powers; such beliefs are ridiculed by our scientists although the radio-astronomers do record vibrations from the planets, which may exert some subtle unknown influence on the human mind. The Ancients had some vital reason for venerating Saturn which we cannot fathom. All the accumulated evidence suggests that Cronus symbolised benevolent Invaders from Saturn who usurped the old Dynasty of the Uranid Space Kings and ruled Earth in a Golden Age.

Zeus-Pater (Jupiter) derived his name from the Indian God, Dyaus-Pitar (Deva – God, Pitar – Father), the Sky Father worshipped by most peoples of the ancient world millennia ago, suggesting domination of our Earth by Spacemen. The Vedas associate Dyaus with 'dazzling brightness' and 'lightning' evoking a shining Spaceship. As 'Heavenly Father' he was worshipped like a benevolent King dwelling in a wondrous city in the sky with that same awe with which in those golden days of the British Raj some simple coolie in the slums of Bombay regarded his 'Father', King Edward VII, presiding at banquets in Buckingham Palace. Memory of this Sky-Father persists in human consciousness to this very day. Most Christians pray to 'Our Father which art in Heaven' and picture some benign jovial Gentleman basking on a cloud just waiting to help them; this in fact is how the Sky-Father did appear to the unsophisticated peoples of the Golden Age, when he winged down to their aid like some Missionary bringing golden trinkets to the Hottentots. The early Greeks regarded Zeus as the Supreme God particularly responsible for celestial phenomena, lightning, thunder and the weather; he was portrayed with an eagle as the patron God of flight. Zeus held a feudal Court above Mount Olympus whither he would summon lesser Gods and Goddesses and lay down his divine Law. The Greeks never seriously believed that Zeus lived on Mount Olympus, no tourist climbed to the top to shake hands with God; there were no hordes of pilgrims like the Mahomedans visiting Mecca. Mount Olympus was not far from Macedon, home of Alexander the Great. Had that hero imagined for one moment that Juno and Aphrodite were cavorting on top of Mount Olympus he would have raced his army up the hill instead of trailing to India! Why did lofty cloud-capped Mount Olympus in the North in remote Thessaly exercise such fascination, even reverence for the Greeks when they knew no Gods lived there? The Chinese, the Egyptians, the Babylonians, Ezekiel and observers today, all describe the Spaceships as coming from the North apparently approaching Earth through the Van Allen radiation-belts, opening near the North Pole. Zeus gave the Cretan laws, to Minos on Mount Ida, Shamash gave the law to Hammurabi on a mound in Babylon, Jehovah gave Moses the Ten Commandments on Mount Sinai, Ahura-Mazda inspired Ormuzd on Mount Sabalan. Archangel Gabriel showed Mahomet a golden tablet on the hills near Mecca. In all lands throughout history the Gods are associated with sacred mountains, whither they would summon their Prophets to receive divine instructions. Such veneration of Mount Olympus would suggest that Zeus in his sky-chariot or Spaceship often landed there.

Aeschylus in 'Prometheus Bound' develops Zeus into an omnipotent Ruler of the universe sternly inspiring lofty morality and censuring the follies of fallible Man; as Supreme Lord he was greatly concerned with divine justice and the destiny of the human race. The Greek tragedians elevated Zeus to a transcendent Deity just as, about the same sixth century BC, the Hebrew prophets transformed their tribal Jehovah into an omnipresent, invisible God the Spirit sustaining all Creation. The average Greek ignoring theology loved to think of Zeus as a dignified middle-aged Personage in well-earned retirement after those rumbustious days of his youth, when he fought Gods and Sky-Dragons, destroyed civilisations and seduced every wench in heaven and earth with a virility which made those naughty girls of Athens shudder with desire. Zeus still gloried in a somewhat sedate sex-life; no longer did he disguise himself as a hot-blooded bull, many were the maidens who conceived heroes to the genial Lord on Mount Parnassus. The Priests of Babylon who knew him as Marduk thoughtfully provided a room on a top floor of his Temple, containing a large elegant bed and a golden table, a sanctuary none dared enter save the Bride of the God.[38] The Israelites made a tabernacle designed to Jehovah's own specification,[39] richly furnished, which He could visit in secret; the Bible is discreetly silent on who entertained Him there. Lest such divine lust scandalise all pious believers, it must be mentioned in extenuation that Zeus, alias Jupiter, Marduk or Baal, is now regarded not as a single Entity but as a generic name for Spacemen from the planet Jupiter or one of its Moons, just as American soldiers from Germany to Japan are known to all their dames as Joe.

Jupiter, largest of all the planets with a diameter of 88,700 miles, rotates around the Sun 483 million miles away in nearly twelve years. Astronomers believe the huge globe consists of hydrogen with some ammonia and methane around a layer of liquid metallic hydrogen surrounding a small iron-silicate core. Pioneer 10 in November 1973 photographed Jupiter and telemetered valuable data, confirmed by Pioneer 11 about a year later. Surface temperatures are thought to be about minus 70 degrees Centigrade, although the Pioneer probes detecting strong radiation suggested an enormous heat capacity of the Jovian atmosphere and confirmed an important source of internal heat. Since 1878 Jupiter has been noted for its famous Red Spot 30,000 miles long and 7,000 miles wide; this crimson oval may be some localised atmospheric turbulence. Could the Red Spot be an intelligently controlled asteroid? Dr. G. H. Williamson and Lyman Streeter in 1952 claimed radio-contact with a Jovian Intelligence known as Ankar-22, who lived in Adee, the capital city of Etonya,[40] the native name for the planet. Dino Kraspedon denies life in the rarefied atmosphere of Jupiter but stresses that many of the thirteen Jovian satellites, notably Io and Ganymede, about the size of our own Moon, have atmospheres and conditions similar to Earth with inhabitants like ourselves. The Aetherius Society teaches that ages ago at the time of the explosion of the neighbouring planet Maldek, the inhabitants of Jupiter had reached such a high state of spiritual culture that the planet was used as a reception-centre for the Interplanetary Confederation. Radio-astronomers are particularly intrigued by powerful emissions from Jupiter, which arouse romantic speculation as to whether these bursts of radiation signify intelligent signals or indicate tremendous utilisation of electrical energies by its peoples analogous to the radio-aura which has intensified around our Earth in the last few decades. Some of the Ancients associated Jupiter with great cataclysms such as the submergence of Lemuria and Atlantis, legends say the planet gave birth to Venus causing the phenomena described in 'Exodus' enabling the Israelites to cross the Red Sea. Whatever the truth, the fact remains that the peoples all over the Ancient World regarded this brilliant planet with much more awe than we do. Perhaps they believed that in ages past from Jupiter or its Moons winged down those virile Spacemen to destroy the Golden Age of Saturn and dominate Earth.

Science insists that life evolved from protoplasm in primeval seas, developing throughout vast ages into fishes, mammals and ape-like humanoids, which eventually mutated into monkeys and Man, although after a century's search this 'Missing Link' is still missing. Anthropologists teach that for millions of years Men lived like beasts, then somewhat belatedly chanced to kindle fire, fashion flint tools, hunt, domesticate animals, grow corn in a primitive culture, then suddenly in a few millennia the human race spurted from savagery to our sophisticated selves today. This plausible theory fails to convince Students of Space, who with reasonable logic now believe that Earth was first colonised by Extraterrestrials as we too plan to colonise Mars. Suggestions of a series of civilisations ruled by Spacemen from different planets, a Golden Age, interplanetary wars and the degeneration of mankind to barbarism from which Man is slowly emerging, outrage the scientists, who swear our twentieth century is the loftiest peak in human evolution. Regression from civilisation to savagery contradicts the theory of slow but sure evolution, although in Central Africa it would appear that we today are actually witnessing the degeneration of once-hopeful societies; rule by Spacemen infers that Men mastering super-science not only live on other worlds but in far Antiquity dominated Earth, a hypothesis our scientists seldom consider. The Golden Age is scoffed at as some ancient Utopia, nostalgia for those 'Good Old Days' which never existed, the dream of romantic poets and glib politicians; our Socialists promise a Golden Age tomorrow – or the day after.

Were the Dynasties of the Gods and the Golden Age sung by Hesiod and Ovid restricted solely to Greece, they might be dismissed as local legends; if, as these writers affirm, their sway was world-wide, then independent confirmation should come from countries of which the Greeks had little knowledge. The Divine Dynasties of Uranus–Cronus–Zeus in Greece were chronicled in India as Varuna–Indra–Dyaus, in Babylon as Anu–Enlil–Marduk, in Israel as God–Yahweh–Jehovah, in Iran as Vaya–Ahuramazda–Mithra, in Phoenicia as God–El–Baal, among the Hittites as Anu–Kumarbi–Teshubi, in Egypt possibly by Atum–Osiris–Horus and in Mexico by Ometeotl–Quetzalcoatl–Huitzilopochtli. All over the world myths, though sadly confused, appear to agree that Earth was ruled by three distinct and separate races of Celestials apparently confirming the same three Divine Dynasties in the same epoch remembered everywhere by different names!

Our complementary studies of Spacemen in the Ancient East disclose an Age of Wonder and Wars long ago narrated in ancient Eastern literature without any reference to the myths of Greece. Indra, the War God of India,[41] attended by his warrior Maruts in their golden cars, overwhelmed Varuna and waged war with the giant Asuras, destroying their cities with thunderbolts like nuclear-bombs; later he was supplanted by Dyaus and exiled. Cronus usurped Ouranos and fought the Titans, then was defeated by Zeus and imprisoned in Britain. Those wonderful epics, the 'Ramayana' and the 'Mahabharata' both mention the influence of Indra on Rama and Arjuna, brilliant descriptions of exotic Court life, wars in earth and sky with fantastic weapons, suggest these fascinating scenes depict those fabulous days in prehistoric India during the Golden Age. Sanskrit tales such as the 'Brihat Katha', the 'Harscha Charita' and the 'Panchatantra' tell sparkling romances of

Celestials wenching and warring in that vivacious civilisation beyond the Himalayas, unequalled until the Italian Renaissance. Rama and his descendants ruled India for eleven thousand years, analogous to Divine Dynasties in Tibet, whose first King Shipuye was followed by Seven Heavenly Khri (Thrones) and Two Upper Teng (High Ones), Six Middle Legs (Good Ones), Eight Earthly De (Worldly Monarchs) and Four Lower Tsan (Mighty Kings);[42] folk-lore like 'Gesar of Ling' describes fantastic wars against evil Demons with all the wizardry of those conflicts between Cronus and Zeus.

The Chinese Classic 'Huai-nan-tzu' (Chapter 8) rhapsodises over an idyllic age, when men and animals lived in peace and beauty amid a benevolent climate, injury and crime were unknown, a state of perfection described almost word for word like Hesiod's own account of the Golden Age. The 'Spirits' frequently descended to teach men wisdom but mankind degenerated to wickedness. The 'Shoo-King' (4th part. Chap. XXVII) describes how the Lord Chang-ty (a King of the Divine Dynasty) instructed Chang and Lhy to sever communication between Heaven and Earth. Chinese legends[43] gloat in horrific details of tremendous aerial battles between fire-breathing dragons symbolising Spaceships waged with death-rays and lightning-darts shrivelling the cities of Earth to ash. Stone reliefs on the Wu-Lieng shrines about AD 150 depict the Celestials Fu-hsi and his Consort, Nu-kwa, with human bodies merging into serpents' tails intertwined together; serpents or dragons were associated with Wise Teachers from Space. When the world was convulsed with fire and flood and monsters devoured the stricken people Nu-kwa brought universal peace, the 'Feng-su-tung-yi' describes Nu-kwa as creating men from yellow earth. The 'Lung-heng' or 'Critical Essays' of Weng Ch'ung, first century AD, mentioned a cosmic war between the legendary King Chuan-hai about 2500 BC with King-kung, a human rebel, later described as a horned monster with serpent's body; enraged by failure, King-Kung crashed into Mount Pu-chan in the North-West smashing this pillar of heaven to change the orientation between earth and sky. Some legends state that the hero Yu 'came down from on high' on a winged dragon to rebuild civilisation after the great floods, suggesting a Spaceman. Yu is said to have held a great assembly on a mountain; this Celestial visited the peoples of most of the world; at his command two officials measured the Earth and found it to be a perfect square roughly 77,833 miles and 75 paces on each side, hardly the precision expected from Spacemen. All the Emperors of China believed themselves to be descendants of the race of Divine Kings who according to the manuscript 'Tchi' ruled for 18,000 years.[44]

The Mikados of Japan claim direct descent from Amaterasu, Goddess of the Sun. The 'Kojiki' and 'Nihongi' delight with Celestial Divinities Izanagi and Izanami descending in a Heavenly Rocking-Boat to the cherry-blossom islands of Japan; the diverting quarrel between Amaterasu and her boisterous brother, Susanowo, seems a polite reference to War in Space. A wall-painting in a Chip San tomb shows an ancient Japanese King welcoming Seven Sun Discs, terra-cotta figurines called Jomon Dogus resemble the famous Martian of the Tassili rock-paintings and suggest Oannes the Being who taught civilisation to Babylon.

The Ancient Egyptians believed in the 'First Time', when Ra, the greatest of all the Gods, ruled the Lands of the Nile; in this Golden Age of universal peace and beauty, the Gods and Goddesses governed Egypt in the same manner as the Pharaohs with whom they were more or less acquainted. Osiris taught the Egyptians civilisation then journeyed to many lands to civilise other people, suggesting a world-wide culture; after his murder by Set, his son, Horus, waged war in Earth and Sky against Set flying a winged Sun-disc or Spaceship, aided by magic weapons from Thoth, possibly a Spaceman. Hathor once took the Divine Eye (a Spacecraft?) and devastated the Earth, presumably confirming the cosmic War of the Greek Classics. The Egyptian 'The Book of the Dead' teems with references to the 'Shining Ones', the 'Spirits of Light' who fight the 'Sons of Darkness' with magical light-beams and annihilating rays evoking the fantastic conflict in the skies of Old India and China. When the Divine Dynasties were followed by human Kings, each Pharaoh imagined himself as the Son of Ra and regarded his mother's husband as his father in name only. For thousands of years the divinity of Pharaoh, the God-King, was the fundamental creed governing every aspect of Egyptian life; all the Egyptians believed their divinely-born Pharaoh to be physically perfect transcending their mortal selves; somewhat embarrassing for Pharaoh since he was obliged to relieve himself in secret. Manetho in his 'Aegyptica' states that the first God-King was Hephaestus, succeeded by his son, Helios or Ra (Sun God) then Cronus, Osiris, Typhon (Set) and Horus; after the Gods came the Demi-Gods, Kings and Spirits of the Dead (Spacemen?) in periods totalling 26,000 years. Simplicius in the sixth century AD wrote that the Egyptians kept astronomical observations for 630,000 years, Diogenes Laertius mentioned 48,865 years. Panodorus, an Egyptian Monk, stated that the Egregori (Watchers or Angels) descended to Earth, Syncellus quoted Egyptian tablets called 'The Old Chronicles' declaring that Helios (Ra) ruled for three myriads of years; Berossus detailed six Dynasties of Gods.[45] Egyptian Priests told Herodotus that after Heracles and other Gods, there were three hundred and forty-one generations of Kings ruling for eleven thousand and three hundred years. The Priests of Sais described to Solon how Egypt was threatened by the Atlanteans twelve thousand years ago. Herodotus records the startling revelation by the Egyptian Priests that 'the sun had removed from his proper course four times and had risen where he now setteth, and set where he now riseth', confirming cataclysms mentioned by the Hindus and the Chinese, also the degenerating Ages of Mankind described by Hesiod. If the Gods ruled Egypt, they would surely rule not only Greece a few hundred miles away but all the Middle East.

The Sumerians believed in a Golden Age when Earth was ruled by Gods, then Heroes and superhuman Kings.[46] The Sumerian King List mentions eight antediluvian Kings reigning 241,000 years, confirmed by similar Persian traditions teaching that before Adam the world was ruled by wicked Atlantean Giants then by beneficent Peris, Sons of Wisdom, possibly Spacemen. Proclus in 'Timaeus' Book I states that the Assyrians preserved memorials of Kings for 270,000 years. A cryptic text[47] in Babylonian and Assyrian from the Library of Assurbanipal describes how Etana, one of the first Kings after the Flood, was carried to heaven by an eagle; another version is interpreted as revealing that King Etana was transported to the Moon, Mars and Venus in a Spaceship then returned to his palace. Berossus describes Oannes, a Being with a body like a fish but human feet, having beneath a fish's head, a human head, presumably signifying a Celestial in a space-suit, who taught the early Babylonians agriculture, science, letters and art; he was followed by 'semi-daemons' called Annedotus, Evadocus, Evengames, Ennebalus and Anementus, possibly Space-Teachers. The Gods, Anu, Enlil and Merodach (Marduk) probably paralleled the Space Kings known to the Greeks as Ouranos, Cronus and Zeus; Merodach like Zeus fought a Sky Monster. The Genesis story of Babel when the Giants tried to storm Heaven is not mentioned in any Babylonian tablet extant to us, it may refer to the War between Zeus and the Titan, Prometheus. Those wonderful poems in Sumerian telling of Ishtar's love for the murdered Tammuz recall the Egyptian legend of Osiris and Isis, also the plaintive Greek myth of Aphrodite mourning slain Adonis; the adventures of Gilgamesh which enchanted Babylon resemble the exploits of Kret of Ugarit and the wanderings of Ulysses, suggesting common origin, perhaps that ancient civilisation was ruled by the Space Kings.

Canaan (as Syria and Palestine were then known) was a land-bridge between Africa, Europe and Asia, a focal point between Minoan Crete, Greece, the Hittites in Anatolia, Egypt, Babylon and India far beyond. The discovery in 1929 at Ras Shamra in Syria of texts in Ugaritic script reveal astonishing similarities between early Greek and early Hebrew literature, having affinities with the cultures of Egypt and Babylon, which for many centuries influenced the whole Levant;[48] intriguing parallels could be traced to the Sanskrit epics of India. Adam alone in the Garden of Eden seems symbolism for the men of Hesiod's Golden Age, who lived in an earthly paradise without wives or daughters; the 'Talmud' states that Adam was married to Lilith, a 'demoness', possibly a Spacewoman. The Creation of Eve, the 'Lord's' expulsion of Adam and Eve from Eden to a harsh world probably parallels the decline to the Silver Age. 'Genesis', Chapter III, v 24 states that the 'Lord' drove out Adam and placed at the east of the Garden of Eden Cherubim with flaming swords; such display of force shows that Adam did not leave Eden peacefully of his own free will. What man today basking in sunshine on perpetual holiday in sweet indolence dallying with a beautiful wife would willingly forsake it all to till the soil with the sweat of his brow? Reading between the lines of 'Genesis', Adam feared Eve more than the 'Lord'. This 'Lord' was no intangible 'Spirit' but a powerful Space Being, who had to summon a squadron of Cherubim, winged globes or fiery wheels, to drive Adam from Eden with flaming swords, symbolism for fantastic weapons. The conflict between the 'Lord' and Adam evokes some confused memory of the War between Cronus and Zeus. 'Genesis' VI, v 4 mentions the Giants on Earth in those days, also the Sons of God who came unto the Daughters of Men. The Sons of God, the Ben Elohim, most revered Beings in Jewish traditions recalling the Els, Sons of Wisdom, engendered Nephilim or Giants, who like the Titan, Prometheus, challenged the 'Lord' himself. The 'Book of Enoch' complains of the 'Fallen Angels' seducing women and teaching men magic; an intriguing reference in the 'Dead Sea Scrolls' suggests that a 'Watcher' or 'Holy One' consorted with Methusaleh's daughter-in-law, Bathenosh, and fathered Noah.

Hesiod surely tells the same 'Genesis' story in his 'Theogany'.

'Now all the Gods were divided through strife; for at the very time Zeus, who thunders on high, was meditating marvellous deeds even to mingle storm and tempest over the boundless earth and already he was hastening to make an utter end of the race of mortal men, declaring that he would destroy the lives of the Demi-Gods, that the children of the Gods should not mate with wretched mortals, seeing their fate with their own eyes; but that the blessed Gods henceforth, even as aforetime, should have their living and their habitations apart from men. But those who were born of Immortals and of mankind, verily Zeus laid toil and sorrow upon sorrow.'

The 'Lord' and Zeus may be identified with the Chinese Lord Chang-ty, who instructed Chang and Lhy to sever communication between Heaven and Earth. The Spacemen possibly influenced by political difficulties on their own planets, realised the difficulty of ruling rebellious Earth and like the British abandoned their Empire; thereafter they restricted their surveillance to solitary visits to inspire chosen Initiates guiding civilisation.

Evidence of a Golden Age ruled by Divine Kings followed by change of climate, cataclysms devastating our Earth and plunging Man to barbarism, is world-wide; it will suffice to summarise corroboration from countries not previously considered. In Britain Celtic bards sang of proud Angels driven forth from Heaven, who fathered men, Gods mounting sky-dragons, wielding magic weapons; the Norse scalds recited sagas of Odin, the Sky Father warring against the Mountain Giants, Thor and his mighty hammer; Freya, Goddess of Love; all similar to those myths of Greece. Aborigines in Australia tell of an idyllic 'Dream Time'; the Polynesians of Malekula remember 'winged women' from the skies; natives of the Caroline Isles describe Wondrous Beings in flying-machines. Hawaiians talk of solar-boats; Eskimos smile of Great White Spirits; the peoples of Vietnam evoke their Divine Kings; in Cambodia the ruins of Anghor Wat bear sculptures depicting Beings like Oannes, the Space Teacher of Babylon; the sands of the Gobi are said to enshroud a fabulous civilisation inspired from the skies. North American tribes in British Columbia boast of war waged against the Sky People when the Indians tried to climb a ladder of arrows storming a hole in the sky recalling the Tower of Babel. The Mayas remember four World Ages destroyed by disasters and the benevolence of their culture-hero, Quetzalcoatl; in Guatemala the 'Popol Vuh' describes feathered serpents, Gods flying down to Earth.[49]

All peoples in all parts of the world treasure oral traditions of an Age of Wonder in far Antiquity, which agree with the evidence advanced for those great civilisations of Lemuria and Atlantis long ago. It is fascinating to realise that had all those marvellous myths of Greece been lost, we could have fabricated them from the legends of other countries. The Greek myths were not unique, the Gods of Greece existed under other names in other lands; Hesiod and Ovid merely repeated the same tales told all over the world.

Viewed in perspective of world-wide race-memories and our present awareness of Extraterrestrial visitations, Uranus, Cronus and Zeus, with those Ages of Gold, Silver, Bronze, now Iron, emerge from that miasma of myth into shining reality. The Gods of Greece now live for us with all the splendour of Spacemen.

Chapter Four
Ancient Athens

The War between Atlantis and Athens twelve thousand years ago recorded by Solon and retold by Plato poses implications so profound that scholars completely deny its reality since acceptance must surely revolutionise our whole conception of European culture. Solon, universally honoured as one of the greatest sages in Antiquity, influences our laws even today; Plato with his lofty philosophy has enlightened thinkers until our Space Age. These two great Minds symbolising the genius of Greece are justly extolled for their wisdom, idealism and intellect, which down the centuries inspire the civilisation of the West, yet by some fantastic aberration in human thought, their most fundamental contribution, Atlantis, is rejected.

In his 'Timaeus' Plato quotes the Egyptian Priests at Sais, who told Solon that in about 10,000 BC Kings of Atlantis with great and marvellous powers ruled Libya and Europe as far as Italy then launched immense onslaught on the lands of the Mediterranean, attacking Egypt and Greece.

'And then it was, Solon, that the manhood of your State showed itself conspicuous for valour and might in the sight of all the world. For it stood pre-eminent above all in gallantry and all warlike arts, and acting partly as leader of the Greeks and partly standing alone by itself, when deserted by all others, after encountering the deadliest perils, it defeated the invaders and reared a trophy, whereby it saved from slavery such as were not as yet enslaved and all the rest of us who dwell within the bounds of Heracles it ungrudgingly set free.'[10]

Such Churchillian oratory recalls those proud and perilous days in 1940 when the victorious Axis Powers overran these same lands and Britain, abandoned by her Allies, faced the might of Germany alone to save the world.

Comparison between the Atlantean invasion of Europe

and the Nazi blitz-krieg twelve millennia later across the same countries may not be so fanciful as it probably appears. Psychics believe that both wars were waged by the Powers of Darkness, the victories won by Athens and Britain, Saviour of Civilisation, were inspired by the Angels of Light. Atlantis was totally destroyed, the evil spirit of the Third Reich exorcised. Strategists sceptical of occultism and Atlantis, agree that if the Atlantean War really did happen as Plato asserts, the conflict must have borne a startling resemblance to our own struggle against Hitler. The grandiose design to conquer a continent demanded dynamic leadership, meticulous planning, political genius and military skill backed by arrogant ideology, powerful armaments, organised industry and civil mobilisation presupposing advanced technology. Theopompus of Chios quotes Silenus as estimating the Atlantean armies as ten million men, a fantastic force, transport from their island in the middle of the Atlantic to assault the shores of Europe surely parallels the American G.I.s assembled for D-Day. Plato credits the Kings of Atlantis with 'great and marvellous powers', presumably weapons not available in his own fifth century BC. Could he have meant the flying-machines, death-rays and nuclear-bombs described by the occultists and those ancient writers of the 'Ramayana', which the old Indians are believed to have inherited from the Lemurians and Atlanteans? Though Plato in all his other erudite works reveals no technology, his 'Phaedrus'[51] does discourse on Winged Gods descending to Earth and working wonders, possibly traditions of aerial craft; like all Greeks he was superstitious of the lightning and thunderbolts of Zeus. Perhaps we should not be too critical of Plato, in his fascinating though incomplete account of Atlantis, he paints a more inspiring picture of 10,000 BC than all those depressing views of our modern historians.

If the Atlanteans wielded such armed might, what powers were possessed by the Athenians, who routed the invading hordes in titanic battle, then pursued the fleeing enemy across North Africa to the Western Sea? Did some Athenian Montgomery win an ancient battle at Alamein?

Athens, the dominant State in Greece, possibly led a Confederation of Balkan countries, her alliance with Egypt suggests considerable political and cultural prestige, her successful defiance when fighting alone, then her subsequent defeat of the Atlanteans surely prove her spiritual and martial heroism, anticipating Marathon and Salamis, which freed Europe from the invader. This great war like those conflicts in the 'Ramayana' and 'Mahabharata' would be waged with contrasting weapons, some more primitive, others more advanced than our own today. Our twentieth century is characterised by the internal combustion-engine, oil is the life-blood of our modern world, and has dominated the politics and social structure of our times. The last two wars, deprived of tanks, lorries and aeroplanes, would have been fought by cavalry, like Waterloo, in conjunction with frightful electrical weapons since science would probably have developed in a different direction. Aircraft in far Antiquity were apparently motivated by radiation devices. Immanuel Velikovsky claims that all our terrestrial oil rained down from the hydro-carbonaceous atmosphere of Venus during that planet's approach to Earth as recently as 1500 BC, so the ancient world could have no technology like our own. Traditions insist that Initiates of Atlantis and presumably Adepts in Athens utilised static-electricity by techniques not known to us now; they are believed to have probed into the subtle forces of the universe and developed sonic, vibrational and disintegrating weapons including terrible sidereal-bombs. Science in most ancient times evolved on mental planes unlike our physical materialism. Initiates mastered psycho-magical powers, possibly learned from their Space-Teachers; remnants of this cosmic wisdom still persist among the shamans and witch-doctors of primitive peoples, degenerate descendants of those proud civilisations of the past.

The Sanskrit Classics, recording traditions of that Golden Age when Gods mingled with men, glow with enchanting descriptions of aerial-cars, annihilating-darts, anti-missile-missiles, laser-beams like heat-rays, presupposing sophisticated guidance-systems controlled by a few Initiates; the footmen and cavalry used slings, javelins, swords, bows and arrows; similar weapons existed in Atlantis and contemporary Athens. Such contrast in arms is not so incredible as it may appear; in armies today nuclear-weapons are restricted to a specialist élite and are not standard issue to all soldiers like rifles. Gunpowder was known in Ancient India as in China and probably in Atlantis and old Athens too, but its use was limited by the devastating annihilation-bombs. Society in Antiquity consisted usually of a small ruling caste isolated socially by a vast gulf from the uneducated populace, possibly modelled on the earliest civilisations when the Divine Dynasties or Space Kings ruled the peoples of Earth. The 'Bundhasvamin Brihat Katha Shlokasanigraha', a wonderful Sanskrit romance from old Nepal telling entrancing tales of Divine Beings winging down from the skies, wenching and warring in the exotic lands of the Himalayas, reveals that aerial chariots and Space-cars were built with surprising ease but the secret of their construction was restricted to a few Adepts who jealously guarded it from the masses. The 'Brihat Katha' discussing the manufacture of aerial craft states that 'As for flying-machines the Yavanas (the Greeks) know them'. The 'Harschá Charita' of Northern India mentions 'Kakavarma, being curious of marvels, was carried away, no one knows whither, on an artificial aerial car made by a Yavana (Greek) condemned to death.' It intrigues us to learn that the peoples of Ancient India should attribute the knowledge of building Spaceships to be a secret of the Greeks. Surely there must have been some reason for this belief, now lost to us?

Plato in the 'Critias' states that once upon a time the whole Earth was shared among the Gods or Spacemen. Poseidon took Atlantis. Hephaestus and Athene in their love of wisdom preferred Greece. Athene on the craggy rock of the Acropolis founded Athens, city of the arts and elegance.

Philologists agree that the name 'Athene' is pre-Grecian, it may be Mycenaean or even pure Cara-Maya, the language of lost Lemuria. If Athene was a Space Being, her name might echo the language of another planet. It is surely significant that the name of immortal Athens springs from some ancient tongue not Greek. The oldest representations of Athene were the 'palladia', stones which were said to have come from the sky, later these stones were replaced by statues in wood which had the same celestial origin. The writer, Giuseppe Aprile, quotes Apollonius as stating, 'This ancient statue measured three cubits (1.32 metres), its feet united, it held in the right hand a lance and in the left a spindle, like an image of death and destiny.' Peter Kolosimo[52] cites the suggestion that this space-device represented a terrible 'Palladium-laser' capable of causing immense destruction. In 708 BC during the reign of Numa Pompilius an 'ancile' or 'bronze shield' fell from the sky and was revered by the priests of Rome.

The prehistory of Europe still has surprises. Soviet archaeologists have discovered near Vladimir, north of Moscow, two tombs about twenty-seven thousand years old. The grave at a depth of three metres contained the bones of two boys. Among the remains were the remnants of garments apparently establishing that in that distant epoch men wore shirts, leather trousers, boots lined with fur and headgear 'sewn with little pieces of bone'.[53] Cave-drawings at Lussac-le-Château in France show people wearing clothes. Should we be surprised?

The 'London Mirror', Vol. 36, 4th July, 1840, discussing ships embedded in the Earth states that in 1462 men in a mine near Berne, Switzerland, found a ship a hundred fathoms deep in the ground with anchors of iron and sails of linen with the remains of forty men.[54]

This conception of an advanced civilisation in Europe at about 10,000 BC does not necessarily invalidate the conventional panorama painted by prehistorians of a desolate continent peopled by nomadic hunters, isolated lake-dwellers and primitive cave-men. Geologists support the Greek legends telling of vast earthquakes ravaging Libya and driving the waters from Lake Trithonis, presumed birthplace of Athene, to form the Sahara Desert. At the same time the Atlas and Spanish peninsulas collapsed, Atlantis submerged and the great Mediterranean Lake cracked open at the Pillars of Hercules. Europe too must have suffered immense devastation. With their civilisation destroyed, Neanderthal Men hunted bison with flint-tipped spears near the retreating sheets of ice, in the South-West the broad-skulled, impressively intelligent Cro-Magnons and Aurignacians enchanted their cave-walls with those magical paintings of animals and medicine-men, some of the sketches like the Tassili frescoes vaguely resemble Spaceships and Spacemen.

Plato suggests that after the devastation Greece was almost uninhabited. Prehistorians teach that Neolithic Villages appeared about 5000 BC,[55] but civilisation is generally ascribed to the Sesklo tribes who two thousand years later surged into the Peloponnese from Asia Minor. This opinion seems somewhat doubtful in view of the highly civilised site of Cata Huyuk on the high plateau of Anatolia in Central Turkey which apparently enjoyed a highly sophisticated society as long ago as 6800 BC. Soon after 2000 BC Indo-Europeans invaded from the North bringing the Greek language; about 1600 BC settlers from Minoan Crete established the wonderful Mycenaean Bronze Age, destroyed by the virile Achaeans from the North-West, possibly impelled by some cosmic cataclysm ravaging Hyperborea; in 1200 BC[56] these heroes of Homer's 'Iliad' sacked Troy. Archaeologists admit to much dispute regarding the early settlement of Greece and its links with Minoan Crete; perhaps the decipherment of the Cretan Linear A script and new discoveries will considerably revise present opinions. About 1000 BC hordes of Dorians swept down from the Danube; the newcomers brought the use of iron from the Hittites, borrowed the alphabet from the Phoenicians and soon built their famous cities, Athens, Sparta, Corinth, Thebes, to grace Antiquity. The history of classical Greece, whose great playwrights, philosophers and poets still inspire our Western civilisation, spanned a surprisingly short period from the First Olympiad in 776 BC until conquest by the Romans in 133 BC.

It is strange that Plato, whose transcendent philosophies inspired the scholars of the West for so many centuries, should be completely ignored when he narrates the history of his own country; today two thousand years later we assume we know Ancient Greece better than he did. Let us hearken to this noblest of all Greeks extolling the glories of his ancient land!

In the 'Critias' Plato describes how the Gods (Spacemen?)

'... planted as native to the soil men of virtue and ordained to their mind the mode of government. And of these citizens, the names are preserved but their works have vanished owing to the repeated destruction of their successors and the length of the intervening period. For as was said before, the stock that survived on each occasion was a remnant of unlettered mountaineers, which had heard the names only of the rulers and but little besides of their works.'

Plato goes on to stress, what we should well know, that after each cataclysm the scattered survivors for many generations were too occupied rebuilding society to worry about the former civilisation destroyed.

'For legendary lore and the investigation of Antiquity are visitants that come to cities in company with leisure, when they see that men are already furnished with the necessities of life and not before.'

The statement of Solon, quoted by Plato, asserted

'... that the Egyptian Priests, in describing the war of that period mentioned most of those names (of the Ancients) ... such as those of Cecrops and Erectheus and Erictonius and Erysichton and most of the other names which are recorded of the various heroes before Theseus ... and in like manner also the names of the women.'

About a hundred years later Egyptian Priests told Hecateus of Miletus, a most distinguished historian and geographer, and afterwards Herodotus, whose History is surely the most fascinating travelogue in all Antiquity, that they could trace the Kings of Egypt back for eleven thousand three hundred and forty years. The Priests revealed that in the eleven thousand years prior to Herodotus the axis of our Earth became considerably displaced; four times the Sun twice appearing to rise in the West, probably only national pride made the Egyptians swear that their own country was not affected.

The tragic destinies of the House of Pelops, grandson of Zeus, who gave his name to the Peloponnese, proved a favourite theme for classical poets. Atreus, son of Pelops, was usurped by his brother, Thyestes, who seduced his wife, Adrope, and seized the throne of Mycenae. Apollodorus in 'Epitome' II, 10-3, states

> 'But Zeus sent Hermes to Atreus and told him to stipulate with Thyestes that Atreus should be King (of Mycenae) if the sun should go backwards and when Thyestes agreed, the sun set in the east; hence the Deity having plainly attested the usurpation of Thyestes, Atreus got the Kingdom and banished Thyestes.'

Ovid in 'Tristia' ii, 391, and 'Ars Amatori' i, 32, Hyginus, Fab. 88 and 258, Seneca, 'Thyestes' 776, and Martial, iii, 45, all claimed that the sun reversed its course in the sky not in order to demonstrate the right of Atreus to wear the crown but in horror at the King for murdering his two young nephews and serving their flesh at a banquet for their father, Thyestes; the interpretation of Sophocles in his lost tragedy 'Atreus' or 'The Mycenaeans'. Servius in his learned Commentary on Virgil's 'Aeneid' suggested that Atreus was an astronomer, who first calculated an eclipse, thus surpassing his less scientific brother, Thyestes, a rationalist explanation for the apparent contrary revolution of the sun in ancient times.

The insistence by Plato in the 'Critias' that repeated convulsions had devastated our Earth confirmed the ancient traditions of World Ages taught by the Hindus, Mayas, Irish and other peoples of Antiquity.

In 250 BC Berossus in 'Babyloniaca' described the Divine Kings of Babylon; Manetho in 'Aegyptica' lists the Divine Dynasties of Egypt; they probably allied with the Athenians to resist the onslaught of the Atlanteans.

Greece about 10,000 BC was a most excellent land with great abundance of water, retentive loamy soil, great forests on the mountains and boundless pasturage for flocks of sheep in a benign climate of well-tempered seasons. Plato excuses the present barrenness of his country by explaining with persuasive conviction

> '... since many great convulsions took place during the 9000 years – for such was the number of years from that time to this – the soil which has kept breaking away from the high lands during these ages

and these disasters, forms no pile of sediment worth mentioning, as in other regions, but keeps sliding away, ceaselessly and disappearing in the deep. And just as happens in small islands, what now remains compared with what then existed, is like the skeleton of a sick man, all the fat and soft earth having wasted away, and only the bare framework of the land being left ..."[87]

Athens twelve thousand years ago was a spacious city, though somewhat austere, since display of gold and silver was forbidden; people avoided luxurious ostentation and meanness, they built pleasant houses inhabited down the generations by their descendants completely unaltered. The military class were originally set apart from the general community by the Divine Heroes (Spacemen?) and dwelled on the exclusive upper slopes of the mountain around the Temple of Athens and Hephaestus, which may have been a landing-place for Spaceships.

In our present age of alarming birth-rate it chastens us to learn that the ancient Athenians

'... watched carefully that their own numbers, of both men and women, who were neither too young nor too old to fight, should remain for all time so nearly as possible the same, namely about 20,000 ...'

Plato delights in concluding that the old Athenians

'... were famous throughout all Europe and Asia, both for their bodily beauty and for the perfection of their moral excellence, and were of all men then living the most renowned.'

Like Atlantis the greatness of ancient Athens was swept away by cataclysm.

'... the action of a single night of extraordinary rain has crumbled it away and made it bare of soil, when earthquakes occurred simultaneously with the third of the disastrous floods, which preceded the destructive deluge in the time of Deucalion ...'

The earthquakes devastating Jugoslavia, Greece and Turkey during our own times support Plato's complaint.

In the 'Timaeus' the Egyptian Priests of Sais stated

'You are ignorant of the fact that the noblest and most perfect race amongst men were born in the land where you now dwell, and from them both you yourself are sprung and the whole of your existing city, out of some little seed, that chanced to be left over, but this has escaped your notice because for many generations the survivors died with no power to express themselves in writing. For verily at one time, Solon, before the greatest destruction by water, what is now the Athenian State was the bravest in war and supremely well-organised also in all respects. It is said that it possessed the most splendid works of art and the noblest polity of any nation under heaven of which we have heard tell.'

Deucalion was son of the hero, Prometheus, the Titan, who warred against the Gods and stole fire from heaven in a hollow tube and taught civilisation to men. Our new knowledge of Spaceships suggests that Prometheus stole nuclear secrets, possibly from the planet Jupiter, then returned to defend Earth against invading Spacemen. Later cataclysm ravaged Earth, destroying almost all mankind; Deucalion and his cousin, Pyrrha, built a ship like Noah and floated to safety; their son, Hellen, became a King in Thessaly, his descendants gave his name to Hellas, that ancient land of Greece.

This wonderful story of Athens told by Plato seems confirmed by legends all over the world, recalling a great civilisation long ago, when men on Earth fought Invaders from Space, then suffered calamitous destruction.

What has been, shall be again! In ten thousand years, time will prehistorians deny our modern London or swear we did not exist?

Man is much older than historians imagine. Dr. Louis Leakey, the noted anthropologist, whose discoveries of most ancient fossils in Kenya are revolutionising our conception of Man, believed that the split between ape and 'near'-man from a common ancestor occurred between forty and fifty million years ago. Eleven fossilised jaw-fragments from nine individuals found in Kenya have been dated by Mr. Jack Miller of Cambridge University as between nineteen and twenty million years old. Hominids of the Oligocene period, twenty-five million years ago, have been excavated by American anthropologists near Fayum in Egypt. For a million generations Man has lived on Earth; the first men may not have evolved from an ape-like ancestor as generally believed, cultured Beings could have landed here from some advanced planet to colonise our world or have been 'ship-wrecked' here and marooned like those ill-fated Dropas in the mountains of China.

If Evolution does proceed by infinitely slow progression and not by sudden mutations caused by cosmic cataclysms or fluctuations in cosmic radiation, then in a few hundred generations our descendants, a little wiser, perhaps a little sadder, will differ only slightly from ourselves. Our ancestors twelve thousand years ago in physique and mentality must surely have closely resembled us; it seems absurd for historians to suggest that for millions of years men lived like animals then suddenly ascended from caves to Space-capsules. Millions of years ago great civilisations could have flourished all over the Earth; continents suffer constant change, are we to deny early Man merely because our archaeologists cannot excavate his cities now under the sea?

In 1962 Professor Walter Matthes of Hamburg University announced a sensational discovery revolutionising current theories of human antiquity. Near the River Elbe German prehistorians found five hundred stones with flint drawings of men's heads at least 200,000 years old depicted with an artistry quite different from the cave-paintings of late Neanderthal times; some of the sketches showed animals of the Ice Age. Rock pictures on cave walls in the Val Cosmonique and the Swiss Alps resemble human beings in space-suits and helmets with antennae, breath-filters or night-sight devices. Similar drawings or figurines like the Japanese dogu have also been found in Australia, Ferghana, Uzbekhistan, and near the city of Navoi in Soviet Central Asia, all suggest association with Oannes, the Teacher of Babylon, and the famous 'Martian' of the Tassili frescoes in the Sahara. Such prehistoric drawings or sculptures evoke those intriguing carvings of noble faces on the lofty desert plateau of Marcahuasi in the Andes and the fascinating petroglyphs in the Grand Canyon recalling some vanished civilisations of the past, perhaps Visitants from the stars.

Some of the peoples of far Antiquity had an astonishing sophisticated knowledge of the Earth vastly surpassing the narrow horizon of the cavemen. One of the most exact sciences must be cartography; the making of precise maps demands detailed geographical, mathematical and astronomical study presupposing keen, enquiring, adventurous minds, which had already explored the world and mastered the difficult art of mapping it.

It is generally agreed that Christopher Columbus was inspired by a map of the great cartographer, Toscanelli, a fascinating drawing which showed from right to left the coastline of Europe and the unknown Western Ocean extending to the islands of Japan, China and India, inviting adventurous mariners to seek the fabulous Indies by sailing West. After years of frustration Columbus finally persuaded Queen Isabella of Spain to provide him with three small ships, and in 1492 with a cut-throat crew he braved the Atlantic to re-discover America. Startling evidence now suggests that though Toscanelli's map did not show America, Columbus was aware of that continent's existence, a secret shared by a few Initiates and scholars. Columbus is said to have been greatly influenced by Seneca's 'Medea' describing the voyage of Jason and the Argonauts for the Golden Fleece with fascinating geographical traditions.[58]

In the early sixteenth century, Piri Reis,[59] a popular Admiral of the Turkish fleet sweeping the Mediterranean to challenge Christendom, wrote his memoirs, 'Bahriya', the 'Book of the Sea'. Piri Reis was a cultured and accomplished nobleman, who spoke many languages and developed that astonishing versatility, so characteristic of his more famous contemporaries in Renaissance times; a great seaman, he contributed heroically to the rise of the Ottoman Empire; today he is honoured as a scholar and cartographer, whose astounding maps are suddenly revolutionising our whole conception of Antiquity. We in the West forget that during the Middle Ages science was fostered by the Arabs, who inherited the learning of the Greeks; the capture of Constantinople in 1453 which drove scholars westwards to promote the Renaissance, left the Turks in possession of all the treasures of Byzantium, the greatest libraries in the world with the old and erudite manuscripts from Greece and the countries of Asia. In his 'Baḥriya', which contained picturesque descriptions of Mediterranean ports and 215 exquisitely drawn maps, Piri Reis claimed to possess about twenty secret and most ancient maps[60] including some from the East, of which only he in the whole of Europe had knowledge. Piri Reis possessed a map actually made by Columbus himself, acquired from a slave who sailed with Columbus but was later captured by Piri's uncle, Kemal Reis.

In the 'Baḥriya' Piri Reis stated that Columbus knew precisely where he was going, hence his sublime confidence when his crew nearly mutinied and begged to turn back; Columbus was inspired by an ancient book which depicted the Mare Tenebrosum, Sea of Darkness, bounded by islands in the west; this knowledge had prompted him to beseech aid from most of the monarchs of Europe. The Turkish Admiral claimed that this famous book dated from Alexander the Great, it mentioned that the natives were fond of glass trinkets, so Columbus duly pacified them with such gifts. The Egyptian and Greek Mystery Schools probably did preserve maps of the world before and after the destruction of Lemuria and Atlantis; Initiates of the Secret Wisdom would surely possess some map showing America. Seafaring traditions from ancient times told of a vast continent called by the Greeks 'Antichtone', the land of the Antipodes, now Antarctica. The Phoenicians, those great mariners of Antiquity, must surely have reached America, today the Atlantic has been crossed in rowing-boats. Hyatt Verrill and other prehistorians claim to have found many traces of Phoenician influences on the coasts of North and South America. Discovery of America is now generally credited to the Vikings.

The celebrated Map of Gloreanus dated 1510 in the Library at Rome shows not only both the Americas from Canada to Tierra del Fuego but also the North and South Pacific, posing speculations difficult to resolve without admitting world-wide navigation long ago.

Piri Reis, a meticulous and erudite cartographer, drew two maps of the world, one in 1513, the other in 1528 in the reign of Soliman the Magnificent, compiled from those rare and ancient maps in his collection. The Reis Maps on coloured parchment are adorned with fascinating sketches of strange peoples, monsters and ships, annotated in elegant Turkish script; more startling to our modern eyes are the precise delineations of North and South America with mountain-ranges in Canada and Alaska, most astounding of all the coastline of an ice-free Antarctica. Both these maps were preserved in the Museums of the Topkopi Palace at Istanbul for hundreds of years, apparently lost until 1929 when fragments were found by M. B. Halil Eldem, Director of the National Museum. In 1953 a Turkish naval officer presented a copy to the United States Hydrographical Bureau, where for many years it was studied by Arlington H. Mallery and I. Walters, specialists in ancient maps.

The mapping of the spherical Earth on a flat surface poses highly technical problems in trigonometry, the excellence and accuracy of the Piri Reis map proved that its original compilers possessed great geographical and mathematical knowledge equalling our own. Years of research were required by Professor Charles H. Hapgood at the State College of Keene in New Hampshire before the map's co-ordinates could be resolved and the map re-orientated to the Mercator projection adopted today. Amazed at the uncanny accuracy charting continents believed unknown so long ago, Professor Hapgood extended his studies; maps of the great Ptolemy (AD 140) showed Greenland half-covered with ice though Germany had glaciers unknown in historical times; the Map of the Brothers Zeno in AD 1300 revealed Greenland as ice-free with rivers actually named, confirmed by a 12th century Chinese map hitherto thought fabulous. After consideration of world-wide legends Professor Hapgood published his findings in 'Maps of the ancient Sea-Kings, Evidence of advanced Civilisation'; he concluded that these maps were made by a highly cultured people, whose civilisation was destroyed about ten thousand years ago by a cataclysm displacing the Earth's axis, a disaster ascribed by Hans Hoerbiger to the capture of our present Moon destroying Atlantis and the brilliant civilisation at Tiahuanaco in Peru; possibly the same catastrophe mentioned by the Egyptian Priests to Herodotus.

Radio-carbon analysis proves that the advance of the ice occurred about 11,000 years ago, previously this maximum period had been assumed to date from about 25,000 years ago, reported by P. Johnson and W. F. Libby in 'Radio-Carbon Dating' (University of Chicago Press, 1952).

The Piri Reis Map depicted the Andes with llamas, animals then unknown to Europe, and mountains in now frozen Canada only recently discovered. Such landmarks far from the sea could be mapped only from the air, the world must surely have been surveyed by aircraft or Spaceships.

The Great Pyramid was built exactly in the centre of the Earth's land-mass, its position could have been determined only from Space.

Evidence confirming the astonishing geographical and mathematical knowledge in far Antiquity is given by Dr. Livio C. Stecchini in his remarkable essay 'Astronomical Theory and Historical Data'.

> 'I was fortunate enough to come across a set of Egyptian documents well-known but neglected, that prove that by the time of the first dynasties (5000 BC) the Egyptians had measured down to the minute the latitude and longitude of all the main-points of the course of the Nile from the equator to the Mediterranean Sea. Following this first result I have traced a series of texts (all earlier than the beginning of Greek science) which, starting from Egypt, provide positional data that cover most of the Old World, from the Rivers Congo and Zambesi to the Norwegian coast, from the Gulf of Guinea to Indonesia, including such unlikely places as peaks of Switzerland and even junctions in Central Russia. The data are so precise that they are a source of discomfort. I have desperately tried to ascertain errors but I have never been able to establish an error of latitude greater than a minute or an error of longitude greater than possibly five minutes in ten degrees.'[91]

Such fantastic precision presupposes scientists with immense erudition after millennia of civilisation yet Egyptologists stress that the Egyptians had little mathematical skill. The Rhind Papyrus, 2000 BC, describes the Egyptians doing simple sums but complex mathematics was beyond them. Sir Leonard Woolley states that the Egyptians had no scientific knowledge of algebra, geometry and arithmetic, their methods were childishly imperfect, it is difficult to explain how they could calculate the volume of a pyramid.[62]

Perhaps the Egyptians of historical times were degenerate descendants of that great civilisation twelve thousand years ago, which according to Plato partnered heroic Athens to smash Atlantis?

The mapping of the Earth from the River Congo to Norway, Guinea to Indonesia, surely suggests an aerial survey from a Spaceship. This description parallels the remarkable account in 'Ezekiel' Chapter XXVII in which the 'Lord' describes the ports and commerce of the Mediterranean and the Middle East, from Tarshish to Arabia, Tyre to Persia, as though the vast scene were viewed from the air.

Colonel James Churchward declares that the original Greeks emigrated from Mu, the Motherland in the Pacific, to Central America, Atlantis, then finally settled in the Grecian Archipelago; they spoke the Cara-Maya language, both Homer and Herodotus referred to the earliest inhabitants of Greece as Carrians, a warlike, sea-faring people. A recital of the Greek alphabet from Alpha to Omega according to Churchward tells in pure Cara-Maya the destruction of Mu by earthquake and flood, a suggestion fantastic but feasible. The letters of the Greek alphabet were re-arranged during the archonship of Euclid in 403 BC, possibly by Initiates, who wished to preserve a record of the lost Continent. Philologists teach that Greek was derived from Sanskrit, but Sanskrit and Cara-Maya must have been closely related, both originating from the world-language of Mu. The distinctive Greek Cross is said to have been taken from the royal escutcheon of Mu, the Empire of the Sun, an identical cross is found all over Central and South America. Mythology and early literature state that the ancestors of the Greeks originated from the Saturnian Continent in the West, from Atlantis. Many thousands of years ago, great migrations swept across the whole world, the comparison of ancient languages, the rediscovery of old trade-routes and the probability of cataclysms changing the climate, prove that for ages mankind was on the move, the early Greeks surely shared that world-wide culture sung by their Poets, the glorious Golden Age.

Plato did not romance when he praised the high civilisation of Athens twelve thousand years ago, he distinctly states this was destroyed by catastrophes millennia later. Primitive peoples built Neolithic villages in Greece excavated by our archaeologists, history began again.

Ancient Athens defeated Atlantis to save the world until Destiny destroyed her too. Surely those heroic Athenians were inspired by Spacemen!

Chapter Five
Spacemen in Ancient Greece

The most fascinating stories of Spacemen shine not in our chill Science-Fiction but in those warm, colourful, passionate tales told long ago in Ancient Greece, inspiring the classical poets of Antiquity to delightful romance. Awed by the beauty and perfection of wondrous Creation, the Greeks described the universe as 'Kosmos' meaning 'Ornament' revealing their reverence for the sublime splendour of Heaven and Earth, which the Gods made for them.

Man amid those bare hills and perilous seas felt attuned to Nature in silence and storm, around him brooded cosmic mystery, the secret spell of things unseen; he lived in realms of magic expecting miracles. Life was harsh and dangerous, when sorrows troubled, his anxious eyes would supplicate the Celestials in those golden ships sailing the skies beseeching the immortal Gods to come to his aid. Despite afflictions Man rejoiced. Earth belonged to the animals, to the uncomprehending beasts of the field; some inspiration within his soul told Man he was a stranger here, his true home shone beyond the clouds; when life was finished, there to yon wonderland he would return. Awareness of Man's divine heritage, knowledge of his nobler self, promoted morality, the quest for perfection, the triumph of good over evil, the ascent from darkness to light inspiring religion, the search for Truth. Those glorious Gods from Space transmuted Man's mind to wonder and turned his thoughts aspiring towards the stars.

To the peoples of Antiquity the Universe felt mysteriously alive, over hills and vales brooded grandiose spirits, the woods hid satyrs in rustic revelry, the mountain streams babbled the frolics of water-nymphs, above all beyond the blue sky brooded Wondrous Beings watching the follies of Men. To the North on cloud-capped Mount Olympus dwelled Father Zeus with his celestial family of Gods and Goddesses, temperamental personalities whose escapades enlivened all Heaven and Earth; their conflicting moods and colourful manners prompted playwrights and poets to immortalise their exploits in classical literature enchanting the civilisation of the West.

We who soar into Space without surprise simply cannot comprehend the awe with which the Greeks regarded the heavens, reading omens in the glittering stars and larding their very speech with oaths to the Gods. Those dauntless Athenians defied the might of Persia to save the Western world but quivered panic-stricken during an eclipse of the sun and dreaded calamitous events when a comet fell from the sky; despite that shrewd commonsense which reasoned Democracy like all ancient peoples they feared the stars as if dreading invasion from Mars. On these wild hills of Hellas Spaceships had landed, though in the scanty literature left to us no description is found, surely in all those lost writings some poet must have penned a vivid picture more lucid than the garbled tale of Ezekiel weeping by the waters of Babylon. The gay vimanas which graced India would surely span the Himalayas; those Wondermen wearying of Elijah in troubled Israel must certainly swoop for more amorous adventures with the women of Greece.

Stories of gallant strangers appearing in secret haunts to inspire some hero or seduce some willing wench might amuse sophisticated sceptics though few cynics dared scoff; many unmarried mothers swore their babies heaven-born, bastards boasted descent from the Gods, that popular name 'Diogenes' meant 'sired by Zeus'. Politicians would preach democracy while acknowledging imperial Zeus, simple peasants saw Celestials materialise in their midst, sailors in superstition propitiated Deities of sea and sky before leaving shore; even those great philosophers spoke guardedly of the Gods as though they lived next door.

Today our astronomers squint at the stars and solemnly swear they are sterile though some broad-mindedly do admit to bug-eyed monsters light-years away. The Greeks would surely marvel that scholars should spout such nonsense;

they knew the whole universe throbbed with life, all around invisible realms teemed with spirits, satyrs, nymphs, eager to snare some mortal in their spell. Now in our Space Age satellites circle the Earth, astronauts assault the Moon, the bored public hardly bother; UFOs haunt our skies day and night seen by everyone but scientists. Adamski wrote of his trip in a Spaceship and of meeting a Cosmic Master; all over the world people report humanoids manifesting among us, these wonders are ignored even ridiculed by folk who still pray to those Angels helping Abraham so long ago. Religions were founded by Spacemen in Israel, when they land today we laugh them to scorn. We on the threshold of Space challenging the stars care less about the Gods than those Ancient Greeks.

The dim cave of prehistory descends through labyrinthine depths to pools of darkness; glimmers of light illume wild paintings on cavern walls, glimpses of the magic past, but of those vast ages of humanity, the joys and sorrows of multitudes, the epics of peace and war, events eclipsing heaven and earth, no memories remain. Those moss-covered ruins of Antiquity stand mute and forlorn, the people who frolicked there in love and light have fled to the shadows for ever, does the lack of written records prove that nothing happened? What can we ever know of the infinite experience of Man? History cannot mirror the past only distort what truly happened; those dusty volumes merely record the moods of the historians selecting their facts. Do those garrulous gossips so assiduously chronicling the trivia of our own times deign to mention the UFOs haunting us today? All the voluminous reports in the Parliamentary 'Hansard' show not one 'Saucer' in the sky. What will future historians fathom of our own century?

Sometimes a chance comment will illumine a whole Age. Mongolia is noted for its mules not its myths, no legends titillate us with the love-life of its Gods yet a passing comment by the German mythologist, Jacob Grimm, two hundred years ago revealed that strange land in new wonder. In his 'Deutsche Mythologie' the learned Grimm mentioned casually 'To the Boruat Mongols beyond Lake Baikal fairy-rings on the grass are where the Sons of the Lightning have danced.' Sons of the Lightning! At once we think of the Lords of the Flame, the Elohim, Indra, Horus, Jehovah, Zeus himself. Genghis Khan worshipped the Sun. Surely Mongolia was visited by Spacemen! Fairy-rings in Britain, Ireland and Italy now find tongue singing of Gods from the skies. Did those 'Sons of the Lightning' dance in Arcadia? If a random remark about old Mongolia conjures Celestials descending to Earth, what wondrous revelations shine in the literature of Ancient Greece?

Scholars ignored Plato's description of a flourishing Greece about 10,000 BC and agreed with Thucydides writing in 400 BC that Hellas was not settled until recent times, since the nomadic inhabitants were constantly harried by invaders they built no cities.

> 'Before the Trojan War, Hellas, as it appears engaged in no enterprise in common. Indeed it seems to me that as a whole it did not yet have this name either but that before the time of Hellen, Son of Deucalion, the title did not exist and that the several tribes the Pelasgians most extensively gave their own name to the several districts.'[8]

The Romans called the peoples of the Peloponnese 'Graeci' but even today they know themselves as 'Hellenes', proof of proud antiquity. In the ancient world Hellas meant a way of life, a whole civilisation.

In Athens philosophers discoursed with aery eloquence on the Golden Age of the Gods and moralised over the sorry decline of mankind; not one of them ever dreamed of digging up his own olive grove for relics of the past. It was left to Heinrich Schliemann and our archaeologists to resurrect the glories of Greece. Thucydides, a model historian, marshalled his facts with scholarly precision, he dismissed prehistory in one paragraph and concentrated on the Peloponnesian War. Our learned professors educated in the Classics scoff at the bizarre suggestion of Spacemen in Ancient Greece millennia ago and are content to quote Thucydides, conveniently forgetting that like all his contemporaries in the absence of written records and archaeological research, he was understandably ignorant of events in the past.

After the destruction of Atlantis and the subsequent downfall of Athens, Greece is believed to have suffered a Dark Age for thousands of years being overrun by migrations from East and North-West; recent discoveries are illuming this gloomy panorama. In Yugoslavia at Lepenski Vir[64] near the Iron Gates of the Danube, Professor Dragutin Srejovic of Belgrade and other archaeologists found remains of forty-one houses of an hitherto unknown trapeze-shaped design apparently planned set on a hill beside the Danube, a settlement dated about 6000 BC. Beside well-built hearths lay skeletons as though the people had fallen asleep with their hands resting under their heads; with each body was a stone sculptured in a sophisticated fashion, there were no graves, they had presumably been overcome by some disaster. Professor Srejovic hopes to find a market-place, evidence of a sophisticated community in Yugoslavia 8,000 years ago, 5,000 years before the Siege of Troy, nearly 6,000 years before Thucydides and Plato. New archaeological discoveries are constantly unearthing older and older civilisations, having now dug back 6,000 years can we honestly doubt the likelihood that in a few decades our archaeologists will proudly discover some Greek remains dated 10,000 BC and agree at last with Plato's tale of ancient Athens?

Archaeologists have long been puzzled by the absence of ancient cities on the Peloponnese, ignoring Plato historians concluded that in early times Greece was therefore uninhabited. The Lamont Geological Observatory, New York, has shown that the floor of the Eastern Mediterranean has compressed like a concertina between Africa and Eastern Europe; Dr. Nicholas Fleming of the Institute of Oceanography has found that over the past few thousand years the Peloponnese has submerged by between three and twelve feet from north to south while the islands to the south, Kythera and Antikythera have emerged from the sea by as much as ten feet. This sinking of the Greek coast explains the apparent lack of ancient settlements; they did exist but were submerged from sight. In a two-month survey of the Greek coast Dr. Nicholas Fleming has found nineteen drowned cities belonging to Classical times and one,

Elaphonisos, dated back as far as 2000 BC; this latter city covers twenty-one acres, consisting of a complex of houses and streets; it had never been noted before: its sudden destruction may have been due to the great volcanic explosion of Thera erupting about 1450 BC, which some experts believe to have caused the sudden collapse of Knossus and the Minoan civilisation of Crete. Thucydides knew nothing of these drowned cities, although Plato does not mention them, he infers in the 'Critias' that such cities did flourish millennia before and through earthquakes were engulfed by the sea.

Pottery found at Fourth Millennium Greek sites has affinities with pottery in Mesopotamia around 3500 BC; Sargon, 2400 BC conquered Cyprus and extended Babylonian influence to the Aegean. Egypt had historic links with Greece, particularly during the tragic times of Akhnaton, 1375 BC, whom Immanuel Velikovsky[65] has provocatively identified with Oedipus.

On Minos, the legendary King of Crete, Thucydides wrote

'Minos is the earliest ruler we know of who possessed a fleet and controlled most of the Greek waters. He ruled the Cyclades, and was the first coloniser of most of them, installing his own sons as governors. In all probability he cleared the seas of pirates so far as he could to secure his own revenue.'

Dionysius of Halicarnassus in his 'Roman Antiquities', Book 2 – 61 states that Minos like Lycurgus, the great legislator of Sparta and Numa Pompilius of early Rome, received the Laws from the Gods. Minos claimed to hold converse with Zeus, at once evoking those famous conversations of Abraham and Moses with Jehovah.

In prehistoric Athens was born the genius Daedalus, who claimed descent from Erechteus, a God-King of Athens, possibly an Extraterrestrial, killed by Zeus with a flash of lightning at the request of Poseidon. The Greeks honoured Daedalus as a great engineer and architect, inventor of plumbing and carpentry, the saw, the axe, the masts of ships and the magnifying-lens. Daedalus seems more than mortal, sired and inspired by a God, he devised figures which opened their eyes, moved their arms and walked about, the first automaton. His affinity with the divine Leonardo da Vinci many centuries later is assured by the coincidence that for their patrons they both built reservoirs and fortresses, dissected dead bodies and experimented with man-made flight, though Daedalus left no paintings his artistic talents found expression in architecture and sculptures on temples for which he was famous.[66] When his young nephew Perdrix put two pieces of magnetised iron together to invent the compass, Daedalus, like most geniuses intolerant of talented rivals, tricked him into climbing a high tower then pushed him off. Legend relates that Minerva changed the falling boy into a bird bearing his name, the partridge which avoids heights by flying close to the ground. Ignoring this alleged miracle Athenians summoned Daedalus to the Areopagus, the ancient criminal court, charging him with murder; to escape execution he fled to Crete.

The magnificent ruined palaces at Knossos with their colourful vivacious frescoes of youths and maidens vaulting over bulls, wrestling together or relaxing in sunny sea-green salons of iridescent loveliness enchant us even today; at its golden zenith the civilisation of Crete must have allured all the Mediterranean. On this idyllic isle was born Zeus according to cherished tradition intimating perhaps that the Space Gods landed on this focal site between the countries of the Middle East and those fabled Lands of the West. Like Leonardo Daedalus soon found scope for his many talents planning elegant buildings and fortifications, he constructed the famous Labyrinth, a maze of winding paths from which there was no escape until Ariadne helped Theseus with a ball of thread to find his way out.

Daedalus for the protection of the island invented Talos, a giant bronze robot, invulnerable except in one ankle, programmed to hurl rocks at hostile ships. When Jason and the Argonauts, voyaging for the Golden Fleece sailed along the coast this huge mechanical man promptly appeared and threatened to sink them with a huge rock. Medea knelt and prayed to the Hounds of Hell to come and destroy him; as the bronze giant lifted an immense stone to hurl upon them he grazed his ankle, blood gushed forth, he sank down and died. Theseus, one of the heroes of Jason's famous expedition, during his imprisonment on Crete would probably learn the mechanism of Talos and would surely plan its destruction. The blood may have been the well-known Cretan oil. Theseus may have struck the ankle of Talos with a spear and burst the valve allowing the oil to flow out rendering the monster impotent. A tall tale, perhaps, but no more fabulous than the legend of the Golden Fleece itself.

The ingenuity of Daedalus sorely strained by King Minos was further exploited by his nymphomaniac Queen Pasiphae, who like those naughty girls in Copenhagen today craved abnormal sexual delights and demanded intercourse with the sacred bull. Undaunted by his bizarre task Daedalus fashioned a life-size cow from real hides, duly scented with sexual fluids having a suitable orifice over which Pasiphae inside crouched at the required angle. The lusty bull mounted the 'cow' and impregnated the Queen, who promptly conceived and duly produced the Minotaur, half-man, half-bull. Minos ashamed of this unnatural progeny confined it in the Labyrinth where it roamed feeding on human victims. Minos made war on Athens and forced the Athenians to send seven youths and seven maidens as yearly tribute to be devoured by the Minotaur. Prince Theseus volunteered to accompany the doomed youths, aided by Ariadne he slew the Minotaur and escaped in triumph; as his ships approached the Attica coast he neglected to hoist the white sail which was to have been the signal of success; his father, Aegeus, thinking the young Prince had perished, cast himself into the sea giving his name to the Aegean. Theseus became King of Athens and led a notable expedition to the Caucasus to capture Antiope, the Amazon Queen, whom he married; in revenge her Warrior-Women invaded Greece and stormed Athens meeting final defeat. The Theseus legends tell of a civilised Athens, contemporary Knossos and those brilliant Cretans who sailed the Mediterranean and the Black Sea long before recorded history, as Plato insists.

The enraged Minos imprisoned Daedalus and his son,

Icarus, in the Labyrinth forgetting that genius like love will always find a way. Barred by land and sea Daedalus turned to the air; he carefully studied the flight of birds then laid down a row of feathers beginning with the small ones and gradually increasing their length, so that the edge seemed to slope upwards, these he fastened in the middle with thread and at the bottom with wax, then rounded them in a gentle curve to look like real birds' wings. After hovering in the air mastering the technique of flight, this mastermind made a pair of wings for Icarus and instructed him to follow a course midway between earth and heaven in case the sun should scorch his feathers, the water made them heavy, if he went too low; he was to pay no attention to the stars.[87] Father and son soared in the air and to the amazement of sundry shepherds and fishermen flew out to sea, gliding beyond Delos and Paros between Samos on their left and Labinthus on their right over the Aegean. Icarus swooped and soared on air-streams attracted to the blazing sun, the wax melted, his wings fell off. By tragic oversight Daedalus had omitted to invent the parachute, his son suddenly discovered the laws of gravity and crashed into the sea and drowned. Daedalus flew on to Italy and landed at Cumae near the future Naples, abode of the prophetic Sibyl, where he built a temple to Apollo; later he found shelter in the Court of Cocalus, King of Sicily.

Still smarting at the escape of Daedalus, Minos thought of a clever ruse to find him; he offered a princely reward to anyone who could pass a thread through the intricate convolutions of a sea-shell, a problem to baffle even our bright boys today, knowing only one man in the world could solve it. Daedalus told the Sicilian King to fasten a thread around an ant to be introduced into a hole pierced in the shell; the ant finally found its way through the maze and duly emerged. Instead of the prize he had promised, Minos invaded Sicily with an army and demanded the surrender of Daedalus. By strategems not vouchsafed to us, the daughters of Cocalus surprised Minos in his bath and heartlessly filled it up with boiling water, mighty Minos turned pink, scalded to death like a lobster. Zeus took compassion somewhat too late and made Minos a Judge of the Dead in Hades. No man knows how Daedalus died.

Even the great Leonardo and our technicians today have failed to solve the problem of man-powered flight; the alleged aeronautics of Daedalus so long ago are scoffed at as myth. Ancient Chinese records assert that about 2250 BC[68] the Emperor Shun escaped from captivity by making himself wings like a bird. Geoffrey of Monmouth in his 'History of the Kings of Britain' mentions that the Bronze Age King Bladud, 'a right cunning artificer', fashioned wings and tried to 'go upon the top of the air', when he fell upon the Temple of Apollo on Lud's Hill in the city of Trinaventum (London) leaving his throne to his son, Leir, the King Lear of Shakespeare.

The 'Koran' recalls Nimrod soaring to the skies on the back of an eagle whose wings were singed by the sun. A popular Babylonian tale tells how shortly after the Flood the childless King Etana ascended to heaven on an eagle to seek counsel from the Gods; some time after his return to Earth the Queen bore him a son. The man-bird, Garuda, is featured in the Classics of Ancient India.

It is natural for us today who believe flight started only this century to dismiss all tales of flying in Antiquity as childish fancy, poetic yearning of primitive man. Study of the literature of the Ancient East astounds us with the aerial chariots of India, flying-horses in Tibet, dragons over China, heavenly rocking-boats over Japan, solar-boats in Egypt, winged wheels in Babylon, the 'Power and Glory' of the 'Lord' inspiring Israel; we become suddenly conscious that flying-machines did exist in ancient times. Surely those craft must have flown over the Mediterranean to land in Greece and Crete?

Minos and Daedalus are shrouded in mystery yet for thousands of years their deeds are remembered. The human mind can imagine events only in terms of its own experience; the peoples of Antiquity conceived of flight in the likeness of birds. Does the story of Daedalus and Icarus preserve some memory of Spacemen?

The Minoans were a literate people; Knossos lasted for

many hundred years. If only we might unearth some Library!

The sudden downfall of Knossos in about 1400 BC at the zenith of its glory, when that gay and brilliant civilisation dominated the Mediterranean, remains a mystery. Sir Arthur Evans attributed the smoke-stained ruins to earthquake followed by terrible conflagration consuming the city; a theory challenged by J. D. S. Pendlebury, who argued that in the absence of gas and electricity-mains earthquakes seldom cause fires, moreover the grand-staircase would have been split by earth-tremors; in fact it survived for a long time. Dr. Angelos G. Galanopoulos, Professor of Geophysics at the University of Athens, suggests that Knossos might have been destroyed by the explosion of Santorin Island to the north, which he equates with Plato's Atlantis, which erupted in the fifteenth century BC dropping a thick layer of ash over central and eastern Crete rendering these regions virtually uninhabitable for many centuries. Controversy still rages! The intriguing suggestion has been made that the advanced technology of the Cretans possibly utilised petroleum, the famous Greek fire of future centuries, perhaps the oil-tanks exploded in flames. The obvious cause would appear to have been invaders from Greece, symbolised by the legend of Theseus and the Minotaur, who devastated Knossos and the neighbouring cities; however Thucydides stressed that Minos ruled the sea, it is difficult to imagine what coalition of the Aegean Powers could have launched an armada to smash the powerful Cretan fleet and lay Knossos waste, its splendour desolate. Centuries later the Romans tore Carthage to the ground and ploughed over its ruins but history does not record any country overwhelming Crete. Today in our Nuclear Age the sudden destruction of a city at once evokes memories of Hiroshima and the annihilation of Sodom and Gomorrah possibly by Spacemen. The 'Mahabharata' is generally supposed to describe the Bharata War in Northern India about 1400 BC; this wonderful epic gives most fascinating descriptions of aerial warfare and annihilating-bombs. Extraterrestrials apparently interfered in world affairs throughout the Second Millennium BC, they would surely have taken special interest in Crete where Daedalus, Icarus and others were building flying-machines. Archaeologists find that the ancient city of Hattus in Asia Minor appears to have been destroyed by some weapon generating terrific heat, its calcined walls resemble granite battlements of fortresses in Ireland apparently fused by aerial bombs. Every disaster in ancient times cannot be attributed to the activities of Extraterrestrials yet it is highly significant that the Babylonians, Britons, Hindus, Chinese, Mayas, all the peoples of Antiquity, kept radar-like watch on the heavens. Did they fear attack from the skies? Invasion by Spacemen? Destruction like Knossos?

Thucydides little dreamed that Knossos had been suddenly destroyed a thousand years before he was born; its brilliant civilisation probably began about 3400 BC. This home of the Minotaur had close links with Egypt, inscriptions from the 12th Dynasty, 2000 BC referred to Crete as 'Keftiu' or 'Caphtor', legendary origin of the Philistines; the recent discovery of the drawings of a labrys or double-headed axe on a trilithon at Stonehenge associates Crete with the Britain of 1800 BC. In the 'Odyssey' Book XIX Homer marvelled at the rich and lovely land of Crete with ninety cities, great Knossos and King Minos, friend of Zeus; this vivid description was wonderfully confirmed by excavations of Sir Arthur Evans at the beginning of this century revealing the colourful, enchanting Minoan civilisation lost to history. In the palace of Phaistos Sir Arthur Evans discovered a terracotta disc, four inches in diameter, with spiral ideograms which seem identical to prehistoric symbols found in South America, suggesting world-wide communications promoting the Sun religion evocative of Spacemen. Scholars were long baffled by two strange scripts, Linear A and Linear B, on baked clay tablets found in the Palace at Knossos for which there was no bilingual key. For decades archaeologists studied them in vain until in 1952 Michael Ventris with brilliant logic deciphered Linear B and announced to an incredulous world that this Minoan script was archaic Greek written many decades earlier than experts had imagined.[69] Similar scripts were found on the mainland at Mycenae proving that the Dark Age of illiteracy taught by the historians must in actual fact have been a time of culture and learning; this revelation extended the civilisation of Greece back to 2000 BC.[70]

The Greek myths are attributed to the Mycenaean period from 1600-1200 BC, although affinities with legends of the Ancient East suggest all sprang from some common source millennia before. After excavating Troy Heinrich Schliemann inspired by the plays of Aeschylus began to search for the tomb of Agamemnon and the treasures of Atreus in the cyclopean ruins of Mycenae which had staged the murder of Agamemnon, Clytemnestra and Electra in the greatest tragedies of Greece. According to Homer Troy was rich, Mycenae even richer.[71] In 1876 Schliemann found five royal graves, later Stanistakis a sixth, and unearthed the skeletons of nineteen men and women and two small children surrounded by golden treasures unequalled in opulence until the opening of Tutankhamun's tomb. Over each man's face shimmered a golden mask modelled to his features, on his chest shone a breast-plate, the women wore golden frontlets, one a magnificent gold diadem, the children lay wrapped in sheets of gold. The wives had toilet-boxes of gold, superb necklaces, earrings, jewellery, even cosmetic adornments shaming our modern millionaires. In Ancient Greece 3,500 years ago!

Writing, cyclopean cities, goldware of exquisite artistry, alluring jewellery, coquettish cosmetics, all show a highly sophisticated society possessing great imaginative, technical skill. The invention of writing communicating ideas pre-supposes philosophy and logic of lofty intelligence maturing through vast millennia. Transcending all perhaps were the religious ideals, belief in an after-life, persuading the Mycenaeans to bury such golden treasures with their dead.

In 1901 some sponge-divers off the island of Antikithira, between Cythera and Crete, fished up a metal box covered with coral which was found to contain an assemblage of wheels, balances, cylinders and dials comprising an ancient astronomical clock dated by experts between 80 and 50 BC, which gave the signs of the Zodiac, the orbits of Mercury, Mars, Jupiter and Saturn, the solar year, the months and the time of day. A fascinating, mechanical masterpiece!

Recent discoveries at Alaca Huyuk where tombs disclose an extraordinary profusion of elegant silver and golden objects of art, prove that about 3000 BC a brilliant civilisation flowered in Central Turkey. The noted archaeologist, Henri-Paul Eydoux,[72] believes that the culture of Troy, Maecenae and Hellas originated from Turkey not from Egypt as Herodotus had claimed. The Trojan War was not the beginning of Greece, rather was it the end of a great civilisation around the Bosphorus possibly thousands of years old. Such revelations of a flourishing culture in Asia Minor so long ago adds credence to the insistence by Solon that about 10,000 BC Athens and her Allies smashed the invasion by the Atlanteans from the West.

Thucydides in his austere Athens with few written records could hardly appreciate the remote past. Dark Ages recurred periodically throughout Greek history as in our own. Since Roman days Britain has been invaded by Saxons, Danes, Normans, now Asians, all influencing our way of life. After AD 410 when the Roman Legions left, learning and culture were preserved for centuries by solitary monks. About 10,000 BC old Athens was destroyed by earthquakes, Greece suffered invasion by Pelasgians, Achaeans, Dorians, nomads from North-East and West. Plato in 'Critias' frequently stressed 'repeated destruction' and 'intervening periods' when these 'unlettered mountaineers' knew little of the Works of the past. Most of the wisdom of Atlantis and prehistoric Athens became lost but basic knowledge was handed down by Initiates for generations; the country blossomed into temporary brilliance until invading tribes again brought ruin. This ebb and flow of history was surely watched by Extraterrestrials worshipped as Gods, studying our Earth then as they do now.

Last century those great Greek scholars, Jebb and Porson, denied the real existence of Troy; not long since professors taught that Hellas began in 776 BC with the First Olympiad, today archaeologists in excitement dig up the Helladic Stone Age, tomorrow will the experts admit that Ancient Greece knew Spacemen?

The literature now left to us suggests that about the Second Millennium BC Extraterrestrials interfered in human affairs more directly than today; their landings in various countries would logically include visits to Greece remembered in those glowing traditions of the 'Gods'.

'Truth is beautiful and enduring.'[73]

The early Greeks were unsophisticated souls living among hills, seas and open skies, awed by the sublime grandeur of Nature in all her moods, aware of the imperfections of mortal men with all the frailties that flesh is heir to; their logical minds knew there must be some ideal harmony to which men could aspire. The spirit of Hellas yearned for universal simplicity, aesthetics marvelled at the wholesomeness of things, freedom, beauty, goodness and truth. Greeks viewed human life against the complete universe, conscious of the greater grandeur, limitless expanse of Eternity. Those sublime tragedies of Athens revealed in heroic language the nobility or baseness of Man, the virtues or wickedness of Woman, not as character-studies holding up the mirror to earthly mortals but in emulation of those Personages larger than life, the 'Gods' in the skies. The Greeks staged no 'kitchen-sink' drama or plays about perverts, though Athenian morals seemed worse than our own; their sculptors carved no queer shapes, nor did painters torture their pictures with psychological symbolism, they depicted the world in simple perfection, men and women not as they were but as they should be. The golden rule meant moderation, perfect balance, clarity and freedom, pursued with energy even passion. The Olympic Games and the open-air Theatre promoted a healthy mind in a healthy body. Socrates campaigned as a common soldier, the athlete winning the Marathon might declaim a Victory Ode. Aristotle with his universality would have pitied a scientist, specialist in one field but stupid in others; much as the Greeks praised athletes, they would never have admired a man running a record mile if he had only the mind of a Moron.

The Greek ideal, beauty in mind and body, was probably inherited from ancestral memories of those golden Strangers from the skies, who after millennia of spiritual enlightenment and scientific diet on planets with highly evolved civilisations had developed the human form to perfection. Our own cosmonauts are most carefully selected from the very cream of a nation's manhood, each undergoes most prolonged and rigorous training, extending their mental and physical perceptions to new powers, wondrous potentialities latent in Man; these superb specimens will be sent to the skies representing our peoples of Earth. Those Celestials who landed here long ago to rule our world would surely be the most perfect Beings from their own planets, models of intelligence, grace and beauty far transcending common Man. Legends from every country in the world marvel in awe at the 'Gods' descending in celestial chariots, their radiant features and magnetic personalities enchanting the unsophisticated peoples to wonder and adoration inspiring worship.

The most handsome of the Greek Gods was Apollo, sometimes identified with Helios, the Sun; poets sang of his birth on the island of Delos, son of Zeus and Letos twin-brother of Artemis, the Roman Diana. Delos was a floating island drifting from place to place until Zeus chained it to the bottom of the sea. Some occult traditions allege that Apollo was born on a sidereal island called Asterid, 'the golden star island', the 'Earth which floats in the air', known to the Hindus as 'Hiranyapura'. Reference to a 'God' from a sidereal or floating island coincide with our modern conception of Extraterrestrials landing from huge Spaceships. Zeus, presumably a Spaceman, married Leto, daughter of Coeus, one of the Titans, that ancient stellar race of Uranids. Apollo was known as 'Phoebus' meaning 'brilliant' or 'shining', apparently suggesting the Sun, yet we are reminded that the countenance of the 'Angels' appearing to the Israelites also shone with radiance like the faces of the Spacemen alleged to be landing today. Glorious

Apollo had most wonderful influence on the mind of Hellas like Osiris in Egypt and Oannes in Babylon; he taught early Man all the arts of civilisation, music, healing, delighting in the founding of towns; mystics venerated this radiant God with Christ-like qualities symbolising those Celestials of supreme beneficence said to inhabit the Sun, who inspired Initiates on Earth. Sudden death was believed to be the effect of Apollo's arrows, the God sent plagues into the camp of the Greeks besieging Troy.

Apollo like other Greek Divinities was often depicted with a circle of rays around his head; his son, Aesculapius, the great Healer, also had a nimbus analogous to the haloes of the 'Angels'. The hats of Castor and Pollux emanated sparks evoking the globes surmounting those intriguing figures in the Tassili frescoes; today we find ourselves wondering whether such crowns symbolised the helmets of Spacemen. Around the head of the Scandinavian God, Thor, artists showed a ring of stars; certain Slavonic idols were crowned with circular rays; Xenocrates associated the planets with the Gods; the likening of the Gods to radiant luminaries of heaven symbolising divine beauty and grace does suggest that these Celestials were not mere figments of imagination but actual Supermen from the skies.

The Gods sped through the skies mightier and swifter than mortals; Poseidon traversed an immense distance in only three steps like the Indian Vishnu, who crossed the three worlds in only three strides. With such swiftness the Gods suddenly appeared and disappeared at speeds beyond attainment of Man in far Antiquity, streaking through the skies like shooting-stars. Hera like Indra travelled swift as thought, Hermes and Athene glided down on winged sandals, Athene like Odin was sometimes portrayed in flight like a falcon; Zeus appeared to Leda in the form of a swan, perhaps descent from a Spaceship. Zetes and Calais, the Boreades, two of the Argonauts, who drove the Harpies, evil winged-maidens, from Thrace were said to have long hairy shoulders covered with golden scales and wings on their feet. Poseidon gave Pelops a winged chariot, even when it ran through the sea its axles were not wet recalling that car of burnished gold driven by the twin Aswins who flew from Space to rescue the Indian Bhujya from the sea. Zeus bound Ixion to a fiery wheel entwined with writhing snakes similar to those discs with feathered serpents depicted in Mexican portraits of Quetzalcoatl which evoke Spacecraft emitting radiation. The Centaurs, said to be born from a cloud, descendants of Ixion, son of Ares (Mars), have been equated with the Vedic Gandharvas, followers of Indra, living in a city in Space; they were depicted as half-man, half-horse, perhaps to symbolise speed. Chiron, the Centaur, educated by Apollo, instructed Aesculapius in medicine and taught the young Achilles, after Hercules struck him with a poisoned arrow he gave his immortality to Prometheus then Zeus placed him in the constellation of Sagittarius.

Demeter made a chariot of winged dragons for Triptolemus and gave him wheat which he wafted through the sky and sowed the whole inhabited Earth. Vengeful Medea murdered her two children by Jason and fled to Athens in a car drawn by winged dragons like those Gods of Ancient China and the Celtic Goddess, Keridwen, of Wales. Eros had wings, the Roman Bellona flew like a bird, Plato in 'Phaedrus' describes Zeus, the mighty leader, holding the reins of a winged chariot driving across the heavens with his Gods; Woden and Thor occasionally drove star-chariots followed by winged Valkyries; Indra and his Maruts raced in celestial cars, all remembered by Christians as the Archangel Michael and his Heavenly hosts. Homer in the 'Iliad', Book V, gives a wonderful description of Minerva in her blazing car drawn by ethereal courses cutting the liquid sky speeding high over Greece to land near Troy recalling that picturesque flight of Rama and Sita from Ceylon beyond the Ganges, so colourfully narrated in the 'Ramayana'; all surely suggestive of a world-wide domination by Celestials.

The motion of the Gods through the skies in shattering splendour struck awe into the marvelling Greeks just as half an hour later the Patriarchs in Israel would gaze in wonder at those same Spaceships, the 'Power and Glory' of the 'Lord'.[74] The driving of Zeus or Thor awoke thunder in the clouds; mountains and forests trembled beneath the tread of Poseidon evoking our own jet-planes breaking the sound-barrier, some Celestials, Hermes and Iris famed as Messengers, traversed the heavens in silence. The older Divinities of the Greeks, Zeus, Apollo, Athene, Demeter, like their Indian rivals, drove in sky-chariots, only the lesser Gods, Perseus, Theseus, the Dioscurii, rode on horseback; Bellerophon and Oceanos flew on winged horses. It may seem absurd to construe any significance in such development yet the change could imply that the new generation of Celestials flew in single scoutships.

The Gods would suddenly appear or disappear as though they had travelled with the speed of light, recalling those fascinating descriptions in the Sanskrit Classics and the Egyptian 'The Book of the Dead' where people marvelled at the materialisation of the Spaceships just as we do today. Often the Deities remained invisible, shielded in mist they intervened in battle to save their favourites. Athene[75] threw her aegis around Achilles, Apollo[76] snatched Hector from that hero's sword, Venus[77] flung her protective veil around hard-pressed Aeneas, later in North Africa the Goddess conveyed Aeneas in a cloud to Dido[78] sighing by the waters of Carthage. Legend asserts that Venus appeared to Hippomenes[79] in his race against the fleet-footed Atalanta, invisible to all save the youth himself, she gave him three golden apples; he dropped them one by one, Atalanta tarried to pick them up, so Hippomenes won and married his lovely prize. Sanskrit texts, Chinese myths, Teutonic legends, all tell of cloaks of invisibility; we ridicule such tales as nonsense flouting our laws of Physics yet as we consider the accumulating evidence of Extraterrestrial interference in human affairs, like the Greeks of old we wonder.

The Gods often had a golden staff with wonderful powers similar to the vril rods possessed by the Adepts of Atlantis, which were said to radiate sidereal forces causing apparent miracles. The 'Talmud' declares with some improbability that Moses found in the Midianite garden of Jethro, his father-in-law, the very staff which was carried by Adam out of Eden and passed down to Abraham, Noah, Isaac and Joseph; with this rod Moses discomforted the magicians of

Pharaoh and smote the rock in Horeb to obtain water for the thirsty Israelites. Circe,[80] the enchantress, waved her magic wand and transformed the companions of Ulysses into hogs; Athene[81] with her wand of gold withered wandering Ulysses to miserable old age, in this disguise the hero returned home to Ithaca, there the Goddess[82] with another wave of her wand restored him to graceful youth to the astonishment of his son, Telemachus. Hermes usually carried a caduceus, a wand of power, which he had received from Apollo wreathed with serpents, symbol of occult force.

The Druids were said to have wielded rods controlling Dis Lanach (Lightning of the Gods) and Druis Lanach (Lightning of the Druids) with which they shrivelled their enemies. The bow of Apollo transmitted plagues; the Vedas mention Indra's magic bow, Odin wielded a wondrous spear. There is reason to believe that Initiates in these great civilisations of the past mastered a psychic science, possibly learned for their Space Teachers; the powerful staff seems to have radiated some electrostatic force still unknown to us. Remnants of this occult science persisted down the ages preserved by wizards and witches all over the world, who carried wands of power or wishing-sticks hoping to work transformations flouting our own Physics. It is fascinating to think that the golden staff of the Gods, the vril rod of the Spacemen, is perpetuated today in the royal sceptre of the Sovereign.

The Ancients supposed that the Gods actually did descend to Earth and lived among men. Plautus[83] the celebrated comic poet of Rome, in about 211 BC, expressed general belief in his Prologue to 'Rudens'; Arcturus declares that at night he was a bright, shining star in the sky, by day he walked among mortals appointed as a spy by the great Jupiter to observe the deeds and characters of men. In another play 'Amphitryo', Plautus brought the Olympians down to the streets of Grecian Thebes; Mercury dressed as a young slave explains that Jupiter likes to have inspectors patrolling this theatre of Earth. St. Paul enjoined the Hebrews, 'Be not forgetful to entertain strangers, for thereby some have entertained Angels unawares.'⁸⁴ People often did not realise until later that they had met Celestials just as we ourselves, it is alleged, may speak to Spacemen living among us yet never know. The Gods sometimes revealed their identity before departing, as Poseidon left Ajax and Venus her son, Aeneas. Zeus and Hermes visited the aged Philemon and his wife, Baucis, then drowned all their evil neighbours in a flood, paralleled by the appearance of Jehovah and His Angels to old Abraham and Sarah before the 'Lord' destroyed the wicked Sodomites with fire from Heaven.

Orpheus was contemporary with Moses five centuries before Homer and thirteen centuries before Christ. Greece was greatly divided both as regards her religion and her political life. In Thrace the solar and lunar cults were disputing for supremacy, two religions and two social organisations absolutely opposed to each other. War to the death between priests of the Sun and priestesses of the Moon raged with bitterness. Orpheus, son of Apollo, appeared in Thrace, his melodious voice had strange charm, he created Mysteries and became the soul of his country, he is said to have descended to Hades vainly for Eurydice, traditions say he was torn to pieces by wild Bacchante women.⁸⁵

The belief of God materialising in the Middle Ages was preserved in Jubinal's 'Nouveau Recueil de Contes', Vol. 2, pp. 377-8, which tells how the Lord God having fallen sick descends from Heaven to Earth to get cured and comes to Arras; there minstrels and jesters receive commands to amuse Him, one manages so cleverly that the Lord bursts out laughing and finds Himself rid of all his ills.

Today some 'Contacts' claim that Extraterrestrials are actually landed by Spaceships to live in most countries; they seem indistinguishable from ordinary humanity and report developments to the Rulers of their own planets. Our egocentric minds find such claims incredible yet certain mysterious personages, notably Count St. Germain, seen on Earth from the 17th to the 20th century do suggest that Spacemen may have always lived among us. George

Adamski writes of meeting Venusians who took him for a trip in a Spaceship; Truman Bethurum lyricises over the beautiful Aura Rhanes from Clarion,[86] and Howard Menger claims to have met Saturnians.

Perhaps the 'Gods' really did descend to Ancient Greece?

Chapter Six
Helen of Troy

> 'Achilles' wrath to Greece the direful spring
> Of wars unnumbered, heavenly Goddess sing.'

These opening lines of the 'Iliad' telling of the Siege of Troy heralded the literature of Antiquity to inspire our civilisation of the West. Homer's wonderful epic poem, still unequalled in sublime events, glows with human, passionate men and women caught in fateful drama between the conflicts of mortal life and the judgement of the Gods. Such age-old stories of love and war transcend all the struggles of history; techniques may change but the basic emotions of men and women, nobility, heroism, suffering, sorrow, ambition, defiance of destiny, must ever illumine the human spirit. These entrancing tales of Ancient Greece, the seduction of beauteous Helen, the anger of Achilles, the outraged majesty of Agamemnon, the wily Ulysses, effeminate Paris, brave Hector and his heroic wife, Andromache, grim battles, tremendous duels, funeral games, manly valour, womanly grief, overshadowed by the Gods; all led to the grandeur of Greek tragedy linking Antiquity with our troubled world today. The heroes and their courageous women experienced all the trials of humanity, fighting the enemy and each other, depicted in brilliant scenes and colourful imagery; their lofty ideals and moral precepts enshrined this poem like the Bible in the hearts of the Greeks inspiring the spirit of Hellas to civilise the world. The common people quoted the 'Iliad' like sacred texts almost with the force of laws; even philosophers like Plato bowed in humility to the divine vision of Homer. Poets and scholars down the centuries have plundered such treasure to create our European culture; today this epic of the Gods and men shines in startling significance suddenly illuming our Space Age.

Who Homer was and when he lived, no one knows. Even Herodotus who knew everything about everybody, supposed uncertainly that he probably lived about four hundred years earlier in the ninth century BC. Tradition accepts that this greatest of Greek poets was born not in Greece but in Ionia, Asia Minor, about 850 BC; in his old-age Homer was blind and poor. The Achaeans led by Agamemnon besieged Troy near the entrance to the Dardanelles towards the end of the Mycenaean Age about 1200 BC; for centuries wandering minstrels sang lays about the Gods and the Heroes, which Homer finally collated into one intellectual and artistic unity giving vivid descriptions of life in the Bronze Age. Scholars have argued that 'Homer' was in fact a corporate name for perhaps six authors although academic opinion supports the poet, Matthew Arnold, who maintained that the 'Iliad' has the stamp of genius and must be the work of a great Master. The 'Odyssey' narrating the wonderful adventures of Ulysses returning home to Ithaca after the fall of Troy was thought not to be Homer's but an epic by more than one writer. The Rev. A. Q. Morton and the Cambridge professor, Dr. John Chadwick, a Greek scholar and joint discoverer of Linear B script have patiently conducted a computer analysis of the 250,000 words of Homer and claim to have proved that they must all have been written by one man.

Even more remarkable perhaps than the events of the 'Iliad' are the brilliant language, the sublimity of thought and superb characterisation expressed in picturesque similes and poetic invention, which make Virgil's 'Aeneid' seem an uninspired imitation. Today we boast writers of genius yet it is difficult to conjure any world-figure with the universality of Homer. Such a supreme poem cannot be the work of some ignorant barbarian but the quintessence of many hundreds probably thousands of years of literary tradition. The recent decipherment of Linear B script proves that Greek was written in Mycenaean times; tantalisingly few texts remain, it is likely that a vast literature was lost; the wonder of the 'Iliad' surely suggests that Homer was heir to a great and long-developed culture. The noble ideals and mellifluent language penned with such supreme genius nearly three thousand years ago prove in the 'Iliad' the vast, unfathomable antiquity of Man.

Paris, son of Priam, King of Troy, asked to judge the fairest Goddess, slighted Hera and Athene, he gave the golden apple to Aphrodite, who promised him the most beautiful woman in the world, Helen, married to Menelaus, King of Sparta. The young Prince eloped with her to Troy. The Greeks launched a great expedition led by Agamemnon, brother of Menelaus, to assault Troy and capture Helen; they were joined by all the famous heroes of Greece including invincible Achilles. The Gods took sides in the conflict. Hera, Athene and Poseidon favoured the Greeks, Aphrodite and Ares the Trojans; Zeus and Apollo were neutral. The 'Iliad' begins in the ninth year of the Siege with a quarrel between Achilles and Agamemnon over the hero's slave-girl Briseis. Achilles in anger sulks in his tent, the Gods in heaven take counsel and as the battle against Troy continues frequently intervene to protect their favourites. Finally to avenge the death of his friend, Patroclus, Achilles slays the Trojan Hector. The 'Iliad' ends with the funeral of Hector amid the lamentations of his wife, Andromache.

Soon afterwards Troy was taken following the strategem of the Wooden Horse, and the city sacked in flames, told in Virgil's 'Aeneid', Book 2. Agamemnon sailed home to be murdered by his faithless wife, Clytemnestra; Achilles and Paris were killed. Helen, the alleged cause of this long war, surprisingly enough returned to Menelaus and lived happily ever after in Sparta as though nothing had happened. But did she?

For many centuries scholars extolled the 'Iliad' as a brilliant invention, classic fiction unrivalled in fire and splendour, the source of literature, the summit of genius. The Greeks regarded the 'Iliad' as superbly revealing the Will of Zeus, just as the Jews venerated the Old Testament as enshrining the Will of Jehovah; they did not believe the story to be literally true. Educated people all over Europe for generations treasured this epic of Homer and based their cultured standards on the heroic example of those proud and noble men and women contending for Troy but even the most learned pedants mesmerised by such a marvellous poem laughed at suggestions that the events might have actually happened. People accepted Adam and Eve in the Garden of Eden but Paris and Helen in the palace of Troy was plainly romance. The great nineteenth-century scholar, Professor Max Muller, declared, 'The Siege of Troy is a repetition of the daily siege of the East by the Solar Powers that are robbed of their brightest treasures in the West.' So much for the wisdom of experts!

In 1870 all Europe smiled when Heinrich Schliemann, a wealthy German businessman, whose success from poverty to riches accelerated by mastery of a dozen languages, was already a romance, announced his intention of fulfilling his boyhood dream by finding Troy. With the topography of the 'Iliad' as guide, he excavated the hill at Hissarlik dominating the plain two and a half miles from the Dardanelles. In 1873 after unearthing nine cities below each other, Schliemann saw one day, twenty-eight feet down near the walls of what he wrongly considered to be Priam's palace, a glint of gold, which held him spellbound. Calling to Sophia, his young Greek wife, to send all the workmen home at once, he attacked the masonry with Teutonic vigour and dug out a wonderful, glittering hoard of golden treasures, diadems and brooches, worn, he imagined, by Helen herself. It was not until near his death that Schliemann realised he had dug down past Homer's Troy and had found treasures belonging to a Troy destroyed a thousand years earlier. However Schliemann had discovered Troy, other archaeologists found evidence of destruction about 1200 BC. The Trojan War emerged from myth to history.

As the victorious Greek fleet sailed from burning Troy Athene in anger at the wicked treatment of the ill-starred prophetess, Cassandra, persuaded Poseidon to raise a great storm, many ships were sunk, the others scattered. The hero, Odysseus, better known as Ulysses, eagerly returning after ten years absence to his faithful wife, Penelope, was blown off course almost in sight of Ithaca, for ten long years the wanderer would suffer most fantastic adventures before the Gods relented and finally permitted his return home.

The fabulous adventures of Ulysses anticipate, indeed surpass, our cheerless Science-Fiction. For nearly three thousand years these wonderful tales have inspired the greatest poets, dramatists and artists of the civilised world. Driven by the storm Ulysses came to the Land of the Lotus Eaters, where his men dallied in sunnied ease until forced to set sail to the island of the Cyclops; captured with his companions by the giant, Polyphemus, he made the monster drunk and with a burning pole blinded him in his one eye. On the Aeolian Island King Aeolus gave Ulysses a bag containing contrary winds which when opened swept them to the shores of the Laestrygonians, cannibals who stoned and sank all the ships except the vessel of Ulysses. On the island of Circe the crew were changed by the enchantress into swine. Hermes helped him overcome her and restore his men, then Ulysses arrived at the mysterious country of the Cimmerians and descended to Hades where he conversed with the shades of departed heroes. When their ship skirted the rocks of the Sirens to escape their alluring songs the wily Ulysses stopped the ears of his companions with wax and fastened himself to the mast, then sailing between Scylla and Charybdis the former monster devoured six of the crew. On the island of the Sun they killed some of the God's cattle, in revenge Zeus destroyed the ship with a lightning-blast. Ulysses, sole survivor, drifted on a plank to Oygia, isle of the nymph, Calypso. For eight years he languished in her charms until Zeus ordered her to let him go. Ulysses built a raft, wrecked by Poseidon, battered and naked he was cast on Scheria, Land of the Phaecians, to be found by Nausicaa, daughter of King Alcinous, whose marvellous palace evokes Plato's description of Atlantis. The Phaecians apparently devised robot slaves and animals of gold and bronze in fabulous automation; they grew luxuriant fruit in artificial currents of warm air. The tender love of Nausicaa, the return of the Wanderer to Ithaca, the greeting by his son, Telemachus, his slaying of the suitors of his wife, Penelope, form a dramatic climax to the most immortal epic in all literature abounding with wondrous thrilling adventures destined by the Gods.

In his fascinating 'Odissea Stellare',[87] brilliant Peter Kolosimo retraces the steps of Ulysses collecting cosmic traditions and relating his wonderful adventures to archaeological enigmas from humanity's prehistory world-wide. He concludes that the 'Odyssey' is not a fable, nor is Ulysses a person of legend; the parallels existing between Homer's poem and the most ancient traditions of the whole world, the memories buried in our remote past, the cosmic references are countless. 'The Odyssey must only be from the stars.'

The 'Helen of Troy' theme is world-wide. The 'Ramayana' describes in wonderful imagery how Ravan abducted Sita, wife of Prince Rama, who launched aerial invasion of Lanka, Ceylon, and aided by Immortals fought duels in flying-cars with fantastic weapons. Rama finally slew the giant Ravan, rescued Sita and flew home with her in a sumptuously furnished aerial-machine high across India to Ayodha near the Himalayas. Inscribed tablets found at Ras Shamra in Syria, identified with old Ugarit, dating from about 1400 BC, tell the fascinating Epic of Kret,[88] King of Ugarit, whose betrothed, Hurrai, was stolen by the Son of Pebel, King of Udum. Counselled by the God, El, Kret marshalled a great army, confronted Pebel, rescued Hurrai and married her.

Spacemen haunted our Earth throughout the Second Millennium BC, the old traditions prove this period to have been one of the most wonderful ages in all history.

> 'Was this the face that launch'd a thousand ships
> And burnt the topless towers of Ilium?
> Sweet Helen, make me immortal with a kiss.'[89]

Beauteous Helen had allured the imagination of men for three thousand years, the most seductive sex-symbol in all history. Faust magically restored to youth conjured Helen from the shades, in poetic rapture they produced a son.

> 'Das Ewig-Weibliche zieht uns hinan.'[90]
> 'The Eternal-Feminine draws us on.'

Johann Wolfgang von Goethe, that idealist of the eighteenth century, poured forth his fascination for the fair sex in plays, poems and love-affairs culminating in his great masterpiece 'Faust'. He saw classical Helen as the quintessence of Woman and in matchless verse extolled her charms far surpassing our own synthetic film-stars.

With shrewd insight Homer avoided portrayal of Helen's loveliness, he hinted at elusive beauty beyond description.

> 'They cried "No wonder such celestial charms
> For nine long years have set the world in arms.
> What winning grace! What majestic mien!
> She moves a Goddess, and she looks a Queen!" '[91]

Today sex-equality is still a myth, sought but undesired. Has any Poet ever penned sonnets to a post-wench? Love springs from illusion, woman's elusive mystery, the femme fatale.

The Ancients believed that the Gods winged down to Earth and mated with mortal women, their divine offspring dominated history. Zeus, enamoured of Leda, Queen of Sparta, visited her as a swan; she brought forth two eggs, from one issued Castor and Pollux, from the other, Helen. Pausanias, that Compiler of guide-books to Antiquity, alleged he had seen the actual shell on show in Sparta. Apollodorus, even sillier, swore that lusty Zeus had seduced his own daughter, Nemesis, who laid an egg for Leda to hatch: Hesiod believed that Zeus[92] impregnated a daughter of Ocean, like Aphrodite Helen sprang from the foam. All over the ancient world the Cosmic Egg signified the sudden appearance of Extraterrestrials, the first Peruvians were said to have been born from a gold, silver and bronze egg which fell from the sky, the Egyptians symbolised the 'Egg' as the 'Eye of Horus', the Sumerians believed that their great Teacher, Oannes or Enki emanated from an Egg, the aborigines of Tasmania tell of their 'Man from an Egg', who taught their ancestors, the famous Tassili frescoes show figures like Spacemen emerging from Eggs, which roughly do resemble Spaceships.

The famous beauties of history owed more to their wit and intelligence than to their good looks; true charm means the marriage of twin minds far transcending physical attraction. Helen captivated the greatest heroes in an Age of dominant women; all down the centuries her phantom loveliness had seduced the souls of men. The few facts known of her still tantalise imagination with idyllic dreams. When Helen was an alluring wench, Theseus carried her off to Athens, where she gave birth to ill-fated Iphigenia, and was later rescued by her brothers, Castor and Pollux. On her return to Sparta the noblest Chiefs in Greece sought Helen's hand in marriage; she chose Menelaus and became mother of Hermione. Life with a petty King probably a bandit-chief, disputing for the Peloponnese soon palled for cultured Helen, she eagerly eloped with dashing young Paris and provoked the Trojan War, although those Greek soldiers of fortune would be more tempted by the plunder of Troy than Helen's fabled charms on those topless towers of Ilium. Helen treated Greeks and Trojans with spirited disdain; Homer mentions her romps with lusty Paris, after he was killed she lost no time in marrying his brother, Deiphobus; shrewdly realising the fortunes of war she soon betrayed him to the conquerors and calmly escaped to Menelaus without remorse for her celebrated, costly escapade. While the Trojan Women, innocent of war, were exiled as slaves, Helen lived in surprising happiness with Menelaus; when he died some say she fled to Rhodes and was strangled, tied to a tree; the poets swear she ascended to a star like her Space-brothers, Castor and Pollux.

Euripides in his drama 'Helen' alleges that the real Helen never went to Troy; actually Paris kidnapped her phantom double; Helen herself sought refuge on the Island of Pharos at the mouth of the Nile with Proteus, an astonishingly honourable Pharaoh, who in ten long years made no attempt to seduce his alluring guest. If Euripides believed this tall tale, few Greeks did. Paris seemed well satisfied with his lovely bride. Had this strange story been really true, surely someone should have told those heroes besieging that Helenless Troy.

Four hundred years later during Homer's own life-time, Babylon was ruled by Semiramis, believed to be the daughter of the God, Oannes, and the Goddess, Ataryatis, symbolising Space Beings. This fabulous Queen invaded Egypt, Ethiopia and Libya, then led the greatest army in Antiquity to storm India; the Assyrians said she ascended to the skies and worshipped her as a Goddess. During the same century Elijah was translated to heaven on a whirlwind, possibly a Spaceship. From the hills of Ionia Homer would sometimes see the 'Power and Glory' of the 'Lord' speeding to the prophets in Israel and those Winged Counsellors visiting Shalmaneser II and Assurnazirpal III in Babylon.

For four centuries minstrels had sung of the Gods intervening at Troy; all traditions told of those wondrous Strangers from the skies. Homer believed in the Gods and Goddesses, Spacemen and Spacewomen, above all in Helen, the Space Queen, whom he immortalised in the 'Iliad'.

Chapter Seven

SPACE LITERATURE OF ANCIENT GREECE

The decipherment of Linear B script astounded historians by proving that Greek was a written language throughout two thousand years of the Ancient World; Homer's wonderful 'Iliad', Hesiod's profound 'Theogony', reveal that by 700 BC Greek literature had attained a sublimity unsurpassed, suggesting long development, yet from many centuries of literacy of this period only a few works remain. Spacemen would probably restrict their 'Contacts' to selected individuals like they apparently do today, such disciples would confide their revelations under secrecy to a few trusted friends. Pythagoras, a likely 'Contact' sternly distrusted the written word, his teaching were transmitted orally down generations of Initiates. Secrets of the Gods would be guarded in the Mysteries. Aeschylus was once condemned to be stoned to death for allegedly disclosing the Mysteries in his great tragedies. All the great civilisations of the past suffered immense destruction, only a tiny fraction of the ancient records are left to enlighten or mislead us.

An intriguing reference by Plutarch in 'Agis and Cleomenes' reveals the vital influence of the stars and the Gods on the affairs of Ancient Greece.

'After instructing others to spread these charges against Leonidas, he himself (Lysander) with his colleagues proceed to observe the traditional sign from heaven.

This is observed as follows. Every ninth year the Ephors select a clear and moonless night, and in silent session watch the face of the heavens. If then a star shoots across the sky, they decide that their Kings have transgressed in the dealings with the Gods and suspend them from their office until an oracle from Delphi or Olympus comes to the succour of the King thus found guilty.

This sign Lysander now declared had been given him and indicted Leonidas.'[93]

The Etruscans, Babylonians, Mayas, Chinese, all ancient peoples, anxiously scanned the skies and interpreted heavenly phenomena as betokening the Will of the Gods, surely a race-memory of Celestial interference with life on Earth.

The earliest Greeks like primitive peoples all over the world in far Antiquity worshipped the Spacemen as Sky Gods descending as Divine Kings to teach the arts and crafts of civilisation to aspiring humanity. The Celestials mastered a wondrous science, some Gods were believed to control thunder, lightning, winds, storms, seas and the potent, ever-present forces of Nature. Temples were erected on hills as dwelling-places of the Gods, race-memories perhaps of the secluded abodes of the Space-Kings in ancient days.

Plutarch in 'De Facie in Orbe Lunae apparet', Moralia XII, discussing the rotation of the Moon, writes 'There is reason to wonder then not that the velocity caused a lion to fall on the Peloponnesus but how is it then that we are not forever seeing countless men falling headlong and lives spurned away tumbling off the Moon as it were and turning head over heels. Diogenes Laertius (viii 72) quotes Timaeus to the effect that Heraclides Ponticus spoke of the fall of a man from the Moon.' Was this some memory of Spacemen?

Visitants from space or Etherean Realms may have occasionally appeared in sacred retreats to their Initiates just as in Israel the 'Lord' materialised to His priests within the tabernacle. Veneration of the Celestials in Greece as in China and Japan developed into the deification of heroes, then to ancestor-worship; life after death in the shades was a drab existence, a miserable immortality which the departed Achilles bewailed to Ulysses as worse than slavery.

The annual cycle of the growth of corn without which life would perish, inspired fertility-cults of the Great Earth-Mother associated with Demeter and later with Aphrodite and Dionysius, the 'Son of God'. Worship of the Sky Gods declined before the mystical religions of Delphic Apollo and Orpheus which purified the souls of men.

As actual manifestations of the Spacemen grew more rare,

the domination of the Heavenly Powers became subtly transformed and extended from the physical to the moral universe; Zeus like Jehovah in Israel was spiritualised from tribal God to awesome supernatural Authority ruling Man's cosmic existence. The Will of Zeus was venerated as Moira governing the lives of men. The Greeks vaguely imagined that somewhere in the sky dwelled the three Moiras or Fates; Clotho, represented with a spindle, spun the fates of men, Lachesis assigned to Man his fate and Atropos decreed the fate that could not be avoided. Sometimes the Fates were depicted as aged women or grave maidens spinning the thread of life and cutting it when life is to end. Aeschylus and the poets in their yearnings for divine justice and meaning to mortal life endowed Zeus and Apollo with the loftiest ethics of universal grandeur directing human affairs; Plato associated God with perfection and sublimity later to inspire St. Paul; for most Greeks religion became a personal matter veiled in Eleusinian Mysteries teaching life after death, which was to have a profound influence on Christianity.[94] The powerful logic of the philosophers, the contention between Epicureans and Stoics the appeal of those novel cults from Egypt and Asia inevitably eclipsed the archaic religion of the Sky Gods, despite much scepticism Greeks still believed that the Gods were real Supermen dwelling in the sky, now elderly pensioners perhaps but on due supplication ready to aid mankind.

Plato, the wisest of Greeks in his 'Laws'[95] solemnly reminded the cynical younger generation 'No one who has adopted in youth that the Gods do not exist, ever continued to hold it until he was old.' More than two thousand years later, the Very Reverend William Inge, Dean of St. Paul's, sagely remarked 'The Gods do exist but they are not what men think they are.'

Peasants in Greece like superstitious country folk everywhere depended on the soil, believed in elementals, satyrs, fairies and nymphs animating Nature, whom they invoked or propitiated with spells, charms and bucolic rituals. This belief in benign and evil spirits, ghosts and demons from those vast uncanny realms of the occult conjuring white and black magic finds the closest affinity with popular superstitions in India, China, Babylon, Egypt, Mexico, Britain, echoes of a most ancient worldwide Nature-worship associated with a witchcraft of strange powers which our own once-materialist science now explores. Such demonology from primitive religion confounded the Christian Church baffling the theologians of the Middle Ages into damning witchcraft; even enlightened intellects like Paracelsus accepted denizens from inner spheres, who sometimes materialised to instruct or torment men and women enchanted by their magic.

Since the relevant classical texts are lost, we may perhaps be pardoned for seeking illumination on Spacemen in Ancient Greece by analogy from one of the most remarkable works of the seventeenth century. In 1670 Montfaucon, thirty-two year-old Abbot of Villars near Toulouse, published in Paris his masterpiece, 'Le Comte de Gabalis',[96] based on rare Latin and Greek manuscripts and magical books summarising the secret lore from far Antiquity. With impressive erudition Montfaucon de Villars claimed that the air was filled with a countless multitude of Sylphs in human form, great lovers of Science, whose wives and children bloomed in wondrous beauty; the seas and rivers were inhabited by Undines and Nymphs of surpassing loveliness, the Earth almost to its centre was peopled by Gnomes, the Little People, guardians of treasures; the Salamanders dwelled in regions of fire and inspired Philosophers. In the eighth century during the reign of Pepin the famous Cabalist, Zedechias, advised the Spirits to reveal themselves to men, they appeared in human form in aerial vessels of admirable structure ranged in battle order, their superb pavilions gliding on the breeze; people impressed by this marvellous spectacle thought they must be sorcerers. This aerial pageant of Sylphs evokes the brilliant and gaily-flagged sky-cars of the Celestials attending Rama and Arjuna and the peoples of Ancient India, perhaps even the Gods of Greece.

This most profound mystery of 'Demons' alien to our

modern thought puzzled the greatest minds of Antiquity and tormented the theologians of the Middle Ages; now as we review the old tales in the light of our new Space knowledge we suddenly discern the familiar pattern of UFOs and Spacemen extending from our world today back to dim prehistory. New discoveries in physics appear to confirm worlds of subtle matter interpenetrating our own, the Borderland Scientists[97] and some Sensitives believe the Extraterrestrials materialise from Etherean Realms, the Sylphs of the Middle Ages, perhaps the 'Daimones' of the Greeks.

That most excellent publication the 'Flying Saucer Review' in its special issue 'The Humanoids' analyses about three hundred reports describing the landings of Extraterrestrials all over the world. Some Beings were almost human in appearance, others seemed freaks, even monsters. On 22nd August 1955 the Sutton family near Hopkinsville, Kentucky, saw

'... a small, spectre-like figure approaching the house. It appeared to be lit by an internal source, had a roundish head, huge elephantine ears and a slit-like mouth which extended from ear to ear. The eyes were huge and wide-set. Only about 3 or 3½ feet in height, the creature had no visible neck, and its arms were long and ended in clawed hands. Although it stood upright, it dropped to all fours when it ran...'[98]

UFO literature abounds in well-documented evidence of the landings of non-humans in isolated places particularly in South America; notable experts appear gravely concerned at the invasion. Descriptions of these humanoids often exuding unpleasant odour at once recall those fantastic tales of devils reeking of sulphur, alleged to have consorted with witches in the Middle Ages, confessions under torture seem more than mere hallucinations as our psychiatrists insist, some correspond uncomfortably with apparitions reported by credible witnesses today. Legends of trolls in Norse faery-tales and circumstantial details of dwarfs and gnomes in Grimm's 'Deutsche Mythologie' and his wonderful 'Märchen' reveal a startling similarity between 'non-humans' recorded throughout history and some

Extraterrestrials manifesting today. Such strange creatures are mentioned in the ancient literature of the East.

A commentary in the 'Nihongi' states

> 'The Celestial Dog or Tengu of modern Japanese superstition is a winged creature in human form with an exceedingly long nose which haunts mountain-tops and other secluded places.'[99]

Similar humanoids appeared in Ancient Greece and were worshipped as Gods. Greek countryfolk delighted in the noisy, merry God, Pan, usually represented as a sensual Being with horns, puck-nose and goat's feet, often depicted as dancing and playing his reed flute. He loved the wild mountains and forests of Arcady, where he frolicked with the woodland-nymphs; sometimes travellers were scared by strange sounds in the wilderness. (Dare we compare the eerie UFO phenomena plaguing Warminster today?) which they attributed to Pan, their fear coined our word 'panic'. Pan was a wonderful musician and son of Hermes (Mercury), a Space God. A tortuous though valid argument can be advanced to suggest that Pan was a generic term for humanoids similar to those bizarre Spacemen now plaguing the peasants of Brazil, his association with music in wild country may have been some poetical connotation for strident noises from Spaceships. An admittedly extravagant deduction yet not wholly untenable as the famous sighting of Philippides suggests.

In 490 BC Darius, Great King of Persia, who had conquered much of the Middle East, invaded Greece, the Persians subdued Attica and marched southwards to crush Athens. Herodotus relates

> 'And firstly before they had yet left the city the captains sent to Sparta as messenger, Philippides, an Athenian, who was a runner and had practised this trade and as Philippides himself reported to the Athenians, Pan met him on Mount Parthenium above Tages. And Pan called Philippides by name and commanded him to ask the Athenians wherefore they paid him no attention though he was well-disposed to them and had often helped them already and should do so again. And Athenians believed it to be true and when their affairs had prospered, they founded a temple to Pan beneath the citadel and ever since his message they have propitiated him with sacrifices and with a torch-race every year.'[100]

Philippides ran the seventy-five miles to Sparta in one day. The Spartans refused aid to Athens, the next day he ran back; a feat which would task our own Marathon runners.

The Athenians attacked the Persians on the plain of Marathon winning one of the most decisive battles in world-history. Plutarch in 'Theseus' records that the Greeks claimed that superhuman warriors, Theseus, Athene and Heracles descended to fight with them, victory was won by aid from the Gods.

Herodotus was born only six years after the Battle of Marathon and probably met people who confirmed the tale of Philippides; he would see with his own eyes the Temple of Pan and learn why it was built. Silenus, brother of Pan, a jovial, tipsy old man, was a satyr, possibly a humanoid. Plutarch in 'Sulla'[101] reports that in 83 BC at Apollonia near Dyrrachium in Illyria Sulla's soldiers caught a satyr asleep, 'such a one as sculptors and painters represent'; despite many interpreters this humanoid could not understand, he emitted a hoarse cry like a goat. To us this sylvan creature appears an alien from another world like those green children manifesting from St. Martin's Land in the Middle Ages and the strange humanoids said to be manifesting today.

Surely Philippides must have told a most convincing tale to persuade the Athenians to build a Temple to Pan. Could he have met a Spaceman?

Plutarch relates that in the time of Tiberius, 14 AD, one, Thramm, pilot of a ship making for Italy, was thrice called by name and bidden to give the news that the Great Pan was dead. A tale with UFO overtones?

Since 1942 natives in South Sea islands have worshipped an American airman as the God, John Thrumm, and followed the Cargo Cult. Could not the Greeks have worshipped a humanoid as their God, Pan?

The Persians planned revenge for their defeat at Marathon. Ten years later in 480 BC Xerxes invaded Greece with tremendous land and naval forces numbering according to Herodotus 2,641,610 fighting-men swollen by reserves to 5,282,220 with countless women and concubines. The vast army bridged the Dardanelles, conquered Thessaly and Macedonia then advanced on the disunited South. Leonidas with his three hundred Spartans met heroic deaths defending the Pass of Thermopylae, the Persians swept on to burn Athens; the Athenians had evacuated their wives and children to the island of Salamis. Themistocles cleverly lured the great Persian fleet, partly crippled by heavy storms, to venture into the narrow waters, watched by Xerxes seated on a marble throne on the hill above. The heavier Greek ships smashed the trapped enemy in a glorious victory. The following year the Spartans routed the invaders at Plataea. The Persians were shattered and Greece saved.

Plutarch in 'Themistocles XV' wrote

'At this stage of the struggle they say that a great light flamed out from Eleusis and an echoing cry filled the Thriassian plain down to the sea, as if multitudes of men together conducting the mystic Iachus in procession. Then out of the shouting throng a cloud seemed to lift itself closely from the earth, pass out seawards and settle down upon the triremes. Others fancied they saw apparitions and shapes of armed men coming from Aegina with hands stretched and to protect the Hellenic triremes. These they conjectured were the Aecidae, who had been prayerfully invoked before the battle to come to their aid.'[102]

In 1287 BC Rameses II facing defeat by the Hittites at Kadesh swore the God Amen came to his aid; the Japanese claim that in 660 BC the Heavenly Deities assisted their Emperor Jimmu against the Ainu; Cicero recorded that in 498 BC Castor and Pollux saved the Romans at Lake Regillus. A comet, possibly a UFO, hovered over the Battle of Hastings in AD 1066. Strange aerial lights attended battles during the Hitler and Korean Wars. Did Gods visit Marathon and Salamis? The great dramatist, Aeschylus, probably thought so; he fought there.

The fifty-three years from 484 BC, the year Aeschylus gained his first prize, including the great plays of Sophocles, to 431 BC, when Euripides wrote 'Medea', was a Golden Age of Drama, unequalled until those glorious decades of Marlowe, Ben Jonson, Shakespeare and their brilliant rivals. Aeschylus[103] was said to have been ordered by the God, Dionysius, to write tragedies; Sophocles said Aeschylus wrote without knowing it; others swore he was drunk or inspired by the Gods, his originality and genius were superhuman. Only seven of his seventy tragedies are extant. Aeschylus modestly described his works as scraps from Homer's banquet; like Homer he was inspired with religious awe of the supreme authority of Zeus, his plays sternly upheld moral law, the triumph of good, the punishment of evil; he wrote with concentrated power, dictating human destinies directed by the Gods. The trilogy of 'Agamemnon', 'Choephori' and 'Eumenides' describing the murder of Agamemnon by his adulterous wife, Clytemnestra, the matricide and suffering of their son, Orestes, are mighty tragedies, impressive today. In the 'Eumenides' Apollo advises the guilt-stricken Orestes to go to Athens for the judgement of Athene who acquits him, as though Aeschylus knew that Celestials judged the fate of men. 'Prometheus Bound' concerns the struggle between Zeus and Prometheus, a titanic drama of the Gods; this tragedy could be irreverently regarded as science-fiction though it soars in cosmic grandeur transcending the squalid morals titillating our modern stage.

Aeschylus died at Gela in Sicily in 456 BC at the age of 69. An eagle mistaking the poet's bald head for a stone dropped a tortoise upon it to break its shell, and so fulfilled an oracle by which he was fated to die by a blow from heaven.

Do UFOs drop tortoises on playwrights' bald heads?

Sophocles,[104] thirty years younger than Aeschylus, was a sunny-natured Athenian, trained in music and gymnastics, famed for his handsome physique, the ideal healthy mind in a healthy body. The pleasure-loving pursuits of this gallant endeared him to the Athenians, who soon preferred his lyrical plays to the austere moralisings of his crusty rival, Aeschylus. His astonishing output of 130 plays did not detract from their excellence, only seven are extant. Tragedies like 'Antigone', 'Electra', express deep and poignant emotions with soulful beauty yet Sophocles is profoundly aware of Gods brooding over the destinies of Men. Aristotle considered 'Oedipus Rex' to be the masterpiece of Greek tragedy, a judgement still held today;

dominating the plot was the oracle of Apollo; the Goddess Athene introduces 'Ajax', Heracles as 'Deux ex machina' suddenly appears to conclude 'Philoctetes' directing the hero with divine decree. Lucian wrote entertainingly

'Sophocles, the tragedian, swallowed a grape and choked to death at ninety-five. Brought to trial by his son, Iophen, towards the close of his life on a charge of feeble-mindedness he read the jurors his "Oedipus at Coloneus" proving by the play that he was sound of mind, so that the jury applauded him to the echo and convicted the son himself of insanity.'[105]

The idealism of Sophocles charmed easy-going Athens, he expressed popular opinion in stressing that all men and women, whatever the trials and temptations of human life, are finally subject to the Gods above, the Spacemen.

While Aeschylus was fighting to defeat the Persians at Salamis in 480 BC on that very island was born his distinguished successor, Euripides, whose parents had evacuated from their home in Athens. Close friendship with Socrates and study of the teachings of Anaxagoras, made him break with tradition, he represented men and women as they really are not as they should be, stressing human emotions in theatrical scenes without which drama could never have developed. Such modernity made him enemies. Even Aristophanes, himself a free-thinker, jeered that Euripides was no gentleman since his mother sold cabbages. Euripides was sour-tempered and loathed ridicule, his two wives proved unfaithful. In his old age he left Athens in disgust for exile at the Court of Archelaus of Macedon, a fateful venture for in 406 BC at 75 jealous courtiers contrived for Euripides to be attacked and killed by savage dogs. Of his seventy-five plays only eighteen survive. Despite his unhappy marriages Euripides had surprising understanding of women, creating the brilliant characters of Hecuba, Helen, Electra, Iphigenia and above all the fascinating, revengeful Medea, classic roles long foreshadowing those emancipated women of Ibsen.

Euripides[106] considered it 'good theatre' to bring the Immortals down to Earth. Castor and Pollux appeared in 'Electra' and 'Helen'; Apollo in 'Alcestis' and 'Orestes';

Minerva in 'Ion'; 'Suppliants', 'Trojan Dames' and Artemis in 'Hippolytus'.

Aristophanes born 448 BC wrote fifty-four comedies, the eleven which survive satirise the Gods in burlesque scenes amusing the Athenians. In the 'Birds' Peisthetairus goes to seek his fortune in Nephefcoccuga, a City of Cuckoos in the clouds, there he meets Prometheus, Hercules and Iris. Trygeas in 'The Peace' flies to heaven on a giant dung-beetle and meets Mercury. Hundreds of Greek plays must have been lost, the few that remain suggest that the characterisation of the Gods on the stage was a welcome convention.

The intervention of a God to foretell the future or to give judgement was evidently accepted as vaguely possible, if somewhat improbable. Race-memory had implanted in the mind of all Greeks the reality of the Gods in ancient times; the cynical younger generation probably looked upon them as exiled Royalty living in luxury somewhere in the skies, perhaps even returning occasionally incognito to see their friends. Elderly people no doubt welcomed representations of the Gods confirming their religious beliefs. Today were Christ, Buddha and Mahomet to appear on the stage our theatre-goers would be shocked, could even our greatest playwright give such Illumined credibility were they just figments of imagination and had never existed? The Greek dramatists knew the Gods were not symbols but Supermen larger than life with grandiose moods dominating mortal men. Surely the Gods were Spacemen!

The Greek Classics tell of generals and politicians, philosophers and playwrights, whose genius inspired Hellas. Alexander, Pericles, Socrates, Sophocles, bejewel a galaxy of Immortals shining across the centuries to inspire civilisation of the West. Behind these Colossi bestriding Greece we glimpse in the shadows a few solitary eccentrics who seem more suited to our Space Age. Those Spacemen watching Babylon and Israel must also have landed amid the mountains of the Peloponnese and met some disciples; our knowledge is so tantalisingly vague yet we may imagine the men they would likely contact.

Lycurgus, son of Eunoxus, King of Sparta, visited Spain, Crete, Libya, Egypt and even India in the ninth or tenth century before Christ meeting the wise men of those countries, although Plutarch deplores that concerning Lycurgus nothing can be said which is not disputed since indeed there are different accounts of his birth, his travels, his death. On return to Sparta, a city torn by anarchy and licentiousness, Lycurgus was hailed by all factions as a Saviour, the only man to cure the sorry ills of State. He paid frequent visits to Delphi and said the Laws were given him there by Apollo just as Minos, Hammurabbi and Moses had received Laws from their own Gods. Apollo slew Python, the celebrated serpent after the deluge of Deucalion, similar legends of dragon-slaying in Ancient Britain and China seem to symbolise conflict with Spacemen. Serpent worship all over the ancient world was associated with sky-dragons, a primitive memory of Spaceships. The high-priestess at Delphi, called Pythia, inhaled an intoxicating vapour emanated from a chasm in the Temple floor; her oracle purported to give the revelations of Apollo usually couched in double-talk which left the ancient questioners more confused than before.

The brother of Lycurgus was said to be Polydectes, King of the island of Seriphos, whither floated the massive chest containing the infant Perseus and his Mother, Danae, seduced by Zeus, metamorphosed into a shower of gold. Polydectes fell in love with Danae; when Perseus attained manhood the King got rid of him by sending the young hero off to slay the Gorgon. On his return to protect his Mother Perseus used Medusa's head to turn Polydectes and all his guests to stone, Perseus flew on winged sandals; he apparently possessed some death-ray weapon, the Egyptians worshipped him as a God and told Herodotus he visited them; he closely resembled Balor with the Flashing Eye in Irish mythology and the Aztec Tezcatlipoca with the malignant rays, possibly Spacemen. Whether Lycurgus was concerned in this confusion is not clear; he may have lived contemporary with Homer or even Solomon, when Spacemen were active on Earth. The belief that Lycurgus was inspired by Celestials was strengthened by the tradition that after giving the Laws to Sparta he left to end his life in voluntary exile just as Laotse after teaching Taoism to the Chinese was last seen climbing a mountain towards the clouds. The Cretans claimed Lycurgus died in Pergamus, some say he died in Cirrha, others in Elis, no one really knows. Centuries later the Spartans believed that Lycurgus was not a man but a God and built a temple to him with yearly sacrifices and the highest honours. Like Quetzalcoatl, Law-Giver to Ancient Mexico, was Lycurgus translated to the skies?

About the sixth century BC lived the poet, Aethalides, a herald, the son of Mercury, to whom it was granted to be amongst the dead and the living at stated times; he was said to have travelled in Hades and above the Earth, reminiscent of Enoch. This ancient Adamski penned his revelations in a poem unfortunately lost. Pythagoras claimed to be a reincarnation of Aethalides suggesting the poet was an Initiate receptive to Spacemen. Only tantalising fragments remain of those exquisite lyrics of Sappho, that supreme, passionate poetess of Lesbos, lilting of love; Anacreon sang gaily of wine, Philoxenus, the great dithyrambic poet, wrote a Rabelaisian poem about the cloudship of Zeus more amusing than our stolid 'Saucer' books. About 400 BC Philoxenus at the Court of Dionysius in Sicily, obliged to listen to the King's bad verse, suggested that the best way to correct it would be to draw a black line through the whole paper; the King somewhat aggrieved sent him to slave in the quarries. Later on release Dionysius recited his poem again to be interrupted by the anguished Philoxenus begging to be sent back to the quarries rather than be sentenced to listen to such rubbish. A stern example to our Television critics!

Pythagoras, the Sage of Samos, who flourished in the sixth century BC, was acclaimed by Diodorus Siculus as a God among men; he possessed not only great eloquence of speech but a temperate character of soul and a marvellous memory. He believed in the transmigration of souls and remembered having been the Trojan hero, Euphorbus, who was slain by Menelaus. Callisthenes said Pythagoras was the first to introduce geometry to Greece from Egypt. The Sage preached a simple life and taught his disciples to eat meat uncooked and to drink only water. Pythagoras called his principles 'Philosophia' or 'Love of Wisdom'; he said because of human weakness no man is wise but all men could become 'Lovers of Wisdom' or 'Philosophers'. Ammianus Marcellinus reported that Pythagoras learned his knowledge from the Hyperborean Druid, Abaris, the Priest of Apollo, who took no earthly food and rode through the air on the 'Arrow of Apollo' suggesting a Spaceman. Suidas told of the presence of Apollo in Athens and Sparta, where he instructed people in the prevention of plagues. The so-called Pythagorean doctrine, according to Suidas, was an adaptation of the ancient British philosophy. Caesar later wrote that the Druids were renowned for their religious and astronomical knowledge, in their famous colleges students studied the Mysteries for twenty years, evidence of profound wisdom. Pythagoras also told of intercourse with the Gods, people believed the Sage to have been miraculously transported around the Earth, hinting at his friendship with Space Beings. When the populace of Crotona burned down the Temple where Pythagoras and his followers had taken refuge, the Celestials must have arrived too late for the Sage perished in the flames.

The mysterious disappearances of people in the present-day and in the past arouses speculation as to abduction by Extraterrestrials. Legends in many countries tell of heroes transported to some Land of Eternal Youth, where they mingle with Immortals in wondrous realms beyond Space and Time, possibly another planet; sometimes they return to find their families and friends long dead and buried, suddenly they age centuries old and die themselves. Epimenides, the celebrated poet and prophet of Crete, when a boy in the early seventh century BC was sent out by his father in search of a sheep; seeking shelter from the heat of the midday sun, he went into a cave and there fell into a deep sleep, which lasted fifty-seven years. On his return he found to his amazement that his brother had grown an old man. In

596 BC Solon invited Epimenides to purify Athens from the plague, there he worked many wonders. His God was the Cretan Zeus, tradition assigns to him a theogony, a Critica and various mysterious writings. The influence of Epimenides must have been most profound for six hundred years later St. Paul in his Epistle to Titus quoted him concerning the people of Crete saying, 'One of themselves, even a prophet of their own, said "The Cretans are always liars, evil beasts, slow bellies." ' Harsh words! The Spartans took Epimenides prisoner in a war with Proconnesus and put him to death because he refused to prophesy favourably. The Cretans believed he lived for three hundred years and worshipped him as a God. Fantastic though it seems, Epimenides' sleep in a cave lasting fifty-seven years might have been his own explanation concealing translation to another planet, where he was taught wisdom to impart to the peoples of Earth: stories of him wandering outside his body ascribed to him powers of astral travelling practised by great Initiates but they could be meant to conceal possible trips in Spaceships. The extraordinarily long life of Epimenides evokes Count St. Germain, who claimed to have lived for several centuries.[107]

Another astral-traveller was Aristeas of Proconnesus, a noted writer quoted by Longinus, who lived in the third century before Christ. He once vanished from Cyzicus, the wealthy city near the Sea of Marmora and reappeared at Metapontum near Taranto to spread the worship of Apollo. He was an authority on the inaccessible Hyperboreans. It is tempting to wonder whether his travels were made in Spaceships.

The scanty evidence would suggest that Lycurgus, Aethalides, Pythagoras, Epimenides and Aristeas, like their contemporaries, the Prophets of Israel, were inspired by Spacemen.

The Philosophers spoke of the Gods somewhat vaguely; perhaps they hesitated to reveal the esoteric teachings of the Mysteries but generally they were much more interested in men. Plato, Aristotle and their followers studied the relation of Man to the Universe, abstract problems of human conduct, love, justice, education and practical conceptions of the ideal State. This was the age of Sophists like Socrates concerned with ethics and the nature of Reality, disputing with the irritated Athenians not speculating about Spacemen. When Socrates spoke of his 'daemon' he usually meant the voice of conscience, his inner self. Plato, however, wrote in 'Laws' 713 AD, 'Daemons are defined as a race superior to men but inferior to Gods; they were created to watch human affairs', suggesting perhaps the existence of a celestial race or Spacemen. In the 'Phaedra' 246 F, Plato describing the divine as beauty, goodness and the like, added

'Zeus, the mighty leader, holding the reins of a winged chariot, leads the way in heaven, ordering all and taking care of all and there follows the array of Gods and Demi-Gods, marshalled in eleven bands.'

This concept would suggest that Plato believed in Celestials speeding across the skies like the Gods in their golden cars so brilliantly described in the Sanskrit classics.

Aristotle was never at a loss for ideas. Unfortunately they paralysed men's minds for nearly two thousand years. In his 'Meteorology' he declared

'The cause of these shooting stars is sometimes the motion which ignites the exhalation.... The flames passed wonderfully quickly and looks like a thing thrown or as if one thing after another caught fire.... Sometimes it is like the flame from the lamp and sometimes bodies are projected by being squeezed out (like fruit-stones from one's fingers) and so are seen to fall into the sea and on dry land both by night and by day when the sky is clear.... These then must be taken to be the causes of shooting-stars and the phenomena of combustion and also of the other transient appearances of this kind.'[108]

This diverting, if mistaken, opinion of the great Aristotle suggests that in his leisure moments, he, too, might have watched UFOs.

Anaxagoras, an intimate friend and teacher of Euripides and Pericles, taught that a Supreme Intelligence was the cause of all things. Pliny wrote in 'Historia Naturalis', Book II, LIX

'The Greeks tell the story that Anaxagoras of Clazomenae in the 2nd year of the 78th Olympiad (467 BC) was enabled by his knowledge of astronomical literature to prophesy that in a certain number of days a rock would fall from the sun, and that this occurred in the daytime in the Goat's River, a district of Thrace (the stone is still shown, it is of the size of a wagon-load and brown in colour.) – a comet, also blazing in the nights at the time – There is also one that is worshipped at Cassandra, the place that has been given the name of Potidaea, and where a colony was settled on account of this occurrence. I myself saw one that had recently come down in the territory of the Vocentii.'[109]

In 1772 Lavoisier and other Members of the French Academy reported that stones do not fall from the sky, a conclusion destined to cause scientists some embarrassment.

Darmiachus in his treatise on Religion wrote that in 468/7 BC an immense fiery body moved erratically in the heavens for seventy-five days then crashed in flames like shooting-stars.

Lysander, the distinguished Spartan General, in 405 BC brought the Peloponnesian War to a conclusion by defeating the Athenian fleet at Aegospotami near the Dardanelles. (Lampsacus, Propontis.) Plutaarch in his 'Life of Lysander' declared

'Lysander had wrought a work of the greatest magnitude with the least toil and effort and had brought to a close in a single hour a war which in length and the incredible variety of its incidents surpassed all its predecessors. Its struggles and issues had assumed ten thousand changing shapes and it had cost Hellas more generals than all her previous wars together and yet it was brought to a close by the prudence and ability of one man. Therefore some actually thought the result due to divine intervention.... There were some who declared that the Dioscuri (Castor and Pollux) appeared as twin stars on either side of Lysander's ship just as he was sailing out against the enemy and shone out over the rudder-sweeps.'[110]

Diodorus Siculus commenting on the fall of Sparta in 372 BC wrote

'A divine portent foretold the loss of their Empire for there was seen in the heavens during the course of many nights a great blazing torch which was named from its shape a "flaming beam", and a little later to the surprise of all the Spartans were defeated in a great battle and irretrievably lost their supremacy.'[111]

Callisthenes[112] recorded that a similar appearance of a trail of fire was observed before the sea swallowed up Buris and Helice, cities in Achaia in 373 BC. Diodorus Siculus also referred to a celestial torch appearing when earthquakes and floods destroyed cities in the Peloponnese. Aristotle, then only eleven years old, swore it was a comet.

In far Antiquity the Ancients honoured the stars as homes of the Gods, those Divine Kings who brought civilisation down to Earth. The psycho-science of the Celestial Teachers taught that the stars radiated potent vibrations influencing the minds of men, a discovery made by our radio-astronomers who monitor radiations which may subtly affect the human brain. Astrology may be glimmerings from some wondrous wisdom which viewed the Universe as the Supreme Thought of the Creator, where each heavenly body had occult influence on all intelligent life. The Greeks like their Indo-European ancestors had superstitious reverence for the stars, scorned by the astronomers devising their intricate epicycles. The constellations moved across the heavenly vault in serene beauty; this perfection convinced Plato of the existence of the Gods; such stately perpetual motion signified divine direction. The Stoic Philosophy propounded by Zeno about 310 BC preached that everything came from God, at the end of a Great Year all returned to God conforming to the Divine Plan. The Stoics believed that God wrote across the heavens the destinies of men in the celestial language of the stars, resurrecting a doctrine thousands of years old. Astrology encouraging determinism, submission to fate, was sternly challenged by Christianity yet superstition is still deeply rooted in the hearts of the Greeks, echoes of the ancient cosmic religion, race-memories of the Spacemen.

With fantastic erudition Madame H. P. Blavatsky[113] traces the symbolism of the Zodiac or Celestial Belt from India to Babylon, Egypt, Israel and Greece. Originally there were only ten Signs known to the public plus two mystical Signs comprehended by Initiates, one of these became Scorpio, later the Sign of Libra was added by the Greeks. Libra, the Balance, has great occult significance typifying the balance of opposite forces to sustain a universe of harmony. Esoteric lore claims that Libra was invented by the Greeks before the Book of Genesis was written, suggesting a wisdom in ancient Greece of immense antiquity.

The significance of astrology to the Ancient Greeks is illumined in an intriguing thesis by the French mythologist, Jean Richter; in 'Géographie sacrée du mond grece'[114] published by Hachette, Paris, M. Richter after erudite research into ancient Greek religious symbolism has apparently elucidated that on the circumference of a circle, radius a thousand stadii (about 110 miles) centred on the sacred shrine of Delphi, centre of the Hellenic world, navel of the whole Earth, are found twelve famous places, each associated with the corresponding Sign of the Zodiac. Cephalonia-Aries, Olympus-Taurus, Sparta-Gemini, Cythera-Cancer, Hermione-Leo, Athens-Virgo, Thebes-Libra, Chalcis-Scorpio, Pelion-Sagittarius, Edessa-Capricorn, Klea-Aquarius, Kassope-Pisces. Temples and coins in each of these districts honour the appropriate zodiacal symbol, an unlikely sequence of coincidence calling for explanation. Our incomprehension becomes completely confounded when M. Richter reveals a similar sacred circle centred on Sardis in Asia Minor, where its circumference intersects the coastline are found the towns of Patra, Xanthus, Side and other notable sites of Antiquity. Such astonishing correspondence between famous cities and Signs of the Zodiac suggests that these cities were not founded to suit local geography and population needs but to conform with the zodiacal Plan of the Divine Powers, a bizarre explanation more outrageous than the apparent facts. Prehistoric earthworks between Glastonbury and Somerton are interpreted by Mrs K. E. Maltwood[115] to signify the Somerset Zodiac symbolising most ancient esoteric wisdom associated with Teachers from Space. In remote times there were apparently surprisingly close links between Greece and Britain. M. Richter's impressive evidence implies the existence in far Antiquity of accurate maps detailing the Eastern Mediterranean necessary for fixing precise sites on the sacred circle, an assumption ridiculed by scholars who believe the Greeks of prehistory to have been a primitive people. Most precise maps actually did exist in ages past. The Piri Reis map depicts an ice-free Antarctica; Ancient Egyptian records from 5000 BC show Norway, Switzerland, the Congo and Indonesia; about 240 BC Eratosthenes, Chief Librarian at the Museum of Alexandria measured the circumference of the Earth at 24,670 miles, which is only about 200 miles short, proving he probably had access to ancient knowledge. The Zodiacal circles centred at Delphi and Sardis, irrational though they seem to our conditioned thought-pattern, possibly copy similar circles elsewhere, the knowledge needed to determine them suggests an advanced civilisation in ancient times and the mapping of our Earth by Spacemen.

Study of the stars in the remote past by priests all over the world may have been prompted by memories of Celestial Visitants and worship of the Sky Gods, such prolonged observations did record data for practical astronomy as well as for the more popular, fanciful astrology. The Great Pyramid built in far Antiquity incorporates surprising astronomical knowledge; about 4000 BC the Babylonians are said to have discovered the difference between the solar and lunar years, in 4241 BC the Egyptians instituted their Sothic Cycle of 1460 years based on the risings of Sirius or Sothis, the 'Dog Star'; in 4236 BC they produced the first practical calendar and by 4000 BC they had named and noted the positions of all the bright stars in the sky. About 3000 BC the Assyrians recorded eclipses of the sun and moon, by 2650 BC the Chinese had mapped the sky and distinguished the twelve Signs of the Zodiac, noted by Hindu astronomers centuries before. Chaldean astronomers by 2000 BC had charted the constellations and discovered the Saros period of eclipses. In 1800 BC the Britons erected Stonehenge as an astronomical observatory of extraordinary complexity; by 1400 BC Hindu astronomers were recording the motions of the moon with extreme accuracy and in 1250 BC the Chinese correctly measured the duration of the year. By 747 BC the Babylonians recorded the ephemerides of the sun, moon and planets and fixed the calendar. There is reason to believe that some of the Ancients used telescopes, about 2000 BC the Assyrians depicted Saturn with a ring invisible to the naked eye but easily seen with optical lenses found in Babylon.

Many of the religious and philosophical beliefs of Ancient Greece originated in India, it seems likely that the Greeks were acquainted with much of the astronomical knowledge of the East. By 600 BC visitations by Spacemen were reduced to rare surveillance, the Gods appeared content to watch men on Earth evolve by their own efforts without interference; soon eclipsed by new, exciting philosophies the Celestials receded to vague myths. Thales of Miletus (656-546) broke with ancient traditions and, rejecting the old mythological explanations, he introduced into Greece the new astronomy and mathematics he had acquired in Egypt and Babylon, which enabled him to predict the eclipse of the sun in 585 BC. Some of the Greek ideas were astonishingly modern. Anaximander (610-547) propounded an endless cycle of universes, worlds created from immense rotations of matter, as suggested centuries later by Laplace, he studied fossils in the rocks and anticipated Darwin teaching that all creatures including Man had evolved from primitive life in the sea. Pythagoras (570-500) stated that the Earth was round, confirmed by Aristarchus (310-230) who anticipated Copernicus and declared that the Earth revolving on its own axis moved around the Sun. Meton about 430 BC established the Metonic Cycle, the relative positions of the Sun and Moon repeated themselves every nineteen years. About 320 BC Aratus of Soli composed his wonderful poem 'Phaenomena'[116] giving the astronomical description of the heavens according to Eudoxus based on Egyptian theories of the celestial sphere, he accomplished this undertaking with such skill and ingenuity in animated verse that critics extolled the epic as equal to Homer or Sophocles; it was popular for centuries and later translated into Latin by Cicero. The detailed knowledge of the constellations revealed by Aratus astonishes us by proving that the Greeks knew much more astronomy than we generally imagine. Hipparchus (190-120), regarded as the greatest astronomer in Antiquity, rejected the heliocentric theory of Aristarchus; he believed our Earth to be the centre of the universe, compiled a catalogue of 850 stars, rediscovered the precession of the Equinoxes and explained the motion of the planets by assuming they moved in epicycles while at the same time circling the Earth.

Pliny in his erudite 'Natural History', Book II, XXIV, wrote

> 'Hipparchus, before mentioned, who can never be sufficiently praised, no one having done more to prove that Man is related to the stars and that our souls are parts of heaven, detected a new star that came into existence in his life-time, the movement of this star in its line of radiance led him to wonder whether this was a fixed occurrence, whether the stars we think to be fixed are also in motion.'

The 'greatest astronomer in Antiquity' would surely not confuse this bright object with the planet, Venus. The favourite explanation of our own Air Ministry that such aerial lights were due to aeroplanes refuelling at night would have astonished the learned Hipparchus even more than it astonishes us.

About AD 1580 Tycho Brahe, the great Danish astronomer, related

> 'One evening, as according to my usual habit, I was considering the celestial vault, to my indescribable amazement, I saw, close to the zenith in Cassiopea, a radiant star of extraordinary size. Struck with astonishment, I knew not whether I could believe my eyes.'[117]

The Russian astrophysicist, Robert Vitolniek, disclosed

> 'As we were watching the ionosphere and luminous clouds at the observation station in Ogre, Latvia, on July 26, 1965, we noticed at 9.35 pm an extremely bright star which seemed to be slowly moving westwards. Through our 8-power binoculars we could discern a small flat spot. The telescope disclosed that it was a lense-like disc about 350 feet in diameter with a small spherical bulge clearly visible in its centre. Around the disc, at a distance of two diameters three balls were slowly describing a circumference. All the four bodies were lustreless pearly-green.'[118]

Did Hipparchus too see a UFO proving the presence of Spaceships over Ancient Greece?

The development of astronomy in Greece was paralleled by speculations into the nature of atoms by Democritus, the great engineering devices by Archimedes, who calculated the number of grains of sand required to make a universe of the size proposed by Aristarchus as 10 to the power of 63, a guess as valid as the contradictions of our cosmologists. Archytas about 580 BC studied the principles of flight and made a model glider in the pattern of a dove; he was said to have invented the screw. Hiero of Alexandria about AD 100 utilised the power of steam anticipating the steam-engine of James Watt which promoted the Industrial Revolution. It is a melancholy reflection that had the Greek spirit of enquiry not been crushed by bigoted Christians, mankind might now be basking in the wondrous technology postponed until AD 3500.

Alexander the Great, whose death in 323 BC at thirty-three left the world and himself unconquered, in masterly campaigns led the Greeks to India; as Napoleon's ill-starred venture to the Nile resurrected the buried glories of Egypt, so scholars accompanying the expedition fertilised the genius of Hellas with the age-old wisdom of the East. A marvelling posterity adulated the hero with prodigies, he actually thought himself to be a God; his dazzling meteoric career certainly suggests powerful inspiration from some inner 'daemon' or other celestial source. Arrian, Ptolemy and Megesthenes depict Alexander's life and death in prosaic detail, later historians embellished him with wonders of doubtful authenticity omitted in the classical histories. Frank Edwards, the noted American UFO reporter, quoting some source unfortunately not disclosed, states 'Intelligent beings from outer Space may already be looking us over.' He exasperates us by claiming

'Alexander the Great was not the first to see them nor was he the first to find them troublesome. He tells of two strange craft that dived repeatedly at his army until the war elephants, the men and the horses all panicked and refused to cross the river where the incident occurred. What did the things look like? His historian describes them as great shining silvery shields, spitting fire around the rims ... things that came from the skies and returned to the skies.'[119]

This remarkable incident was apparently paralleled by an equally fantastic visitation during the Siege of Tyre by Alexander in 332 BC. Quoting Giovanni Gustavo Droysen's 'Storia di Alessandro il Grande', the erudite Italian Alberto Fenoglio, writes in 'CLYPEUS' Anno 111, No. 2, a startling revelation which we now translate

'The fortress would not yield, its walls were fifty feet high and constructed so solidly that no siege-engine was able to damage it. The Tyrians disposed of the greatest technicians and builders of war-machines of the time and they intercepted in the air the incendiary arrows and projectiles hurled by the catapults on the city.

One day suddenly there appeared over the Macedonian camp these "flying shields", as they had been called, which flew in triangular formation led by an exceedingly large one, the others were smaller by almost a half. In all there were five. The unknown chronicler narrates that they circled slowly over Tyre while thousands of warriors on both sides stood and watched them in astonishment. Suddenly from the largest "shield" came a lightning-flash that struck the walls, these crumbled, other flashes followed and walls and towers dissolved, as if they had been built of mud, leaving the way open for the besiegers who poured like an avalanche through the breeches. The "flying shields" hovered over the city until it was completely stormed then they very swiftly disappeared aloft, soon melting into the blue sky.'[120]

The intervention of 'flying shields' from heaven during a siege was chronicled again about eleven hundred years later. In his curious mediaeval Latin Monk Lawrence in 'Annales Laurissenses' wrote how a few years earlier in AD 776 the heathen Saxons rebelled against Charlemagne and having destroyed the castle at Aeresburg marched down the River Lippy to besiege Sigiburg. As the Saxons pounded the castle with great stones from their catapults and prepared final assault against the outnumbered Christians

'... The Glory of God appeared in manifestation above the church within the fortress. Those watching outside in the place, of whom many still live to this very day, said they beheld the likeness of two large shields reddish in colour in motion, flaming above the church (et dicunt vidisse instar duorum scutorum, colore rubeo flammantes et agitantes super ipsam ecclesiam), and when the pagans who were outside saw this sign, they were at once thrown into confusion, and terrified with great fear they began to flee from the castle ...'[121]

The whole multitude of Saxons in panic were driven to headlong flight, later they submitted to Charlemagne. The heathens were so impressed by the power of the Lord conjured down by the Christians, that they begged to be baptised. Monk Lawrence marvelling at this divine prodigy expressly mentions that many eye-witnesses were still alive to confirm its reality.

Such astounding incidents in the times of Alexander the

Great and Charlemagne confound our conditioned thought-pattern, though we solemnly worship those Extraterrestrials manifesting in Israel. Are these celestial interventions really credible? Suppose if next century our cosmonauts visiting Mars chance on some battle being waged beneath! May they not perhaps swoop down flashing laser-rays to aid one side or the other? The victors will worship their Saviours as Gods, the vanquished curse them as Devils. Is that what happened once here on Earth? An intriguing problem for our theologians!

Whatever discourses the astronomers and philosophers might hold on the existence of the Gods, the people of Greece with superstitious awe firmly believed the stars were inhabited by wonderful Eccentrics who might be cajoled to aid mortals on Earth. The most fascinating travelogue in all Antiquity was surely penned by Lucian, the greatest of Second Century Sophists born about AD 125 at Samosata in Syria, whose fanciful 'Science Fiction' contrasted strongly with those austere 'Meditations' of his Emperor, Marcus Aurelius. Lucian practised for some time as a lawyer in Antioch, then went to Greece to teach rhetoric, an audacity to make Demosthenes turn in his grave. This 'Voltaire of Antiquity' satirised philosophy, religion and the culture of his times with a gay buffoonery concealing shrewd commonsense in a style of simplicity even grace, his so-called 'A True Story' anticipating the tales of Jules Verne.

'Once upon a time setting out from the Pillars of Hercules and heading for the Western Ocean with a fair wind, I went a-voyaging. The motive and purpose of my journey lay in my intellectual activity and desire for adventure, and in my wish to find out what the end of the ocean was, and who the people were that lived on the other side.'[138]

Had Lucian listened to old Greek sailors yarning of lands beyond the Western Sea? If Lucian's deeds had matched his words he could have landed before Columbus and claimed the New World for Athens. Charlemagne might have rested his weary feet in Ford cars, smoked cigars and watched colour-television; he would have been too busy in New York borrowing money to bother about the Holy Roman Empire, which as Voltaire said was neither Holy, nor Roman nor an Empire. If Lucian had really sailed west progress would have speeded by a thousand years, today we might be basking on Mars.

In his 'A True Story' Lucian felt obliged to add artistic verisimilitude to an otherwise bald and unconvincing narrative; he excused his failure to land in the West by blaming a sudden whirlwind, which seized the bellying sails and spun the boat aloft for about three hundred furlongs driving it on for seven days and seven nights becalming them at last in a great country resembling an island, bright and round and shining with a great light. Far below them the travellers saw another land with cities, rivers, seas, mountains and forests. They were on the Moon. Lucian and his friends had no time to analyse the atmosphere or to chip off chunks of rock, as true astronauts should, for they were promptly arrested by Dragoons mounted on giant three-headed vultures and conveyed to their King, Endymion, also a Greek, kidnapped from Earth in his sleep. The Moonites happened to be at war with the inhabitants of the Sun; their fascinating though ineffective forces included archers who flew in the air simply by allowing the wind to blow through their baggy tunics and carry them along like boats. Phaeton invaded with hordes of winged ants nearly two hundred feet long, Dog-faced men naturally enough from the Dog Star, and Sky Dancers slinging huge radishes coated with mallow poison, however his secret war-winning weapon was the eclipse; the Lord of the Sun suddenly plunged the Moonites in darkness and forced their surrender. Endymion agreed to pay the Sunites a yearly tribute of ten thousand gallons of dew and to collaborate in their colonisation of the Morning Star. On their way home the travellers visited Venus, then apparently sailed off-course for they skirted the Sun, a green and pleasant land, called at Lamptown, midway between the Pleiades and the Hyades, sighted amid the clouds the city of Cloud-cuckootown, and finally touched down in the sea. Happily the sea was calm, so instead of reporting to someone they went for a swim. A good time was had by all!

Lucian swears he had never been known to tell a lie.

Who are we to doubt his True Story? His tale is certainly more diverting than those cheerless reports of our Astronauts.

Unlike the learned Pliny Lucian apparently had not studied the works of Posidonius, who correctly calculated the distance from Earth to Moon as 250,000 miles but underestimated somewhat with 625,000 miles from Moon to Sun. In 'Icaramenippus' or 'The Sky Man' Lucian has Menippus say

'It was three thousand furlongs then from Earth to the Moon, my first step; and from there up to the Sun, perhaps five hundred leagues, and from the Sun to Heaven itself and the Citadel of Zeus would be also a day's ascent for an eagle travelling light.'[123]

Our Astronauts take Space too seriously. Lucian had much more fun!

Chapter Eight
Spacemen in Ancient Italy

The lyrical poets of Ancient Rome dreaming of lost Antiquity sang longingly of yon Golden Age when Saturn ruled their sunny land in peace and plenty, under his benign care all men lived in blessed content, attuned in cosmic wisdom from the stars; death was rare, suffering unknown, the fair Earth blossomed in fruitfulness yielding her treasures in prodigality for all to enjoy. Saturnia basked in idyllic splendour, the Gods winged down from the skies to mingle among men inspiring a wondrous culture to teach mankind. Such a prosperous realm tempted aerial invasion by Jupiter, who waged war with fantastic weapons and exiled aged Saturn to Britain. Soon a dragon appeared in the heavens causing devastation on Earth, after a titanic duel Jupiter slew the monster, symbol for some Space Visitant, perhaps a wandering asteroid which ravaged our planet. The climate grew suddenly harsh, the few survivors in this Silver Age shuddered in caves sighing for those golden glories of the past. Later cataclysms brought forth Heroes of Bronze fighting fabulous battles to be followed at last by Men of Iron, those invincible Legions following the Eagles of Jupiter to conquer the world.

Scholars often assume that the Romans, upstarts of Antiquity, having few traditions of their own, borrowed the golden myths of Greece to bask in reflected glory, poets and politicians, soldiers and philosophers were profoundly impressed by the genius of Hellas; the intellectuals of Rome discoursed in Greek modelling their style on the Wits of Athens yet all were superbly conscious that long ago their own land was ruled by the Gods. Ennius called Latium the 'Saturnian Land'. Varro records that on one of Rome's seven hills was an old town named Saturnia with a temple of Saturn; Junius mentions a Saturnian Gate and ancient houses with Saturnian walls, remains of a remote and proud past.

The legend of Saturn ruling Italy in a Golden Age usurped by Jupiter, when the wondrous civilisation degenerated to barbarism, haunted the imagination of men through many millennia. Such deeply-rooted tradition burning for generations in race-memory was more than a pleasant myth to beguile the mind, to the Ancients it was precious history. Were this tale confined to Rome it might be dismissed perhaps as poetic invention to boost morale, although it is doubtful whether Julius Caesar and Augustus would have boasted descent from the Gods had they not firmly believed in such Celestial Supermen. All the peoples of Antiquity worshipped Wondrous Strangers from the stars, who taught mankind, then after tremendous wars and cataclysms returned to the skies leaving Men to rebuild their shattered world.

Ovid discussing the antiquity of Man quoted Pythagoras, who stated he had seen what once was solid earth now changed into sea and land created out of what was once oceans; sea-shells lie far away from ocean's waves and ancient anchors have been found on mountain-tops. 'The London Mirror', Vol. 35, 11th January 1840, discussing giants mentions a skeleton found in 1548 near Palermo about thirty feet in length, later another thirty-three feet and a third thirty feet long; two even longer were discovered near Athens. In 1705 a skeleton measuring twenty-two feet in length was unearthed near Valencia; the 'Journal Litteraire' of the Abbé Nazari recorded that in Calabria a body was exhumed which measured eighteen Roman feet, each of its grinders weighed on an average one ounce. In the consulship of Lucius Flaccus during the Cretan Wars, 'When the floods were gone, in a great cleft and full of the earth', there was found the carcase of a man of the length of thirty and three cubits or nearly fifty feet.[124] Divine Kings descended to teach the arts of civilisation to Hyperborea, the circumpolar continent. Down the centuries people must have migrated southwards to inhabit that sunny peninsula jutting out into the Middle Sea, many were Giants.

Dr. Louis Leakey dates Kenyapithecus Africanus as twenty million years old, among fossils from early Miocene times are found finely-chiselled flints. In August 1958 Dr. Johannes Huerzeler, a Swiss palaeontologist working in a coal-mine at Baccinelle near Grasseto in Central Italy, about a hundred miles from Rome, discovered amid coal strata 600 feet down, a complete skeleton resembling a man, Oreopithecus, who had apparently lived in Italy during the Carboniferous Age of giant forests; long after he died the great trees were compressed into coal, by some miracle his skeleton became embedded in a seam and preserved. Sceptics may reject this most ancient Italian, could he then have been some Spaceman who landed on Earth in times far remote? Charles Fort records many metallic objects secreted within rocks deep underground; he mentions a block of metal found inside coal mined in Austria in 1885, when it was said to be virtually steel. Analysis in 1966 by Dr. Kurst from the Museum of Natural History in Vienna[125] determined iron with a little manganese and manganese-sulphurs, no nickel, no chromium, no cobalt, therefore with certainty no meteor but cast-iron. Was this metal manufactured in Tertiary times or had it fallen in the primeval forest from a Spaceship? Dr. M. K. Jessup,[126] the distinguished UFO investigator, whose mysterious death is attributed by some of his followers to Extraterrestrial cause, asserts that in most remote Antiquity Earth bloomed in a world-wide civilisation of pygmy men, who are known to have existed since Miocene times approximately 33,000,000 years ago. Jesuit records state there were pygmies living amid the Swiss mountains as recently as the sixteenth and seventeenth centuries, human remains of small stature are found there about 9000 years old.

On the walls of the Thayagin grotto in Switzerland are portrayed reindeer feeding, also a man running beside two horses' heads depicted at least 50,000 years ago; they are brilliantly drawn and would do credit to any modern animal-painter. Cro-Magnon Man millennia later was tall in stature with high forehead, large in brain capacity and apparently superior to many existing races of mankind today, his cave-paintings revealing belief in life after death presuppose a fine intelligence. The skulls of the Cro-Magnons are so majestically developed that it is difficult to believe that they could have descended from the brutish, low-browed Neanderthal Man; it seems likely that some cosmic catastrophe possibly the destruction of the planet Maldek into the asteroids affected our Earth, causing a mutation of species or perhaps the Solar System encountered a new potency of cosmic radiation which had swift and drastic influence on human embryos producing more perfect physical and mental men and women. The Cro-Magnons may have been survivors from Atlantis or even from the planet Maldek; a truly fantastic suggestion, yet millennia hence should our own Earth face destruction it is surely likely that the most superb specimens of the human race will be sent forth into Space to people another planet.

Evidence of ancient civilisations slowly accumulate, Soviet geologists prospecting in the almost inaccessible Tien-Shan mountains in Central Asia were astonished to find heaps of slag and well-worn bronze picks, galleries and pit-shafts dating from the Upper Paleolithic Age showing technical ore-mining about 15,000 BC. Dr. Robert J. Braidwood of the University of Chicago's Oriental Institute excavating at Cayanu near Ergani in South-Eastern Turkey discovered three metal pins or awls almost 9000 years old, he said the site bore evidence of human habitation for at least 100,000 years. The wonderful jewellery, ornaments and swords found in Bronze Age tombs all over the world reveal exquisite artistry, delicate craftsmanship and an advanced metallurgy far superior to the crude relics of the Iron Age, which followed, suggesting a decline in human intelligence and techniques. We can only speculate on the marvels of the Golden Age beyond imagination when Earth was ruled by Spacemen.

Saturn was said to have imprisoned the Cyclops underground, those Titans, the fabulous Els, survivors of the old Uranid civilisation, fashioned wondrous weapons to aid Jupiter. Virgil in the 'Aeneid' repeated traditions of a tunnel from the Cave at Cumae, abode of the Sibyl, to Lake

Avernus, down which Aeneas descended to the lower world. Daedalus after his tragic flight from Minoan Crete landed at Cumae and spent some time with troglodytes, artificers of the subterranean world. The early Christians sought refuge in the catacombs of Rome, an underground labyrinth from remote Antiquity. South American legends tell of long tunnels under the Andes built by some most ancient race, perhaps the Els, descendants of Spacemen, where the Incas of Peru hid their golden treasures from Pizarro and his plundering Conquistadores. Sensitives claim that other tunnels lead down to a subterranean civilisation hundreds of miles beneath our feet called Agharta, peopled by descendants of the Atlanteans, a startling suggestion confounding our conditioned thought-pattern. Dr. Costantino Cattoi, the distinguished Italian airman and archaeologist, discovered gigantic stone figures including monstrous carvings of a Sphinx on a hill near Trepani in Sicily and on Mount Argentario, Orbatello, Italy, which closely resembled those fantastic carved figures on the plateau of Marcahuasi in Peru possibly 100,000 even 1,000,000 years old, evidence of some giant race with great intelligence in ages past associating with Spacemen.

The vast antiquity of Man in Italy is supported by the recently discovered Paleolithic site at Terra Amata, Nice, in south-eastern France; here are found the oldest evidence of man-made structures, wooden huts 49 feet long and 20 feet wide built from 3 inch diameter stakes by prehistoric hunters 300,000 years ago. Digging has unearthed about 35,000 objects, mainly a large variety of stone tools, remains of charred wood, bones of rabbits, bear and an ancestor of the mammoth, also antlers and even fossilised human excreta. When the beach was formed the Mediterranean was 85 feet higher than today, although sea-level had dropped somewhat, the sea covered most of the present plain of Nice.[127]

Near Mt Bego in the Alps amid a bleak lunar landscape of bare rocks and rugged pinnacles opens the Valley of Marvels, on the cliff walls are drawn about 40,000 mysterious signs representing people, horned animals, weapons and a strange menacing Magician; these drawings spread across more than ten square kilometres depict numerous folk apparently praying to the Sun. Similar drawings adorn the Camonica Valley[128] between Milan and Bolzano dated from about 2000 BC. A human figure raised both his hands upwards to a circle with a dot in its centre, another sketch resembles a Flying Saucer landed, a five-fold circle has two leg-like sticks protruding from the bottom side and another wider one from the right bottom. At Caven, Voltellina, are found horse-shoe drawings with linked triangular marks attached outside; several other drawings of circles have attachments such as a cross inside, three protrusions outside, another smaller circle linked by a line and a square protruding. In 1968 Professor Francesco Ranaldi, Director of the Potenza Museum, found in a local hilltop cave known as Tuppo del Sassi important paintings dominated by the figure of a many-headed, multi-eyed monster; he believes the shape may be some kind of divinity and adds, 'But it's certainly the most interesting thing in the painting ... a large masculine being, with six lateral protruberances and one at the head, two trailing legs and a long lizardlike tail.'[129] A human figure with several protrusions from his head resembles cliff-pictures found in the U.S.S.R. and claimed by Alexander Kazantsev to be the ancient Space Visitors wearing space-suits; these prehistoric drawings evoke the famous 'Martian' of the Tassili frescoes in the Sahara, also the pictures of the Chip-San King in Kyushu, Japan, welcoming Seven Flying Saucers, also those intriguing rock-paintings discovered by Dr. Marcel Homet near the wild Amazon. Fascinating cave-paintings of possible Spacemen are found in Scandinavia, Spain, Australia, North and South Africa, showing world-wide visitations. Strange cup-like impressions on a cliff near Lake Como repeated on mountains in Scotland, China, Algeria and Palestine led Charles Fort to wonder in his whimsical fashion whether some electric force from Space was writing on our Earth cosmic records to guide Lost Explorers.

Egyptian priests told Solon that about 10,000 BC the Atlanteans ruled a vast Empire; after conquering Italy and

Libya they attacked Greece and Egypt, finally their onslaught was smashed by heroic Athens, the routed Atlanteans fled back to Poseidon, soon engulfed by cataclysm. The Atlanteans were great mariners and colonisers inheriting their brilliant culture from lost Lemuria which they brought to the Lands of the Mediterranean. Initiates from Atlantis are said to have built the Great Pyramid about 80,000 BC, they would probably build temples and cities in that ancient Land of Saturn; the proud history of Italy may be many millennia older than we imagine. The almost total destruction of records means that the chronology of remote Antiquity is most confused, widely separated events may be coalesced into a single occurrence making precise dating impossible. Confirmation of the Atlantean invasion may come from Dionysius of Halicarnassus, who states that Hercules invaded Europe with a great army probably from Erytheia, a Red Island in the West; Calpe, our Gibraltar, and Abyla opposite on the African coast were called the Pillars of Hercules, presumably some ancient memory of this epic event. Herodotus states that Heracles, God of the Egyptians, lived 17,000 years before his day; the Greeks regarded Hercules as Son of Zeus being born in Boetia, whatever the truth he was generally esteemed as a great culture-hero. Hercules conquered Spain, Southern France and campaigned in Italy, where he was worshipped as a God still immortalised by the city of Herculaneum, which he is said to have founded. This great invasion of Europe from the West would surely attract the Spacemen.

Records from Ancient Egypt, Babylon and Israel, suggest that Spacemen were particularly active in the Middle East during the Second and Third Millennia BC; their Spaceships must have landed in Italy. Megaliths in Corsica closely resemble those intriguing statues on Easter Island, similar immense stone structures are found in Sardinia and the Balearic Isles, evidence of a Stone Age culture probably linked to those grandiose mysterious circles and dolmens in Britain. In remote times[130] Western Europe apparently suffered devastation by a Comet, survivors from this cataclysm fled south to populate Italy; later as the Peoples of the Sea they conquered the Mediterranean and were finally smashed in savage battles on land and sea by Rameses III in 1195 BC, shortly after the Siege of Troy. The 'Gods' who had championed the Greeks or Trojans would enjoy a grandstand view of this other conflict, as they have watched so many wars since.

About 1200 BC Aeneas fled from burning Troy and after dallying with love-lorn Dido by the waters of Carthage, guided by his Mother, the Goddess Venus (Space Being?) he sailed on to Italy, landing at Cumae where he sought his future fortunes from the Sibyl and descended with her to the underworld. With his companions the Trojan hero coasted north and finally dropped anchor in the Tiber, there they were hospitably welcomed by Latinus, King of Latium, said to be third in descent from Saturn. The old King gladly gave his daughter, Lavinia, in marriage to Aeneas, for he had been warned in a dream that from their union would spring a race destined to rule the world. Latinus showed Aeneas the ancient town of Saturnia, there Saturn had ruled in the Golden Age. Virgil's 'Aeneid' vividly describes how the hero killed Turnus, King of the Rutulians, in a duel watched by the Gods (Spacemen?), later he founded the city of Lanuvium named after his wife. Iulus, son of Aeneas, built Alba Longa; there four hundred years later were born Romulus and Remus, founders of Rome. Brutus, great-grandson of Aeneas killed his father hunting and in banishment sailed west to that fog-wrapped island on the edge of the world inhabited by Giants, to which he gave his name, Britain.[131] Such legends conceal a kernel of truth; in the Second Millennium BC there were close links between East and West; the armour and chariots of the Britons were Trojan in design, the beliefs of the Druids had affinities with the early religion of Greece. Can we romantic British trace our ancestry back to Aeneas, Son of Venus, are we all descended from that alluring Goddess of Love, some wondrous Spacewoman?

No text remains from those ancient days to enlighten us now. From the tenth to the eighth centuries BC Spacemen inspired Solomon and Elijah, the 'Power and Glory' of the of fabulous Angkor Wat in Cambodia suddenly vanished to other realms. Such theories exasperate all our archaeologists trying to show that the Etruscans like the noble Orsino, Sir Toby Belch, Olivia and Viola in Shakespeare's 'Twelfth Night' came from the 'sea-coast of Illyria'; we may however perversely suggest that the Etruscans were inspired by Spacemen.

Early Etruscan architecture is said to have closely resembled the cyclopean structures of the Incas, characteristic of huge megaliths all over the world, evidence of the worship of Sky Gods in ancient times, perhaps that Golden Age of Saturn. Many Etruscan cities were built on windy, isolated hills like wealthy Perugia and proud Veii. Why did the founders of Perugia build their famous city in the mountains more than a thousand feet above the Umbrian plain? The obvious advantages for defence seem hardly to compensate for such isolation in the clouds. Mountains in Mexico, Britain, Greece, were crowned with cities or temples. Was Perugia a sky-port for Spacemen? Etruria was once famous for its towers evoking those lofty ziggurats of Babylon, the Etruscans had close cultural links with the Babylonians, they copied their astrology and divination from inspecting the livers of sacrificial victims. In the ancient world towers had cosmic significance, like pyramids, artificial mounds and hills they were probably used for communication with the 'Gods' perhaps as landing-sites for Spaceships, where the Celestials could instruct their Initiates or receive sacrifices, people or food to transport to their own planet. On the summit of the great Temple of Marduk in Babylon was a sanctuary sumptuously furnished, reserved for the 'God' and his 'Bride', a most beautiful woman chosen by the Priests. There is now reason to believe from sexual 'experiments' alleged to be performed by Spacemen today, that intercourse by the 'Gods' was not sensual lust but deliberate eugenics to produce some hero or heroine destined to advance civilisation. For hundreds of years the Etruscan priests scanned the heavens, they must have had some overwhelming reason for such scrutiny, unlike ourselves they did not fear air-attack from any other country, times.

Dr. Zacharie Mayani after thirty years' study claims Etruscan is essentially an Indo-European language and has translated a few phrases based on ancient Illyrian, that equally eminent authority, Dr. Jacques Huergon,[133] states that Etruscan does not belong to the Indo-European family of languages but remains a complete mystery. A few words were borrowed by the Romans. The Etruscan 'histrio' meaning 'actor' gives our 'histrionic', and it is fascinating to find that 'antenna' or 'yardarm' has now entered the language of telecommunications in our Space Age.

The sudden appearance in Northern Italy of a talented race speaking an unknown language with a brilliant culture in a land once ruled by the Gods exhilarates us to fantasy. The Sons of God winged down from the skies to mate with the Daughters of Men, the Hopi Indians say their ancestors came from another world, the Dropa tribe may have descended from survivors from a crashed Spaceship marooned in the Chinese mountains. History mentions so many strange disappearances. An old legend tells how in the hill village of San Lorenzo in Piedmont, Val di Susa, there lived a hermit, a certain Canuto di Beruda. One day he laid his woollen cloak on a sunbeam and on this he flew up far away into the sky.[134] This cosmic translation may operate in reverse, perhaps persons and people are landed even teleported from some other planet. Etruria was long associated with the Golden Age of Saturn, cliff-drawings and stone figures may depict Spacemen, circles of stones like those in Britain may have been built to attract the Spaceships. Alexander Kazantsev describing an Etruscan dish treasured in the Museum at Leningrad says 'some sort of anthropoidal creatures can be seen wearing headgear which could perhaps be space-helmets, they are on board a ship apparently propelled by rocket.'[135] The priests practised psycho-science and scanned the skies. Could those mysterious Etruscans have come from the stars?

Lack of convincing evidence makes it difficult to prove that the Etruscans were whisked to Earth from another world or that two thousand years later the Khmers, builders

The Heavy Child

In the year 1686 on 8th June two noblemen on the road to Chur in Switzerland saw a little child lying on a bank, it was wrapped in linen. One of them took compassion and ordered his servant to dismount and lift the child up, so that they might take it to the next village and that it might be cared for. The servant dismounted, took hold of the child, and wished to pick him up, but he found it beyond his powers. The two noblemen were extremely surprised and ordered the other servant to alight and help him. But both with joined hands were not strong enough to raise him from the spot. After they had tried for a long time pushing it to and fro, the child began to speak and said, 'Let me lie here, for you cannot lift me from the ground. But I will tell you that this will be an excellent and fruitful year but few men will live through it.' As soon as he had expressed these words he vanished. Both noblemen with their servants made a deposition to the Council at Chur.

This curious tale, sworn as true, suggests the teleportation of a dwarf whose weight was apparently tremendously increased by the Earth's gravity. Could he have come from the Moon? His prophecy was hardly inspiring; the fact that he promptly vanished whence he came suggests that his journey was somewhat unnecessary.

Extraterrestrials have surveilled Earth for many millennia; advanced Beings on other planets, who have conquered disease, may be almost immortal with a conception of Time vastly different from our own; to these Celestials an interval of three thousand Earth-years may seem quite short. Should this be so, we might expect Beings like Tages to visit Italy again.

Jacques Vallée,[136] whose brilliant researches throw such enlightenment on this enigma of UFOs, analysed 80 sightings in 12 countries including Italy between 1909 and 1960; of the 153 'Pilots' seen, 44 were dwarfs about 3' 6" tall. Some of the dwarfs wore 'diver's suits' or light respiratory apparatus described as transparent clothing, others did not, the latter were characterised by large heads, hairy faces, flat noses, thick and red lips.

Evaluation of the manifestation of Tages to the Etruscans three thousand years ago may be enhanced by examination of those astounding 'little men' who appeared in Northern Italy in 1947, surely one of the best sightings ever recorded.

aerial invasion as in ages past could come only from the stars. The Ancients were not fools, they did not build high towers and watch the skies for centuries and appease the 'Gods' with sacrifices just for stupid superstition! There was no propaganda from newspapers or television to condition people's minds, therefore some obvious, highly-potent ever-present menace must have existed for many hundred years to instil in priests and public all over the world such dread of those 'Gods' from the skies.

Cicero states that the Etruscans were taught by a Divine Being called Tages. One day in the reign of Tarchon, son of Tyrrhenus, as a peasant ploughed a deep furrow in a field near the city of Tarquinia, there sprang out of the earth a young child with grey hair and wisdom of an old man. The apparition, Tages, revealed that he had been sent by Tinia, the Supreme God, to impart to the Lucumones, Etruscan Kings, the laws, religion and art of divination by examining the entrails of animals. He dictated to the augurs the Libri Tagetici, which formed the Etruscan Bible governing the lives of the Etruscans from the cradle to the grave just as the Books of Moses regulated the daily life of the Jews. The artists of Etruria featured Tages in bronze statuettes or on the backs of mirrors showing him as a small boy with a bald head or like a bearded dwarf.

The Egyptians claimed they were taught civilisation by Osiris, a Celestial from the sky; the Babylonians were instructed by Oannes, an Apparition from the Sea; the Etruscans were inspired by Tages, a Being from the soil. Osiris and Oannes may have been Spacemen. Was Tages teleported or transported in a Spaceship from another planet? The Etruscans worshippd Tages with all the reverence the Jews devoted to Jehovah; they did not doubt his divinity; odd though his advent may seem to our cynical minds could it possibly be true?

The brothers Jacob and Wilhelm Grimm in 'Die Grimmische Sagen' Volume 1, page 15, record a curious story 'Das schwere Kind' which merits resurrection to modern Space literature. In our own translation it reads and gave the two Beings the appearance of caricature, but I believe the sight of their "faces" would have removed from anyone the desire to laugh....

'They had no trace of hair, instead of it they wore a kind of close-fitting, dark-brown cap. The "skin" of their faces was an earthen green.... Their "nose" was straight, geometrically cut and very long. It hung over a mere slit, shaped like a circumflex accent, which I had noticed opening and closing at intervals very much like the mouth of a fish. Their "eyes" were enormous, protruding and round. Their appearance and colour were like the colour of two well-ripened, yellow-green plums. In their centre I noticed a kind of vertical "pupil". I saw no trace of eyelashes or eyebrows, and what I would have called the eyelids was constituted by a ring between green and yellow surrounding the base of those hemispherical eyes just like the frame of a pair of spectacles.'

Signor Johannis, extremely astonished, waved his arm with the pick and asked them in a voice quite different from normal, who they were, whence they came and if he could help them. The dwarfs apparently interpreted his rash gestures as threatening.

'... one of them raised his right hand to his belt from the centre of which spurted something which seemed as though it could have been a thin puff of smoke. Today I think it must have been a ray or something of that nature. However I had no time to get out of the way or make any gesture, I found myself stretched out full-length on the ground. My pick jerked out of my hand as though snatched by some invisible force.'

This forcibly reminded Signor Johannis of a violent electric-shock from a Leyden-jar which he had in 1924 when a student. He felt himself deprived of strength, each attempt to stand up caused him unbearable fatigue. One of the two dwarfs bent down to collect the pick which was longer than he was.

'It was then that I could observe distinctly his green "hand". It had eight fingers of which four were opposable to the others. It was not a hand, it was a paw with fingers without claws. I also noticed the chest of the two Beings quivered like that of a dog panting after a long run.... The two dwarfs arrived beneath the disc, I saw them climb up slowly but surely to the rocky cleft and then disappear behind the disc itself, which was embedded in an almost vertical position.

'A few more minutes elapsed, then the strange object arose in the air shooting up from the rock. A cascade of stones and earth fell down on the stony river-bed. And that was the only sound that broke

On the morning of 14th August 1947 about 9 a.m. Signor R. J. Johannis, a well-known artist and writer interested in sociology and anthropology, with knapsack and Alpine pick, was climbing the wooded hills in the valley of Chiassi rivulet near Villa Santina by the little villa of Raveo in Carnia (Friuli). In graphic and colourful language Signor Johannis described his remarkable encounter in the Italian UFO periodical 'CLYPEUS', May 1964.

Signor Johannis was ascending the steep slope by a long path winding through groves of fir-trees. We translate his revelation as follows.

'Coming out from one of those clumps of fir-trees I noticed on the rocky river bank about fifty metres away a large lenticular object coloured vivid red.... When I arrived at a few paces from the "Thing" I could confirm that it was a disc – apparently of varnished metal like the metal of an ordinary toy – in the shape of a lens with a low central cupola without any aperture. At the top protruded some sort of shining metallic antennae.... The object about ten metres wide was embedded about a quarter of its length in a great transversal cleft of the crumbly rock of the mountain-side at a height of about six metres above the bed of the stream.'

He decided to approach and examine the object, however turning around he saw leaving the same wood through which he himself had passed two 'boys', so they appeared to be at first. He shouted to them.

'When I had halved the distance between us, I stopped petrified. The two "boys" were two dwarfs such as I had never seen before nor even imagined.'

Both stopped a few paces from him.

'I seemed to be paralysed or rather dreaming. However I could observe them at my ease in every particular. And those details have remained impressed on me so indelibly that even now today I could make a picture or statue of those extraordinary Beings. I must confess however at the time my predominant feeling was an enormous astonishment combined quite understandably with a sense of fear.

'They were not more than 90 centimetres tall and were wearing a type of dark-blue overall made from a material I would not know how to describe, "translucent" is the only term suitable to describe it. They wore a collar and rather high belt, vivid red in colour. Even the sleeves and the ankles ended in "collars" of the same type. Their heads were – according to my impression – bigger than the head of a normal man

At the British Museum in London there is a small head in terra-cotta coming from Anatolia originally populated by the fierce Hittites; this head reveals strange lineaments which are met in line and form in no other work of that epoch. Especially the eyes. Enormous, circular, very like two great buttons surmounted by others a little smaller but nothing like human eyes. Then the mouth. A thin cut without lips set in an inhuman smile. Pointed nose. This head does not appear to belong to a man, that is to a man of Earth; it at once evokes the two little men seen by Signor Johannis beside their strange machine at Raveo in 1947; there is a fascinating resemblance between the terra-cotta head and the artist's drawings. Recently two unfortunate bank-clerks in Mendoza were immobilised by two little men in black, who sampled some blood from their finger. The strange manikins who visited the Hittites are haunting Italy today.[137]

On 10th April 1962 Signor Mario Zuccala[138] near Florence, saw an object resembling two bowls put one on top of the other land. A door opened, two Beings alighted, they were about five feet tall, completely covered by an armour of shining metal, two antennae came out of their heads. Signor Eugenio Siragusa on 30th April 1962 on the road from Catania to Etna met two Spacemen each 5 feet 4 inches tall wearing metallic helmets and space-suits. In the yard of a silk-mill in Milan at 2.20 a.m. on 17th December 1962 Francesco Rizzi saw an aluminium-coloured Flying Saucer land, a door opened and a little man about 3 feet and 3 inches appeared. Bruno Ghibaudi said in 1963 that the number of definitely ascertained landings on the Earth then totalled 2,000 and the reported sightings at least 200,000; he quoted 'La Domenica del Corriere' which in 1962 stated there had been at least 200 landings in Italy alone.[139]

Scores of Extraterrestrial landings witnessed by reliable people could be quoted from UFO periodicals in several languages, many describe 'little men' landing recently in Italy. If all this literature becomes lost, our descendants in AD 5000 will have no record of Spacemen in our twentieth the silence of that solitary place. The water of the stream trickled without a sound among the pebbles.

'The disc remained motionless in the air like an enormous "gong" suspended at one end.... The disc meanwhile tipped slowly and receded from the vertical then it grew smaller all at once and vanished.'

Signor Johannis still on his back in pain was suddenly assailed by a tremendous blast of air (was it air-shock?) which rolled him over and over on the ground against the stones in the stream.

'At last I managed to sit up again. I then looked at my wrist-watch. It was 9.14.

'But it was only about midday that I was able to return home. Meanwhile I had even slept for an hour. I felt as though my bones were broken and my legs weak and trembling like after a spree of heavy drinking. I looked in my rucksack for my thermos flask of coffee. I was not surprised to find it smashed to pieces but what did surprise me was not finding any trace of its metal casing. In just the same way had vanished my aluminium fork and a small tin of the same metal which contained my cold lunch.'

'... Now I think my old pick may be found in the museum of another planet. I hope that someone yonder tries to decipher the marks cut in the handle that are nothing more than my name and an Alpine motto with a couple of stylised Alpine "stars" and an eagle. And I hope they are wearing out their brains trying to understand them.

'I end by stating that at the time I tried to interpret my adventure in various ways but all quite foreign to Flying Saucers or to other machines of extraterrestrial origin. At first I thought the "disc" occupied the Campoformido airport in Friuli. Next I thought of a machine of Russian origin. Finally I speculated on a machine belonging to some unknown civilisation still hidden in the Matto Grosso or in some still unexplored region on Earth.... But nothing was satisfactory since nothing could justify the presence of those two little men.... Two months later I sailed for New York. During the crossing I heard for the first time about the Flying Saucers seen by Kenneth Arnold. Only then did I understand that I had seen a Flying Saucer.'

In confirmation an old man and a boy separately stated that on 14th August 1947 they had seen a red 'balloon' in the air.

This experience of Signor R. L. Johannis is quoted in detail not only to chronicle one of the most remarkable Extraterrestrial visitations in modern times but also because it probably describes sightings which appeared in Italy centuries ago to the Etruscans and the Romans.

'Lord' haunting Israel would surely visit Italy.

Seven hundred years before Christ between the Arno and the Tiber flourished the brilliant, sophisticated civilisation of the Etruscans, still veiled in tantalising mystery. Dionysius of Halicarnassus with persuasive rhetoric alleged that the Greeks called the land Hesperia, the natives Oenotria, then Italy after their King Italus. The early Italians lived in walled towns with towers, 'tyrseus' in Greek, hence their name 'Tyrrhenians', although they might have been called after Tyrrhenus, fifth in descent from Zeus; the Romans called them Tuscans. The Etruscans considered themselves the original inhabitants of Italy and called themselves Rasena after a chain of mountains in Tuscany, some scholars speculate they originated from North of the Alps, perhaps from the Danube. Herodotus, greatest gossip in all Antiquity, claimed the Etruscans came from Lydia, modern Anatolia in Asia Minor. His picturesque tale asserts that during prolonged famine the Lydians invented dice, gambled two days out of three and ate on the third day only; after eighteen lean years they wearied of playing dice all day with nothing to eat; finally half the population led by the King's son, Tyrrhenus, sailed west for pastures new. After plundering every island they passed, these pirates explored the west coast of Italy, the young prince giving his name to the Tyrrhenian Sea, finally they settled in the north to till the fruitful soil and mine the rich iron deposits of Elba and Bologna.

The descendants of those starving Irish, who during the great potato famines last century forsook the Emerald Isle for beckoning America still speak their beguiling mother-tongue and shed maudlin beery tears for Old Erin each St. Patrick's Day. The Etruscans did not speak Lydian, follow Lydian laws or worship Lydian Gods;[132] even Herodotus dared not suggest that this gifted people evolved a completely new language, a new culture, a new religion. The language of the Mayas is said to resemble Hebrew, Welsh has affinities with Ancient Egyptian, Greek and English descend from Sanskrit, Sumerian has links with Chinese, evidence of world-wide migrations of peoples in ancient century. Most of the writings from Ancient Rome were destroyed. Marcus Terentius Varro (116–27 BC) wrote 620 books, only two survived, he may have described many Spacemen in his erudite Latin. Alas, we shall never know.

Livy (59 BC–AD 17) hinted that the Etruscans had composed a considerable literature and he regretted that almost all had perished; in earlier centuries it was fashionable for Roman intellectuals to study Etruscan culture instead of Greek. Varro mentions a certain Volnius who wrote plays, he might have rivalled Aeschylus but not a line is left. The scholarly Emperor Claudius studied Etruscan traditions and wrote a history of the Etruscans in twenty volumes, all lost. All the works written by all the Etruscans in a period of four hundred years are missing. Just imagine such a wide gap in our own literature since the birth of Shakespeare to the present day? The few inscriptions on tablets, tiles and funeral wrappings defy satisfactory translation despite the efforts of Dr. Zacharis Mayani and his colleagues; our main knowledge of those intriguing Etruscans is gleaned from a few references by Latin writers.

The Etruscans, a religious and literate people, would surely preserve a detailed record of their Teacher, Tages, and his doctrine in their Libri Tagetici; his deeds and words were preached for centuries by the all-powerful Priesthood who dominated the daily lives of all Etruscans from the cradle to the grave. All we know about Tages now is a tantalising mention by Cicero that he was a child with the wisdom of an old man, who was found in a field and whose teachings so greatly influenced the Etruscan then Roman religions. Those proud and talented Etruscans would never have worshipped any mortal child only half their size; they had intelligent children of their own, none to honour as a God. To capture the awe and the imagination of the Etruscans Tages must have worked wonders, impressed the wisest Priests with his own transcendent wisdom and exhibited a dazzling genius demonstrating beyond doubt that despite his diminutive stature he was indeed an Immortal not of this world come to teach mankind the Will of the Gods. Although Cicero makes no mention of any Spaceship Tages must surely have been an Extraterrestrial resembling those Space dwarfs seen by Signor J. L. Johannis in Italy three thousand years later. Tages himself said he had descended from the God Tinia in the skies. Had Tages lived and died like mortal men he would hardly have evoked much veneration. There is no record whatever of his death, perhaps he was translated to the skies in a Spaceship like Elijah, who lived about the same time.

The Etruscan religion was 'revealed', it was enshrined in Holy Books, ideas quite foreign to Greece and Rome but like that of Israel; contrary to popular belief the Jews were not the only people to have their religion revealed to them by an Extraterrestrial. Christians believe that Christ incarnated on Earth to teach the Love of God, eight hundred years earlier the Etruscans believed Tages manifested to teach the Will of Tinia. We may moralise on the merits of the two religions, the Truth we shall never know. Tinia, God of the sky and storm, was a mountain God like Indra, Jehovah, Zeus and Jupiter, whom we believe to represent Spacemen; he hurled thunderbolts but unlike Zeus required permission from the Celestial Council or Higher Gods to hurl a second or third thunderbolt since this weapon was so devastating like the terrible nuclear-blasts mentioned in those Sanskrit Classics. The Celestial Council seems an 'etruscanised' version of Zeus and his family on Mount Olympus; the Higher Gods are hidden or concealed, perhaps they were Beings ruling other planets, no one knows. An important feature in Etruscan religion was the role played by Geniuses, intermediaries between the Gods and men. Tages had a feminine rival called Vergoia, a nymph like the Sibyl whose Books of Prophecy were preserved at the Temple of Apollo in Rome; whether she was a Spacewoman is doubtful, if not, Vergoia must certainly have been an advanced psychic possibly inspired by Extraterrestrials since for centuries the Etruscans held her in the highest esteem. Like ancient peoples all over the world the Etruscans feared and propitiated elementals, gnomes and nymphs who were believed to meddle in human affairs.

The Etruscans believed in life after death, magic and

astrology sharing much of the cosmic wisdom of the Babylonians. They imagined a sympathy between the macrocosm and the microcosm, the heavens, the earth, the individual, having organs corresponding to one another; a most profound conception of the relation between the Universe and Man, which presupposes a recondite psycho-science of vast antiquity inherited from some ancient civilisation or taught by Spacemen. The haruspices or soothsayers examined the entrails, particularly the liver of victims, any blemish or peculiarity foreboded the Will of the Gods, since the entrails were considered to be the Cosmos in miniature, each part being governed by a particular Deity, its appearance was interpreted by the Libri Haruspicini. This divination practised for thousands of years by the Babylonians confounds us today. Perhaps the Ancients treasured some cosmic secret we have lost? Even our own cynical, scientific century is not without its superstitions.

The pantheon of Etruscan Gods was headed by Tinia, Uni and Menvra, who under the names of Jupiter, Juno and Minerva later became the Capitoline triad at Rome. Pliny quoted Tuscan writers stating the heavens were divided among nine Gods, who manifested their Will by hurling thunderbolts at Earth. The celestial region whence the thunderbolt came, identified the God, his omen depended on the type of lightning and the object struck according to the precepts recorded in the Libri Fulgurales; Pliny himself believed thunderbolts originated from the planets Mars, Jupiter and Saturn. Divination also followed the flight of birds, which may have symbolised Gods or Spacemen, still feared in race-memory as ruling the destinies of men. This concern of the Etruscans with lightning, thunder and birds, celestial prodigies dominating for centuries every detail of daily life, astounds us in our Space Age as some irrational superstition quite astonishing for such a highly sophisticated society; then we realise that during the First Millennium BC peoples all over the Earth scanned the heavens with an anxiety comparable to our world-wide radar-watch today. There must have been some overwhelming reason for such concern with the skies. Had the Etruscans cause to associate thunderbolts with Gods hurling down destruction to Earth like those Celestials in the 'Mahabharata' launching nuclear-like blasts on Old India? In the ninth century BC the 'Angels of the Lord' (Spacemen?) instructed Elijah to meet messengers from the King of Samaria, who worshipped Baal. The Prophet sat on top of a hill to prove he was a 'Man of God', he twice called down fire from heaven, each time to consume a Captain and fifty men. Such destruction from the skies once ravaged Etruria.

Pliny may give the probable explanation for the Etruscan awe of lightning; he states 'Historical record also exists of thunderbolts being either caused by or vouchsafed in answer to certain rites and prayers. There is an old story of the latter in Tuscany, when the portents, which they called Olta, came to the city of Bolsena when its territory had been devastated; it was sent in answer to the prayer of its King, Porsena (508 BC). Also before his time, as is recorded on the reliable authority of Lucius Piso in his Annals I, this was frequently practised by Numa, though when Tullius Hostilius copied him with incorrect ritual he was struck by lightning.'[140] Bolsena, the richest town in Tuscany, was burnt by a thunderbolt evoking memories of Sodom and Gomorrah. Was Bolsena destroyed by Spacemen?

The Etruscans perhaps even more than the Jews were obsessed by concern for the Gods and their divine intervention in human affairs; a fact which may surprise many Christians who believe the Incarnation of Christ to be the unique manifestation of God in all history. Such powerful dominance of Etruscan minds for centuries could hardly have continued without some visible signs of the Gods themselves. Mystics may worship an abstract Deity but it is exceedingly doubtful whether the masses would worship Jehovah and Jesus, obey Buddha and Mahomet, had they never appeared before mankind.

Below the handle of a bronze bucket from Offido, Picena, is a relief of a winged Goddess; in the museum at Tarquinia stands a pair of winged horses found in an Etruscan temple there. Like the Egyptians, Babylonians and Greeks, the Etruscans used wings to symbolise Celestials from the skies;

a winged Goddess depicted a Spacewoman, a winged horse a Spaceship. When the Spacemen eventually do land among us, our own imaginative artists will surely give them wings.

The huge family tombs of the Etruscans were usually frescoed with scenes of feasting, hunting, sport and family life. Though fatalistic, gluttonous and dreadfully cruel, curiously like the Aztecs of Mexico, the Etruscans revelled in almost oriental sensuality enjoying a bacchanalian debauch equalled only by their rivals in luxury, the Sybarites, who according to Athenaeus, invented the chamber-pot so they could drink at public banquets without getting up. The immorality of the Etruscans scandalised the Romans, notorious for their own orgies. Athenaeus, a learned Greek grammarian from Naucratis in Egypt, who later lived in Rome about AD 230, wrote in his most entertaining 'Deipnosophistae'[141] or 'Banquet of the Learned', a classic account of Etruscan licence as the nobles lounged on their exquisitely embroidered couches fingering their heavy silver drinking-cups; his vivid description hardly concerns Spacemen but this barnyard morality of the Etruscans may afford some salutary warnings for our own society today.

'Among the Etruscans who had become extravagantly luxurious, Timaeus records in his first book that the slave-girls wait on men naked. And Theopompus, in the forty-third book of his "Histories" says that it is customary with the Etruscans to share their women in common; the women bestow great care on their bodies and often exercise even with the men, sometimes also with one another; for it is no disgrace for women to show themselves naked. Further, they dine not with their own husbands but with any men who happen to be present and they pledge with wine any whom they wish. They are also terribly bibulous, and are very good-looking. The Etruscans rear all the babies that are born, not knowing who is the father in any single case. These in turn pursue the same mode of life as those who have given them nurture, having drinking-parties often and consorting with all the women. It is no disgrace for the Etruscans to be seen doing anything in the open, or even having anything done to them, for this also is a custom of their country. And so far are they from regarding it as a disgrace that they actually say when the master of the house is indulging in a love-affair, and someone enquires for him, that he is undergoing so-and-so, openly calling the act by its indecent name. When they get together for companionship or in family parties they do as follows; first of all after they have stopped drinking and are ready to go to bed, the servants bring in to them, the lamps being still lighted, sometimes female prostitutes, sometimes very beautiful boys, sometimes also their wives; and when they have enjoyed these the servants then introduce lusty, young men, who in their turn consort with them. They indulge in love-affairs and carry on these unions sometimes in full view of one another, but in most cases with screens set up around the beds: the screens are made of latticed wands over which cloths are thrown. Now they consort very eagerly to be sure with women; much more however do they enjoy consorting with boys and striplings. For in their country these latter are very good-looking because they live in luxury and keep their bodies smooth. In fact all the barbarians who live in the West remove the hair of their bodies by means of pitch plasters and by shaving with razors. Also, among the Etruscans at least many shops are set up and artisans arise for this business, corresponding to barbers among us. When they enter those shops, they offer themselves unreservedly having no modesty whatever before spectators or passers-by. This custom is also in use even among many of the Greeks who live in Italy; they learned it from the Samnites and the Messopians. In their luxury the Etruscans, as Alcinous records, knead bread, practise boxing, and do their flogging to the accompaniment of the flute.'

Today we watch television!

Dionysius of Halicarnassus marvelled that the Etruscans were distinguished from the rest of humanity by their morals, though they could hardly have been much more licentious than the Greeks. In pagan times people were conditioned by fertility-cults, sexual licence often signified some holy rite, worship of the Earth-Mother untrammelled by morality. Slowly conquered by Rome the Etruscans educated their conquerors giving to the stolid Romans their laws, religion, ceremonies and town-planning to fashion our Western world.

The most civilised man in all Italy was surely an Etruscan. Wealthy Maecenas descended through both his father and mother from the Lucumones, Kings of Etruria, is still honoured all over the world as the Patron of Virgil and Horace, Counsellor to the Emperor Augustus, symbol of gracious living. Such encouragement of the arts, unparalleled until the Princes of the glorious Renaissance, evokes that Golden Age of Saturn, the cosmic culture of the Spacemen, the genius of Italy.

Chapter Nine
Spacemen in Ancient Rome

'The characteristics for which in my opinion the Roman Empire is superior to all others lies in its religion. This which in other nations would be considered deplorable superstition, here in Rome is the very corner-stone of the State.'[142]

Polybius, the Greek historian who watched Carthage burn in 146 BC, was devoutly impressed by the religious feeling of the Romans, not as a morality but in constant awareness of the Gods dominating their daily lives.

A hundred years later Marcus Tullius Cicero, whose literary genius brought Latin prose to perfection, expressed the convictions of all Romans that the Gods really did exist in celestial realms ever ready to influence the affairs of men. In his profound study 'De Natura Deorum' Cicero vowed

'The voices of the Fawns have often been heard and the Deities have appeared in forms so visible that they have compelled everyone who is not senseless or hardened in impiety to confess the presence of the Gods.'[143]

The Romans watched the skies for a thousand years like all the peoples of Antiquity world-wide; from the portents their augurs prophesied the future, proving the profound impression the heavens exerted on everyone's minds. In 'De Divinatione' Cicero recorded prodigies similar to our own UFO sightings today.

'But I return to the divination of the Romans. How often has our Senate enjoined the decemvirs to consult the Books of the Sibyl! For instance, when two suns had been seen or when three moons had appeared and when flames of fire were noticed in the night, and the heaven itself seemed to burst open, and strange globes were remarked in it.'[144]

Today when luminous objects are seen in the sky our own Parliament even in our Space Age dismisses them all as hallucinations, fireballs or the planet Venus. What flaming memories made the Ancients watch such UFOs with alarm?

The Romans believed their Eternal City basked under the divine protection of the Gods; its foundation was attended by Supernatural Powers.

In the ninth century BC the Latin city of Alba Longa was ruled by Tiberinus descended from Aeneas; he lost his life by drowning in a river called Albula, which was renamed the Tiber on which Rome was destined to stand. His son, Amulius, versed in the secret lore of the Etruscans, dabbled with electricity, using techniques alien to us. Dio Cassius states

> 'Amulius, a descendant of Tiberinus, displayed an overweening pride and dared to make himself a God; he went so far as to match the thunder with artificial thunder, to answer lightning with lightning, and to hurl thunderbolts. He met his end by the sudden overflow of the lake beside which his palace was built; it submerged both him and his palace.'[145]

This astounding revelation suggests that about 800 BC Initiates in Old Italy utilised forces like nuclear-bombs! Such a claim evokes our ridicule yet dispassionate reflection recalls those Celestials with annihilation-weapons mentioned in the 'Mahabharata' and the fantastic wars blasting ancient China. Moses probably learned much of his magic from Jehovah. Amulius no doubt attempted to copy the wonders of visiting Spacemen just as our own scientists are striving to do today. Amulius was not the first man or the last to tamper with some cosmic force and in ignorance destroy himself.

Later Alba Longa was ruled jointly by Numitor and his brother, another Amulius. The brothers quarrelled; Amulius wrested the kingdom from Numitor; fearing the latter's daughter, Rhea Silvia, might have children, he made her a Priestess of Vesta, sworn to live unwedded, a virgin all her days. Soon afterwards Rhea Silva found herself with child, fathered, she alleged, by the God, Mars. Vestal Virgins who lost their chastity were buried alive in an under-ground chamber; Rhea Silvia was spared this fate possibly because she became delivered of two boys in size and beauty more than human, suggesting divine parentage. Amulius more fearful than ever ordered the twins to be put into a basket and thrown into the Tiber; they drifted down stream and were washed ashore near a fig-tree, where they were found and suckled by a 'she-wolf'. The Latin 'lupa' also meant 'prostitute', the 'she-wolf' probably referred to Larentia, wife of the shepherd, Faustulus, who adopted the infants.[146]

On attaining manhood Romulus and Remus returned to Alba Longa, killed Amulius and restored the city to their grandfather, Numitor. With fellow-adventurers the twins decided to found a city of their own amid the scenes of their childhood. Today our own town-planners seek guidance from those Deities in Whitehall, in ancient times the founding of a city was a most solemn enterprise needing the blessing of the Celestials in the skies; some societies buried prisoners alive with the foundation-posts to appease the Gods. Recognition that the building of a new city first required the goodwill of the Gods was no vague superstition; this belief proved the Ancients to be instinctively conscious that affairs on Earth were always dominated by Overlords in the stars, who could – and sometimes did – destroy their cities. Romulus chose the Palatine Hill, Remus, the Aventine; like the Etruscans they agreed to settle their argument as to precise place and name of the projected city by divination from the flight of birds. Remus first saw six vultures on his left, then Romulus saw twelve, although some people alleged he had cheated. The brothers quarrelled. Remus is said to have taunted Romulus by jumping over a trench he was digging, Romulus in wrath killed him, although Ovid in 'Fasti' IV attributes the deed to Celer, friend of Romulus.

On 21st April 753 BC Romulus founded Rome!

The city soon became filled with a mob of pioneers and outlaws like those future townships of the American Wild West; women were scarce so Romulus invited his Sabine neighbours to a festival; suddenly at his signal young Romans rushed among the guests with drawn swords and ravished away the Sabine maidens. Plutarch adds that since the Sabine women were carried into their new homes by force Roman husbands continued to carry their brides over the threshold, a custom followed by bridegrooms ever since. Romulus championed the cause of the people against the grasping patricians; beloved by the soldiers he became greatly honoured. In 716 BC while Romulus was delivering judgement on the Palatine Hill thunder and lightning rent the skies, a black cloud blotted out the sun, when the storm ceased the assembly were astonished to discover that Romulus had vanished from their midst, miraculously transported to the skies. Ovid poetically describes how Mars with Jupiter's consent swept down in his chariot to carry Romulus to heaven; later Juno sent her Messenger, Iris, on a gaily coloured rainbow to seek Romulus's wife, Hersalis; together they ascended the Palatine Hill, a star fell from the sky then bore her to Romulus among the stars.

Shortly afterwards Julius Proculus,[147] a man of noblest birth, swore by the most sacred emblems before all the people that he had seen Romulus suddenly descend from the sky and appear to him radiantly transfigured in bright and shining armour. The hero told Proculus that it was the pleasure of the Gods that after founding a city destined to be the greatest on Earth, he should dwell in heaven. The Romans all fervently believed this miracle and honoured Romulus as their God, Quirinus.

Apollodorus mentions that Hercules was translated to the skies like Enoch and Elijah.

'Hercules proceeded to Oeta in the Trachinian territory and there constructed a pyre and mounted it. When the pyre was burning, it is said that a cloud wafted him to heaven.'[148]

Galenus in his 'Commentary to the Apothegms of Hippocrates' remarks

'It is generally known that Asclepius was raised to the Angels in a column of fire, the like of which is also related with regard to Dionyses, Heracles and others who laboured for the benefit of mankind.'

Ascanius, son of Aeneas, vanished from sight being seen no more alive or dead and he was honoured as a God among the Romans.

So many heroes transported to the skies! Can the Ancients have seen it happen?

Born to a Virgin, Fathered by a God. Guided by divine

omens. Translated to heaven. Resurrection to inspire his followers. Worshipped for centuries as a God. Does the story of Romulus not startle us by its similarity to the Wonder of another Saviour seven hundred years later?

Pagan philosophers not unreasonably complained that Christians worshipped the supernatural events in Israel yet rejected similar happenings about the same time in Italy as superstition; wonders performed by Jesus were miracles, the same wonders wrought by Apollonius were tricks. The Jews believe that Elijah was whisked to heaven in a whirlwind but scorn the tale of Romulus only a few hundred miles away being transported to the skies in a cloud. The dispassionate seeker for Truth finds it odd that throughout the centuries it apparently never occurred to the Jews and the Romans that perhaps Jehovah and Jupiter were the same God, the prodigies in Israel parallel those marvels in Italy. Christians condemned as blasphemy the Roman belief that Romulus, born of a Virgin, was Son of God, dispensed justice and after translation to heaven resurrected in glory; many centuries later the very same supernatural attributes accorded to Jesus became revered as divine Truth, the source of Christianity. When the Christians shrewdly celebrated their festivals on the old Roman feast-days and the Church borrowed the ancient rituals, pagans suddenly found themselves to be Christians; the Gospels in new words told the same old tale, the Descent of God among men, His teachings, then his return to heaven. Beneath the Catholic pomp and propaganda Rome in essence is probably as pagan today as during the reign of Romulus; this is most certainly no insult, if the Romans now worship the Gods in the reverent spirit of their ancestors as symbolising the Creator of the Universe in Whom all men live and have their being, they must be truly religious.

Our cynical scientific Age ridicules stories of Romulus and similar heroes as stupid superstitions. Virgin births cannot happen, Gods do not exist, men are not suddenly whirled to the skies. Science deals strictly with facts. Does it? Scientists have dissolved so-called solid matter into atoms, atoms into particles, particles into electric potentials,

potentials into pure thought, physicists in confusion are finding fact to be fiction. Can the Mystics be right? Is Reality insubstantial as a dream? The Dream of God?

Christianity has conditioned us to believe the story of Jesus without question, the Church has so long insisted that God incarnated only once in human history that any wonders surrounding Romulus centuries before could never have occurred. Gospel writers told the truth, pagan historians not being Christians told lies. Today Science shuns the supernatural, scientists suspend comment on alleged miracles.

Without blind faith or wishful thinking our rational minds reject wonders transcending experience; when some new knowledge suddenly expands our comprehension we marvel that those miracles were merely facts we could not explain. The advent of the UFOs surpassing our Science brings novel awareness opening our minds to new dimensions; in the language of cybernetics our mental computers are becoming programmed to novel thought-patterns, we see with startling clarity the solution to problems perplexing our souls. The Gods of Antiquity were surely Spacemen. Could the tale of Romulus possibly be true?

We are not alone in the universe, astronomers now proclaim countless inhabited worlds, many with civilisations much more advanced than our own; UFOs are seen haunting our skies; Spacemen have apparently landed on our Earth. Sensational stories tell of humanoids haunting people in America. On the night of 15/16 October 1957 near Sao Francisco de Sales in Brazil Antonio Villas Boas, a young farmer, was taken aboard a bird-like machine by four aliens in grey, he was stripped naked then examined and allured into intercourse with a nude blonde. On September 19th, 1961 Barney and Betty Hill were spirited from their car near Lancaster, New Hampshire, U.S.A. into a Flying Saucer where Spacemen subjected them to sexual examination.[149] In California a young woman claimed to have been seduced by an Extraterrestrial from a UFO; subsequently she gave birth to a still-born baby of hybrid appearance.[150] Spacemen are said to be living among us hardly distinguishable from ourselves fantastic though it seems, they may be procreating children with superior intelligence to speed our civilisation; these aliens could have some sinister plan to dominate our Earth.

Spacemen today illumine the Gods of old in wondrous revelation; those notorious lusts of Zeus which titillated story-tellers, now seem deliberate eugenics creating supermen and superwomen to improve the human race. Amorous seductions may have really happened between Gods and mortals, next century our sex-starved cosmonauts will probably mate with wenches on Mars. Belief in a divinely-begotten Saviour who taught mankind is the oldest religion in the world; people in Antiquity honoured bastards and believed their heroes fathered by the Gods. Before ridiculing such superstition we should remember that for two thousand years millions of Christians have worshipped Jesus as the Son of God.

In ancient times peoples all over the world offered the fairest of their maidens as Brides to the Gods, who appeared to them in secret on mountains, in temples or tabernacles; such a custom could not have continued so long without some evidence of celestial intercourse. About 775 BC a Spaceman personified as Mars may have descended to impregnate Rhea Silvia, the noblest maiden in Alba Longa fathering the hero, Romulus, destined to create that great and historic Roman people who have shaped our civilisation. Fifty years earlier Oannes, God of Wisdom, and Ataryatis, the Fish Goddess, possibly Space Beings, gave to Babylon their famous Queen, Semiramis. There is a similarity among the great culture-heroes which is truly intriguing, suggesting some common origin. Romulus and Remus floated down the Tiber in a basket; Sargon, King of Babylon, drifted down the Euphrates in a basket; Moses was found in a basket of bullrushes on the Nile; the infant Cyrus of Persia was exposed then saved by a herdsman, later like Romulus he grew up to rule his people with benevolence. Folk-lore abounds with similar tales. The sexual adventures of Spacemen today confirm their amorous exploits in Antiquity; the divine birth of Romulus far from being idle myth now becomes possible fact.

Two thousand years later another great Italian, the Supreme Genius of the Renaissance, was born without a father. Was Leonardo da Vinci, whose secret ambition was to learn to fly, sired by a Spaceman?

The sudden disappearance of Romulus in a thick cloud while addressing an open-air assembly amazed the Romans; the multitude remembering many legends of the translation of heroes to the skies believed he had been transported to heaven as a benevolent God, reward for having been a good King. Romulus strove to establish his new city with dignity and justice, winning the respect of foreign ambassadors, even of the powerful Etruscans; a brilliant general, he showed unusual clemency to the vanquished, which ensured Rome forty years of peace. The King was revered by the army especially by his bodyguard of three hundred young men; his land-reforms made him popular with the Commons and consequently disliked by the Senate. Some cynics accused the nobles of murdering Romulus, cutting his body into pieces secretly destroyed, then fooling the people with the tale of the King's translation to heaven. The Patricians probably did want Romulus dead but it is difficult to imagine a more audacious plot than murder of the King surrounded by his devoted bodyguard in full view of the people; there must surely have been easier opportunities. No conspirator ever confessed, no one appears to have benefited, his successor, Numa Pompilius, was not living at Rome, this Sabine philosopher needed much persuasion to accept the throne which he at first refused. Perhaps the Spacemen who had planted Romulus in Italy to build Rome, when his mission was completed decided to remove him like their other protege, the fabulous Semiramis of Babylon, a few years before.

Christian writers ridicule the translation of Romulus as pagan superstition but piously accept the disappearance of the body of Jesus as the very basis of Christianity, although the dispassionate seeker of Truth might judge the evidence, slight as it is, as good for one as for the other. Commonsense admittedly does insist that Romulus must have been murdered, science swears that men do not suddenly vanish into thin air. Unfortunately for our peace of mind such consolation may not be true. The writings of Charles Fort and many other investigators today chronicle several bizarre disappearances of people, apparently only explained by teleportation or kidnapping by Spacemen. Many disappearances could be quoted, it may suffice to mention a baffling abduction[151] in Brazil. On the evening of 19th August 1962 two glowing red spheres, the size of footballs, were seen hovering over Duas Pontes near Diamentina; during the night strange humanoids only eighteen inches tall entered the hut of Rivalino Mafra da Silva, a poor diamond prospector, and surveyed the family in bed. Soon after dawn his twelve-year-old son found two odd balls on the ground outside, each had a tail and spike. The father came out to look at them; suddenly the balls joined together and enveloped him in a cloud of yellow smoke. Senhor Mafra da Silva vanished. The affair remains a mystery. Romulus too vanished in a cloud.

After his translation Romulus appeared in an aura of light to Julius Proculus like those other bright 'Angels' manifesting about the same time to the Kings of Israel. Centuries later the Resurrection of Jesus was announced to Mary Magdalene and the other women at the empty sepulchre by two men in shining garments.[152] Apollonius of Tyana, the miracle-worker who some people regard as the real Jesus, was said by the Cretans to have ascended to the skies at the age of a hundred in AD 97. Shortly afterwards he materialised to one of his followers and discoursed on the immortality of the soul. The Romans built a temple to him; Emperors worshipped Apollonius as a God.[153]

Most Romans believed that Romulus did ascend to the skies in his physical body, a phenomenon we today associate with Spacemen.

If the true greatness of Kings is measured by their wisdom, benevolence, piety and pacifism, enhaloed by love for God and Man, then Numa Pompilius in early Rome was surely the greatest King who ever lived. The dream of a Philosopher-King dispensing beneficence to his people, inspiring men to cosmic truth, has long fascinated idealists searching to perfect society. Akhnaton, Solomon, Marcus Aurelius, all with profound compassion sought to establish a social order promoting universal justice and peace. The fault lay in their stars. The world was not ready. Numa Pompilius changed the whole nature of Rome by righteousness without arms or violence; his inspiration influences our own religion even today.

Numa was born significantly on the very day Rome was founded by Romulus, 21 April, 753BC; he lived in Cures, an important town of the Sabines. Unusual in that age of barbarism this young man studied self-discipline and wisdom devoting his leisure to contemplation serving the Gods. For a whole year after the disappearance of Romulus the various factions could not agree on any Roman as King, eventually with one accord they offered the throne to this shy philosopher now nearly forty. To the dismay of the delegates Numa refused stating he lived to serve the Gods not citizens glorying in war. Only when persuaded by the augurs, finally convinced by the divine omen of a flight of birds over his veiled head as he prayed aloud before a vast and silent multitude, did Numa agree that it was the will of the Gods that he must rule Rome. First he disbanded the King's bodyguard scorning all protection, he reorganised the worship of Jupiter and laid the foundations of law changing the warlike mood of the citizens to gentleness and justice. Numa built the famous temple of Janus, whose doors were open in war, closed in peace; apart from two short periods, the doors were open from the end of Numa's reign until Augustus defeated Mark Antony and Cleopatra at the Battle of Actium in 31 BC. He divided the year into twelve months; hitherto the year had only ten, November and December being the ninth and tenth as their names suggest; he also fixed public holidays. During the midwinter festival in honour of Saturn, noted for its sexual licence, Numa allowed the slaves a taste of freedom, for at this feast they were waited upon by their Masters,[154] a custom honoured today in the British Army when officers serve Christmas dinner to their men. The early Church celebrated Christ's birth on 8th January until AD 330 then moved the date of Christmas to the Roman Saturnalia. Even the greatest philosophers look somewhat foolish attempting the impossible. Numa, exasperated by the frivolity of the fair sex, directed that women should be seen but not heard, neither must they meddle or gossip. Centuries of long-suffering husbands know just how he felt.

After his failure to silence women, Numa turned to the easier task of controlling lightning, where he met with success. The Ancients apparently inherited a psycho-science from some advanced civilisation and utilised natural electricity, sonic and possibly anti-gravity, techniques lost to us. The Ark of the Israelites appears to have been a highly-charged battery, the great Temples of Antiquity were protected by lightning-conductors. Initiates called down fire from heaven. Numa anticipated Benjamin Franklin in his experiments with lightning; his discoveries must have been spectacular for Tullus Hostilius tried to repeat them, like Amulius a century earlier the King must have used the wrong formula, a thunderbolt consumed Tullus and all his house.

Numa forbade the Romans to worship God by a graven image, the sacred shrine held no statues, the Deity could be conceived only by mind, a mystical conception of sublime significance. Sacrifices approached Pythagorean worship without bloodshed or costly ostentation. The Temple of Vesta with the sacred fire was built by Numa in the form of a circle to represent the Earth, which he knew to be round. Later generations believed Numa was a disciple of Pythagoras forgetting he lived two centuries before the Sage from Samos, like Pythagoras Numa probably learned much of his philosophy from British Druids visiting Rome; unlike many ancient philosophers Numa did not seek wisdom in other lands; he would certainly study the secret teachings of the Etruscan soothsayers. The Romans believed Numa could call down Jupiter from the skies, snare demi-Gods with spring-water drugged with wine and honey, and converse with nymphs. Could Numa have been taught by Spacemen?

The few records extant from the seventh century BC

suggest that Extraterrestrials were particularly active on Earth. In 670 BC the 'Angel of the Lord' annihilated the army of Sennacherib; in 660 BC 'Heavenly Deities' assisted the Japanese Emperor Jimmu against the Ainu; about 630 BC Zoroaster beheld 'God' amid fire, probably the radiance of a Spaceship, on Mount Sabalan; a few decades later Ezekiel beheld his famous Wheel.

Dionysius of Halicarnassus apparently confirms this space activity, writing of early Rome he makes a cryptic reference

'Higher up in the clouds two great armies marching.'[186]

The Hosts of Heaven in Hebrew theology are generally imagined as spiritual Angels of Light contending against demonic Forces of Darkness, but even this esoteric vision is probably based on some actual conflict seen in the skies. It is relevant to note that the Second Book of Maccabees, Chapter V, records 'Horsemen running in the air' over Israel in 170 BC, a similar spectacle before the Fall of Jerusalem in AD 70 was reported by Josephus, also by Matthew of Paris, who gives a vivid description of two occasions in AD 1236 when there appeared in the skies over England and Ireland 'armed soldiers superbly although hostilely equipped.' Pliny states explicitly

'We are told that during the wars with the Cimbri (North Germany 113-101 BC). Noises of clanging armour and the sounding of trumpets were heard from the sky and that the same thing has happened frequently both before then and later. In the consulship (103 BC) of Marius the inhabitants of Ameria and Tuder (now Todi) saw that spectacle of heavenly armies advancing from the East and the West to meet in battle, those from the West being routed.'[188]

Dare we emulate our Science-Fiction writers and speculate on the fantasy of rival space-fleets pursuing their battle in the skies of Earth? Our critics, who were not there to see them, would no doubt raise objections more bizarre than the spectacle suggested.

Many centuries earlier the Ramayana and Mahabharata brilliantly described celestial wars in the air above Old India.

The Etruscans and their contemporaries all over the

Earth anxiously watched the skies, there must have been some overwhelming cause for their concern. The advent of the God, Tages, and the career of Romulus suggest celestial intervention in Ancient Italy. The report by Dionysius of Halicarnassus concerning armies in the Roman skies may be more realistic then we imagine.

In 708 BC while Rome was ravaged by plague, an 'ancile' or bronze 'shield' is said to have fallen from heaven. Numa promptly inspired the suffering people, declaring that the Muses had told him the marvel was sent by the Gods, an omen signifying their protection of the City. To lessen the chances of theft, the King ordered his most expert craftsmen to fashion eleven exact replicas, these 'ancilia' were entrusted to the Salii, Priests of Mars, who carried them in religious processions to the chant of hymns and solemn dance. The strange metal object from the skies was obviously manufactured and therefore not a meteorite, it cannot have come alone from space since it would have been incandesced and melted, the 'Thing' must have fallen from a low height otherwise its shape would have been greatly distorted on hitting the ground. Superstitious though the Romans were, such a highly practical and militant people would hardly worship an ordinary shield, standard equipment, any more than we would accept an oil-can as from a UFO if we could buy a similar one from Woolworth's; moreover the Romans must have firmly believed that the Gods actually were flying at that time in their sky and could drop something on the City. Plutarch explains that the buckler was not round nor yet completely oval but had a curving indentation, the arms of which were bent back and united with each other at top and bottom; not knowing what it was the Romans called the thing a 'shield' which it partly resembled. Bronze plates do not fall from the sky unless someone drops them; the Romans never doubted the ancile's celestial origin, therefore they must have been fully conditioned to acknowledge Supermen flying over their City in solid aircraft, just as five hundred years later in 214 BC the citizens of Hadria were astonished to see in the sky 'an altar around which grouped the forms of men in white garments.' Today some wild tribe in the Amazon jungle may be dancing around their latest idol, an empty soup-tin flung from some Brazilian aeroplane. The Romans venerated the 'shield' as sent by the Gods. Surely the 'Thing' must have dropped from a Spaceship.

The early Romans believed the whole universe thrilled with life, like all primitive peoples they lived in a world steeped in magic, dominated by mysterious powers dwelling in earth, sea and sky, whose benevolence must be sought or malevolence averted by solemn propitiation with appropriate rites and sacrifice. The erudite Varro summarised popular belief stating that the universe was divided into two, 'Caelum', 'Sky', and 'Terra', 'Earth', the sky contained 'loca supera', 'upper places', those belonging to the Gods, the Earth comprised 'loca infera', 'lower places', those belonging to mankind. The Romans were conscious of two aspects of existence, 'sacred' opposed to 'profane'; 'sacred' meaning neither good nor bad represented the world of the Gods, the Spacemen, in the sense that today 'royal' signifies the domain of our Queen and her family; 'profane' denoted the everyday world of mortal men. When the Gods descended to Earth, the hills, forests or temples they frequented became 'sacred', subject to taboos and approached only through the priests who jealously conserved this celestial 'apartheid' often to promote their own power. The Old Testament and ancient religions from Britain to Japan all agree that the places of the Gods were holy ground. When Spacemen land in our century it is certain that the Army will at once throw a cordon around the area with maximum security, the spot will be 'sacred' that is prohibited to civilians. Our theologians and mythologists ignorant of the inhabited universe proffer tortuous theories to explain the ancient awe for places 'where the Gods have trod' as some atavistic superstition, oblivious to the obvious fact that the reason why certain spots were sacred to the Gods was simply because the Gods had actually appeared there.

The Romans like the peoples of Ancient India, Mexico

and Ireland, believed in World Ages, cycles of civilisation. In 88 BC during the consulship of Sulla 'out of a cloudless and clear air there rang out the voice of a trumpet prolonging a shrill and dismal note, so that all were amazed at its loudness.'[157] The Etruscan priests said this prodigy foretokened a change of conditions and the advent of a New Age, they taught that there were eight Ages completely different from one another, each lasting a Great Year. Whenever one circuit has run out and another begins, a wonderful sign appears in earth or heaven, and it is clear from those versed in the signs that men of the New Age have come into the world. All things undergo great changes. The Senate took great notice of soothsayers. This belief may have prompted St. Matthew's unconfirmed assertion that a Great Star appeared at the birth of Jesus.

Religion[158] initially had no connection with morality, the very word meant the bonds attaching human action to the realm of the Gods; from a strictly purist point of view Students of UFOs are 'religious' in the sense that they are seeking contact with the Celestials. To the average Roman religion did not mean moral subservience to an inspirational God, salvation through a divine Saviour, his piety expressed an awareness of Man's solemn relation to the Higher Powers in the sky ('Our Father which art in heaven') controlling the universe; such dutiful submission to the Gods evoked their benign intervention visibly demonstrated by their promotion of Rome from rustic village to world-state. Even today in our own cynical century during times of war and crises not concerned with morality, we instinctively look aloft to the skies and pray to God hoping some radiant Superman will wing down and put things right. Philosophers later confused ethics with religion making Jupiter a symbol of divine justice, laws governing the citizens of Rome generally favoured the patricians, Emperors being 'divine' like the Gods were above the law, the slaves having no legal right suffered punitive repressions; basically Roman law controlled the family, property and the State, the law existed to strengthen Rome. Though the Romans realised that all religions were merely different aspects of the one cosmic wisdom and allowed generous tolerance, for patriotic and security purposes they insisted that every citizen gave formal oath to the Gods acknowledging allegiance to the Guardian Genius of Rome; failure to accept the Gods signified treachery, particularly dangerous since for centuries the Romans were waging virtually continuous world-war. The Romans persecuted the Christians not for believing in Christ but primarily because their rejection of Rome's Gods implied rejection of Rome itself, which no patriotic citizen could tolerate.

The Indo-European Sky-Father, Dyaus-Pitar or Zeus-Pater latinised to Jupiter, symbolised the Spacemen; he dominated the Roman heavens, the stars, the sun, thunder and lightning, Ruler of Gods and Men. Sky-worship was the fundamental religion of the Etruscans, Britons, Babylonians and all contemporary peoples, who for many centuries scanned the heavens from lofty towers, ziggurats, Stonehenge and mountains all over the world; lesser divinities, Minerva, Juno, Ceres, Venus and Neptune were assimilated from the Greeks, Saturn, Apollo, Vesta and many others from local cults, towering above them all presided Jupiter aided by Mars, God of War, Patron of Rome, and Quirinus, identified with Romulus, specially associated with corn. Celestial prodigies were interpreted by augurs revealing the Will of the Gods. Worship of the Sky-Father was complemented by the cult of the Earth-Mother, whose licentious rites symbolised fecundity, fruitfulness, prosperity for the Roman race. Man was beset by hostile forces from the cradle to beyond the grave, only proper ritual by the priests secured peace from the Gods, so essential to the well-being of individual and State. There was no absolute gulf between the living and the dead; like ancient peoples world-wide the Romans believed the soul survived death, sometimes departing to bliss in distant realms or hovering earth-bound around familiar haunts influencing their family if not duly appeased. Ancestor-worship and belief in resurrection of the souls imply a very high theology, refinements of thought beyond most Romans and their contemporaries in other countries, suggesting that they were really degenerate descendants from some great world-civilisation many millennia before, that Golden Age sung by the poets. Many of the Ancients like Chroniclers in the Middle Ages called the Celestials 'Spirits' imagining them to be the resurrected dead returning to Earth from a heaven on some wondrous star, such superstition evoked dread of the Spacemen but promoted ancestor-worship. Graves and tombs were protected by invisible Powers propitiated with gifts and flowers, a custom in our own cemeteries today.

Certain mountains, woods and streams were haunted by satyrs, gnomes and nymphs. Immortals from etherean realms, who manifested to men. Today like the Romans we are sadly confused, no longer do we ridicule tales of the 'little people', mindful of those humanoids plaguing South America we wonder whether they were Spacemen and speculate now that those fairy-rings in the forests were evidence of Spaceships. The nymphs recall that well-attested Lady of Fatima who may have materialised from Space. The researches of Meade Layne and his Borderland Scientists allied with discoveries in sub-atomic Physics seem to prove the co-existence of etherean realms from which materialise those Sylphs so vividly described by Montfaucon de Villars in 'Le Comte de Gabalis' three hundred years ago. We are astounded to find that our new awareness of Spacemen is expanding our souls to cosmic wisdom, to the religion of early Rome.

Numa Pompilius sought inspiration in a grove of the Gods watered by a perennial spring, where he could meditate in solitude, free from the clamour of Rome. The King claimed to have been honoured with a celestial marriage to the Goddess Egeria who loved him and in blessed communion endowed him with wisdom. The Romans stood in awe of Numa's power, they accepted his strange revelations and believed nothing incredible or impossible. By the counsel of Egeria Numa surprised the Gods, Picus and Faunus, in their retreat under the Aventine Hill and kept them prisoners until Jupiter appeared in the form of lightning and promised his favours, later confirmed by the famous 'ancile' dropping from heaven. Is it too fantastic to wonder if Numa had somehow arrested two Spacemen, probably with drugged wine, who were subsequently rescued by a Spaceship?

Dionysius of Halicarnassus writes

'They relate also many marvellous stories about him, attributing his human wisdom to the suggestions of the Gods. For they fabulously affirm that a certain nymph, Egeria, used to visit him and instruct him on each occasion in the art of reigning, though others say it was not a nymph but one of the Muses. And this they claim became clear to everyone, for when people were incredulous at first, as may well be supposed and regarded the story concerning the Goddess as an invention, he, in order to give the unbelievers a manifest proof of his converse with this Divinity, did as follows pursuant to her instructions. He invited to the house where he lived a great many of the Romans, all men of worth, and having shown them his apartments very meanly provided with furniture and particularly lacking in everything that was necessary to entertain a numerous company, he ordered them to depart for the time being but invited them to dinner in the evening. And when they came at the appointed hour he showed them rich couches and tables laden with a multitude of beautiful cups, and when they were at table he set before them a banquet consisting of all sorts of viands, such a banquet indeed as it would not have been easy for anyone in those days to have prepared in a long time. The Romans were astonished at everything they saw and from that time they entertained a firm belief that some Goddess held converse with him.'[39]

This delightful tale recalls the 'Satapatha Brahmana' telling of the Apsara, Urvasi, who winged down to Earth enamoured of her lover, Pururavas; also the mediaeval chronicle 'De Nugis Curialium' describing how in AD 1070 the Saxon patriot, Edric, the Wild, fell in love with a beautiful damsel from Space. Such unions between celestial maidens and earthly lovers formed the theme of 'Tannhauser', the 'Swan Lake' ballet, the sylphs and succubi of the Middle Ages and Immortals in mythologies all over the world. In 1952 Truman Bethurum met Aura Rhanes, a Spacewoman from Clarion, who enlightened him on cosmic mysteries. Our awareness of Extraterrestrials today makes Numa's inspiration by Egeria a fascinating possibility, his banquet evokes the 'Arabian Nights'; we wish such a Celestial could keep house for us.

Plutarch rhapsodises on the Golden Age when honour and justice flowed into all hearts from the wisdom of Numa as from a fountain and the calm serenity of his spirit diffused itself abroad. Numa reigned forty-three years during which there were no wars or political strife, he lived in harmony free from vice, perfectly proving the belief of Plato[160] three centuries later that human ills would only disappear when by some divine felicity a philosopher ruled as King. When eighty years old Numa died tranquilly in 672 BC, his funeral rites evoked public lamentations by all his people, rich and poor, mourned not as King but rather as the passing of a dear Friend. Numa wrote twelve books on natural philosophy, knowledge which he had imparted to the priests; convinced that such mysteries should not be made public, he directed that all his writings should be buried in one stone coffin, himself in another. About four hundred years later heavy rains washed away the earth disclosing both coffins. The Senate decided that publication of Numa's writings would reveal the most sacred mysteries of the State religion and ordered all the books to be publicly burned. Today we mourn above all the destruction of those twelve books, which must surely have contained the quintessence of Numa's inspired wisdom; written centuries before Pythagoras, Aeschylus and Plato; their compilation proved that in the seventh century BC there existed in Rome knowledge which might have revolutionised our conception of history, revealed the secrets of the Gods, the Spacemen. We have seen books burned during our own century. The Senate were rough, unlettered men, for whom books seemed magic, while we deplore their vandalism, we wonder if twelve Dead Sea Scrolls became unearthed proving conclusively that Jesus never lived, that the Gospels are fiction, as some people believe, would the Pope not be tempted to destroy them rather than have such revelations rock the very foundations of the Church?

Numa's own coffin was found to be empty! The cave containing the body of Jesus was found to be empty. Many intriguing questions could be asked. Was Numa resurrected or translated by his 'Space-wife', Egeria?

His people, who loved him, believed Numa Pompilius conversed with the Gods. Surely this wisest of Kings was inspired by Spacemen?

Tullus Hostilius scorned Numa's pacifism, seeking martial renown in fierce wars with his neighbours, he completely destroyed Alba Longa built by the son of Aeneas and routed the Sabines. At the height of his glory the King's superstitious soul was disturbed by a rain of stones on the Alban Mount. A mighty voice was heard issuing from the grove on the mountain-top which commanded the Albans to return to the Gods of their fathers, recalling the Voice of the Lord admonishing Abraham and Moses. Wearying of war Tullus made forlorn attempts to propitiate the Gods misusing the electrical techniques of Numa, the Gods grew exceedingly angry and Jupiter destroyed Tullus and all his house with a thunderbolt, as two hundred years earlier the 'Angel of the Lord' destroyed those followers of Baal plaguing Elijah. Though so little is known of this period, it is not unreasonable to conjecture that Numa left disciples probably persecuted by the warlike Tullus, finally one of them in 640 BC called down fire from heaven, aid from Spacemen, to consume the King just as St. Germanus a thousand years later evoked lightnings to shrivel Vortigern. Mysterious cremations, during our twentieth century are associated with UFOs, if hostile Spacemen incinerate people today, it is logical to assume they probably did so in Ancient Rome. Tullus Hostilius incurring the wrath of the Gods could have been killed by Spacemen.

Ancus Martius, grandson of Numa, continued to aggrandise Rome by war with the Latins, his only notable contribution to the City was a prison, which was nearly always full. He was succeeded in 616 BC by an Etruscan, Lucius Tarquinius, remembered mainly for his aristocratic, wealthy wife, Tanaquil, who was most skilled in Etruscan science and augury, thus likely to attract the Spacemen. One day while Tarquinius and Tanaquil were at table, a noble slave-woman, Ocresia, was placing food on burning logs when a phallus sprang to her from the flames; Tanaquil interpreted the prodigy as presaging an extraordinary birth.

The King ordered Ocresia to dress in bridal garments, seated in the heat of the fire she conceived a son, Servius Tullius, noted for his flame-coloured hair. An unlikely tale! This wonder however does recall a story in 'Otis Imperialia' by Gervase of Tilbury about AD 1200 concerning a Mongolian Princess who claimed to have conceived from a light which appeared in her tent. Both alleged incidents arouse speculations regarding conception by the Holy Ghost, Sylphs and Spacemen, so easily ridiculed yet said to occur in fact as well as fiction. A few years later as Servius Tullius lay sleeping, his head appeared to burst into flame; Tanaquil read the portent as prophesying kingship. Servius Tullius reigned from 578 BC promoting the grandeur of Rome; it may be relevant to note that in 538 BC in Babylon the Prophet Daniel was communing with Angels, probably Spacemen. In 534 BC the aged King was stabbed by followers of his son-in-law, Tarquinius Superbus; Tullia, his vicious daughter, ran over her father's body in her chariot, calling down a curse on herself and the new King.

Tarquin the Proud refused his father-in-law a funeral saying that Romulus had also perished without burial, he put to death the leading Senators and organised a reign of terror against rich and poor alike. A bad King in peace, Tarquin was a good General in war; under his sway Rome dominated the Latin Federation: he defeated the Volscians and attacked Cumae, abode of the Sibyl. An old woman came to him offering twelve books prophesying the future of Rome for three hundred pieces of gold. Tarquin refused. She returned with nine declaring she had destroyed three. Again the King refused. The woman destroyed another three and returned once more with six which she threatened to sell to the King's enemies. Tarquin bought the six at the original price; these were consulted by the Senate in times of crisis. The Sibylline Books probably resembled those celebrated couplets of Nostradamus, inspired by some extraterrestrial source. Tarquin's tyrannical rule goaded the Romans to revolt. In 510 BC his son, Sextus, raped his cousin's wife, not quite so amorously as Shakespeare suggests; the noble Lucretia called upon her husband and father to avenge her dishonour, then stabbed herself. The citizens flamed with outrage, they deposed Tarquin and established the long Republic of Rome.

'Lars Porsena of Clusium by the nine Gods he swore
That the great House of Tarquin should suffer wrong no more.'[161]

Lord Macaulay's famous ballad, once learned by every schoolboy, told how brave Horatius held the bridge across the Tiber against all the hordes of Clusium (Chiusi) to save Rome. Like all Etruscan Priest-Kings Lars Porsena studied that strange electrical science, still unknown to us, and communed with the Celestials just as Elijah called upon the 'Angel of the Lord'. In a most significant revelation Pliny recalls that Lars Porsena prayed to the Gods, who hurled thunderbolts to destroy Bolsena, the wealthiest town in Tuscany. Spacemen are not always benevolent; the Sanskrit and Chinese Classics give vivid descriptions of assault from Space. The Bible tells how the 'Lord' destroyed Sodom and Gomorrah, slew the First-Born in Egypt, killed worshippers of Baal, annihilated the army of Sennacherib at Jerusalem (Pelusium?). The ancient city of Hattus in Asia Minor was apparently destroyed with a fantastic heat which even melted the bricks at a temperature of more than 1000° unattainable by conventional weapons suggesting nuclear-bombs. Such centuries-old menace from the Spacemen may explain why the Etruscans, Israelites and their contemporaries so anxiously scanned the skies. Aerial attacks have occurred throughout history, perhaps more often than suspected. As recently as June 1954 an eleven-year-old African boy, Leili Thindi,[162] one night watched strange lights hovering above Mt. Kenya, next morning he learned in horror that the whole population and livestock of the village of Kirimuyu had been seared to death by terrible burning streams of light from glowing objects in the sky. On the night of 3/4 November 1957 a UFO hung over the fortress of Itaipu in Brazil,[163] it suddenly attacked the sleeping garrison with heat-rays cutting out all electrical-circuits and severely burning the sentries. In 'The World at One' broadcast by the B.B.C. on 16 January 1968, that distinguished authority, Mr. Gordon Creighton, disclosed that there had been thousands of visitations by UFOs; some were benevolent, many hostile. If some Spacemen are hostile today, it is logical to assume that others were hostile centuries ago. The thunderbolt attack by the 'Gods' on Bolsena about 508 BC now seem credible. Pliny studied more than two thousand works, almost all now lost, the Admiral possessed one of the shrewdest scientific brains in the whole Roman world, he must have had firm reasons for accepting that Lars Porsena requested the Celestials to blast Bolsena with thunderbolts; he added that Piso in his 'Annals' had mentioned similar incidents. Plutarch writes that Numa Pompilius never worried about approaching enemies, he just sacrificed to the Gods, who he knew would defend him. As Joshua was directed by the 'Lord' to utilise the power of sound to flatten the walls of Jericho, so Lars Porsena called on Jupiter against Bolsena. We can picture UFOs hovering over the Italian town blitzing it with heat-rays leaving that proud city in flames open to the army of Lars Porsena just as in 640 BC they had blasted Tullus Hostilius to death in his own palace. Fantasy? Pliny believed it!

In 503 BC warlike spears were seen glowing in the heavens at midnight; these may have been meteors but Spacemen following the affairs of the infant Republic would be interested in the Sabine onslaught which nearly captured Rome.

> '... And this is not to be imputed to chance or folly but to the frequent appearance of the Gods themselves. In the war with the Latins when Aulus Posthumus, the Dictator, attacked Octavius Manilius, the Tusculan, at Regillus, Castor and Pollux were seen fighting in our army on horseback and since that same offspring of Tyndarus gave notice for as P. Vatienus, the grandfather of the present young man of that name, was coming in the night to Rome from his government of Reato two young men on white horses appeared to him and told him that King Perses was that day taken prisoner (Pydna 168 BC). ... Nor do we forget that when the Locrians defeated the people of Crotona in a great battle on the banks of the river Sagra (6th century BC), that it was known the same day at the Olympic Games. ...'

Cicero in 'De Natura Deorum', Book I, Chapter 2, recorded the firm belief of all Romans that the Gods, Castor and Pollux, had landed to save their City.

For ten years the exiled Tarquin plotted return to Rome. In 498 BC with Allies from thirty cities of the Latin League led by Octavius Manilius, he marched to crush the new Republic. The Romans in alarm appointed their first Dictator, Aulus Posthumus, who confronted the invaders at Lake Regillus near modern Frascati. For hours the battle raged indecisively, the Etruscans fought hard and pushed the Romans back. In desperation Aulus Posthumus neglected no help human or divine and vowed a temple to Castor. In a frantic charge against the enemy two strange horsemen, handsome beyond the stature of Man, appeared in front of the cavalry leading the onslaught. On the same day that evening two young men appeared in the Forum fresh from the fray and gave news of the great victory. They departed and were not seen again. Rome was saved for glorious destiny. Aulus Posthumus built the temple he had vowed on every anniversary on the Ides of Quintilis (15th July), knights clad in purple and crowned with olives rode in the procession from the temple of Mars outside the City to the temple of Castor and Pollux.

Plutarch adds that

'... the first man who met them, where they were cooling their horses, while they were reeking with sweat, was amazed at their report of victory. Then we are told they touched his beard with their hands quietly smiling the while and the hair of it was changed at once from black to red, a circumstance which gave credence to their story and fixed upon the man the surname of "Abenobarbus", that is to say "Bronzebeard".'[164]

The Sanskrit Classics tell of the twin Aswins winging down to aid the heroes of Old India. The Greeks after their epic victory over the Persians at Marathon in 490 BC swore they were aided by superhuman personages like Theseus, Minerva and Athena. Whatever the truth, Pausanias, Plutarch and Herodotus certainly believed the outnumbered Greeks to have been saved by Celestials from the skies, likewise Livy, Cicero and Dio Cassius swore Rome was saved by Castor and Pollux.

Our sceptics would no doubt expect Spacemen to materialise in aluminium suits flashing ray-guns; surely it is more likely that they appeared in the costume with the mannerisms of the Age like those Space Visitants alleged to be living among us today.

This magic land of Old Italy seduces our soul. Those mysterious Etruscans, their Divine Teacher, Tages, revealing religion; King Amulius submerged by his own explosions; God-begotten Romulus translated to the skies then resurrected; wise old Numa married to a Nymph playing with lightnings; a shield dropping from heaven; Tullus Hostilius destroyed by a thunderbolt; Tanaquil the queenly witch; Servius Tullius conceived by fire dying like a dog; Lars Porsena calling down lightning to burn Bolsena; Castor and Pollux fighting for Rome at Lake Regillus; mysterious voices presaging centuries of strange lights in the sky, two suns, three moons, apparitions descending to men.

Suddenly we feel we are reading the Bible, Why must we worship such prodigies in Old Palestine as manifestations of the 'Lord' yet ignore identical wonders at the same time in Italy not far away?

Should we not write a Second Old Testament about Ancient Rome inspired by Spacemen?

Chapter Ten
Space Chronicles of Ancient Rome

For two centuries the virile Republic struggled against hostile neighbours, Aequi, Volscians and Etruscans, whom it eventually conquered and absorbed into that Senatus Populusque Romanus, S.P.Q.R. destined to rule the Western World. The greatest threat came from the North; in 390 BC Brennus crept down with his Gauls to sack the City, only the resolution of Camillus routed the invaders and saved Rome. The Spacemen surveilling the Peloponnesian War in Greece and the tribulations of Israel must surely have watched this lusty city on the Tiber extending its dominance all over Italy. Unfortunately of this vital period little is known.

The vast destruction of contemporary literature greatly restricts our knowledge of Antiquity, particularly of Extraterrestrial influence in ancient times. Scholars and archaeologists have resurrected the past with brilliance but so many fascinating details are missing. Five hundred books by Varro, a hundred by Livy, sixty by Dio Cassius, thirty-five by Polybius, almost all those two thousand learned works consulted by Pliny are lost, all lost. For many centuries the augurs spent millions of man-hours studying the skies, they must have witnessed most intriguing phenomena and even monitored the 'Power and Glory' of the 'Lord' visiting the Jews; their records are lost, all lost. The discovery of a few Dead Sea Scrolls is profoundly influencing our conception of Christianity, resurrection of only a fraction of the lost Classics might completely revolutionise our opinions of Antiquity, especially of the vital influence exerted by Spacemen. Today even in our Space Age we cannot comprehend the awe accorded by the Ancients to events in the heavens. The Romans were practical, unimaginative people obsessed with mundane matters of Earth. Why were they so concerned with prodigies in the skies? Is there some secret our scholars have missed?

Livy, Dio Cassius, Plutarch, Pliny, Cicero, Seneca and other writers seemed acutely conscious of Divinities guiding affairs on Earth; their highly intelligent minds really believed that omens in the heavens were written by the Gods to presage great events. Nothing happened by chance. Two moons in the sky, a lightning-flash, a flight of birds, an earthquake, the birth of a two-headed calf, the lumps on a sheep's liver, all prodigies portended calamities to Man, the substance of history.

Such references to strange phenomena in heaven and Earth so intrigued Julius Obsequens, a writer of fourth century AD of whom nothing is known, that he searched all available histories and listed their erratic facts, Fortean phenomena, in his 'Prodigiorum Libellus'. Obsequens recorded his dates from 'Anno Urbis Conditae', A.U.C., 'from the year the City was built'. The fragments from Obsequens now extant to us date only from 577 AUC (176 BC) until 737 AUC (16 BC). In the sixteenth century the writings of Julius Obsequens captured the imagination of a young priest, Conrad Wolffhart,[165] born in 1518 at Ruffach in Alsace; mediaeval theology taught that prodigies in the skies expressed the Will of God. It was religious zeal rather than the cynicism prompting his modern emulator, Charles Fort, which inspired Conrad Lycosthenes (his surname in Greek) then a deacon at Basle to scour the Classics to restore the work of Obsequens; he also read many Authorities of the Middle Ages and extended his chronicle of oddities in Earth, sea and sky up to 1556. Five years later he died from apoplexy.

In his masterly work 'Piece for a Jig-saw', Leonard G. Cramp[166] suggests that those rains of frogs, fish, flesh, stones, iron and chunks of ice reported by Charles Fort and witnesses today are probably elevated from Earth by Spacecraft powered by a gravitational field, then jettisoned from a very high altitude as unwanted cargo. Such debris fallen from the skies so frequently mentioned by Julius Obsequens would apparently prove the presence of Spaceships over Ancient Rome.

Pliny in 'Historia Naturalis', Book II, LVII, discussing celestial phenomena comments

'Besides these events in the lower sky, it is entered in the records that in the consulship of Manius Acilius and Gaius Porcius (114 BC) it rained milk and blood and that frequently on other occasions there it has rained flesh, for instance in the consulship of Publius Volumnius and Servius Suplicius (461 BC) and that none of the flesh left unplundered by birds of prey went bad, similarly that it rained iron in the district of Lucania, the year before Marcus Crassus (in the battle of Carrhae 53 BC) was killed by the Parthians and with him all the Lucanian soldiers, of whom there was a large contingent in his army; the shape of the iron that fell resembled sponges; the augurs prophesied wounds from above. But in the consulship (49 BC) of Lucius Paullus and Gaius Marcellus, it rained wool in the vicinity of Compsa Castle (now Conza in Samnium) near which Titus Annius was killed a year later. It is recorded in the annals of that year that while Milo was pleading a case in Court it rained bricks.'

During most of the fifth century BC Rome fought incessant wars with her neighbours, the Etruscans, Latins and Samnites, which probably attracted the attention of Spacemen. In 461 BC the heavens were seen to glow and the people saw strange phantoms which terrified them, the forms and voices of the apparitions were dreadful to the eyes and ears of men; this terse description by Lycosthenes recalls those startling accounts of humanoids terrorising the peasants of South America today. These Visitants were accompanied by a rain of flesh like the appearance of snow from the sky scattered in pieces large and small as though torn from every kind of bird flying over before it touched the ground, the remains which truly occurred spread over city and field and lay for a long time neither changed in colour nor smell from old decayed meat. This outrage the soothsayers were unable to interpret; however the Sibylline Books advised that it warned of enemies without and sedition within the City.[167] As so brilliantly theorised by Leonard Cramp rains of flesh apparently originate from animals caught up by the gravitational field of a Spaceship, confirming perhaps that those dreadful apparitions in 461 BC were Spacemen.

Today most UFO reports are explained as meteors, bolides, parahelia, sun-dogs, temperature-inversions, birds or the planet Venus; lack of scientific data makes evaluation of Roman sightings somewhat dubious. The following quotations from various Classics may arouse controversy among our modern sceptics, who were not present at the time to observe the phenomena, but the Romans well-experienced during centuries of watching the skies did believe they had seen something strange and significant worthy of comment. Perhaps some of the UFOs were Spaceships? If we really do believe that Spacemen are surveilling our Earth today, then surely we must accept the possibility that they also visited our planet in Roman times and millennia earlier.

In 344 BC Timoleon, who belonged to one of the noblest families in Corinth, was invited by the Greek cities in Sicily to drive out the Carthaginians who had landed on that island. Plutarch describing his voyage there writes

'And now with seven Corinthian ships and two from Corcyra and a tenth which the Leucadians furnished, he (Timoleon) set sail. And at night, after he had entered the open sea and was enjoying a favouring wind the heavens seemed to burst open on a sudden above his ship and to pour forth an abundant and conspicuous fire. From this a torch lifted itself on high like those on which the mystics bear, and running along with them on their course darted down upon precisely that part of Italy towards which the pilots were steering.'[188]

Timoleon won a brilliant victory and became ruler of Sicily; his campaign possibly attracted Space Visitants.

Four years later the Romans more belligerent than ever coveting the fertile land of Campania were waging war against the Latins. Livy in Book VIII, Chapter VI, reports

'340 BC There in the stillness of the night both Consuls are said to have been visited by the same apparition, a man of greater than human stature and more majestic, who declared that the Commander of one side and the army of the other must be offered up to the Manes and to Mother Earth.'

In 332 BC 'Flying Shields' are alleged to have appeared over Tyre besieged by Alexander the Great and later to have dived on the Macedonians crossing a river in India stampeding the soldiers and elephants with darts of fire; these reports cannot be confirmed.

For two hundred years while the Romans extended their

domination over Italy they kept uneasy peace with Carthage, whose fleets lorded the Mediterranean. When the people of Sicily in 264 BC appealed to Rome to liberate their island from the Carthaginians the Senate dreaming already of Imperial glory were determined to challenge Carthage and began the First Punic War lasting twenty-three years. The century-long conflict between Rome and Carthage with such tremendous consequences for future civilisation would inevitably intrigue any Spaceman surveilling Earth.

234 BC   'At Rimini three moons were seen, meanwhile the Gauls invaded Italy.'[169]

223 BC   'Portents occurred which threw the people of Rome into great fear. A river in Picenum ran the colour of blood in Etruria, a good part of the heavens seemed to be on fire. In Ariminium a light like the day blazed out at night, in many portions of Italy three moons became visible in the night-time and in the Forum a vulture perched for several days.'[170]

The omens proved lucky for Flaminius routed the Gauls back to the Alps.

222 BC   'Also three moons have appeared at once.'[171]

221 BC   'At Rimini three moons were seen coming from the distant regions of the heavens.'[172]

While Rome contended for the mastery of Italy Carthage resolved to resume the war. Hamilcar, Supreme Commander, invaded Spain to collect the treasures of the famous silver mines, at his death in battle near the Tagus he was succeeded by his son-in-law, Hasdrubal, killed by an assassin's knife. Command fell to Hannibal, twenty-six years old, destined to become probably the greatest military leader in all history. A dramatic story tells how when Hannibal was still a boy, his father, Hamilcar, made him swear on an altar undying hostility to Rome, this vow dominated his life. A brilliant General, Hannibal surpassed his own soldiers in exercise of arms on foot or horseback; his bodily powers of endurance allied with personal bravery and sagacity won admiration even from his enemies, although the Romans naturally accused him of cruelty and ferocity though he never broke faith with Rome. Like many great soldiers he was a man of culture and delighted to converse on intellectual matters in Latin and Greek. In 218 BC the Carthaginians besieged Saguntum in Spain, ally of Rome, beginning the long and difficult Second Punic War. Hannibal was now in his twenty-ninth year, about the same age as Napoleon, when the Emperor led the Grand Army of France into Italy. Hannibal's crossing of the Alps with 50,000 foot, 9,000 horses and 37 elephants was one of the epics of history; after mass desertions and attacks by the Gauls the Carthaginians slowly descended from the snow-capped peaks to the sunny Po valley with less than half the men with which they had set out. For the next sixteen years Hannibal ravaged Italy yet never set foot in Rome.

This fateful campaign surely attracted surveillance by Spacemen. Livy in Book XXI, LXII, reports

218 BC 'Phantom ships had been seen gleaming in the sky.... In the district of Amiternum in many places apparitions of men in shining raiment had appeared in the distance but had not drawn near to anyone.'

Forty years earlier during the First Punic War similar apparitions were seen.

217 BC 'The sun's disc seemed to be contracted. Glowing stones had fallen from the sky at Praeneste, at Arpi bucklers had appeared in the sky, the sun had seemed to be fighting with the moon, at Caperne two moons had risen in the day-time. ... at Falerii the sky had seemed to be rent as it were with a great fissure and through the opening a bright light had shone and that lots had shrunk.... At Capua there had been the appearance of a sky on fire, and of a moon that fell in the midst of a shower of rain.' (Livy, Book XXII I.)

Lycosthenes paraphrases Livy and adds

'The apparitions of ships were seen in the sky.... Dreadful earthquakes shook the ground.... In that year Hannibal invaded Etruria. The Romans were routed in the bloody battle at Lake Trasimene.'

With brilliant tactics Hannibal extricated his army from ambush in the wooded hills near Lake Trasimene and smashed the Romans under Caius Flaminius, hardly a man survived. Such a battle would probably attract Spacemen implied by Livy and Lycosthenes.

Rome in panic appointed Quintus Fabius Maximus as Dictator, he hoped to defeat Hannibal by delaying tactics; his name in modern times was adopted by our Fabian Society, whose philosophy was to achieve progress slowly but surely. Never had the Romans met such a dazzling strategist. In 216 BC Hannibal annihilated the great Roman army at Cannae in the most shattering defeat in their history. It was said that 'so great a multitude of Romans fell that Hannibal, the General, filled many bushels and quart measures with the finger-rings of the Generals and the other prominent men and sent them to Sicily.'

Hannibal with Rome at his mercy did not enter the City; like Hitler failing to invade Britain after Dunkirk; perhaps the magnitude of this historic prize daunted his soul, more probably he feared his victorious troops would be trapped. During the next few years he rampaged somewhat frustrated up and down Italy, while the Romans under Scipio won back Spain.

Livy in Book XXIV, X, mentions startling sightings in the skies.

214 BC   'Prodigies in large numbers and the more they were believed by men, simple and devout, the more of them used to be reported, were reported that year. The river Minucius appeared bloody.... At Cales it rained chalk.... *At Hadria an altar was seen in the sky and about it the forms of men in white garments* ... certain men asserting that they saw armed legions on the Janiculum aroused the City to arms.'

An altar in the sky with men in white seems surely a classic description of a Spaceship!

213 BC   'In the river at Terracina forms of warships which had no existence had been seen. In the temple of Jupiter Vicilinus in the territory of Compsa was a sound of clashing arms, the river at Amiternum ran blood.' (Livy, Book XXIV, XLIV).

Hannibal continued to win several victories but lacked the strength to smash Rome; when expected reinforcements were crushed by the defeat and death of his brother, Hasdrubal, in Northern Italy in 207 BC the war for the Carthaginians was virtually lost. For four years Hannibal roamed the mountainous regions unable to launch an offensive, then in 203 BC returned to Africa; a year later he suffered decisive defeat by Scipio at Zama. Rejected by his own people Hannibal fled to Antioch and continued to struggle against Rome; in 183 BC rather than fall into Roman hands this aged lion took poison.

Intriguing celestial phenomena haunted Italian skies.
Livy reports

206 BC   'At Alba they said two suns were seen and at Fregellae that light had appeared in the night.'

204 BC   'Two suns had been seen and at Setia a meteor had been seen shooting from east to west.'

During the same year a curious event occurred which strangely illumines Roman superstition concerning the Gods. While Crassus reconquered part of Bruttium in Southern Italy direful prodigies sent by Jupiter terrified Rome; the decemviri consulted the Sibylline Books which said that something would soon fall from heaven at Pessinus in Phrygia, which should be brought to Rome. Shortly afterwards came the news that the Image of the Mother of the Gods had fallen there. The ship bringing it to Rome stuck in the mud of the Tiber, the soothsayers swore it could only be moved by a woman who had never committed adultery. Claudia Quintia under suspicion for such offence protested her innocence, she called to the ship which freed from the mud followed her, thus Claudia's immoral reputation changed to shining virtue.[173]

This Image from the skies recalled that 'Shield' falling from heaven five hundred years earlier during the reign of Numa Pompilius. Could these objects have dropped from Spaceships?

203 BC   'At Anagnia there were at first shooting-stars at intervals, then a great meteor. At Frusino a halo encircled the sun with its slender circumference and then the ring itself had a greater circle bright as the sun circumscribed about it. At Arpinum in an open meadow the Earth settled into a huge depression.'[174] (See 163 BC and 82 BC.)

Today such sudden depressions in fields arouse speculation as to the landings of Spaceships.

This swift transmission of news apparently by divine Messengers greatly impressed the Roman writers. Cicero in 'De Natura Deorum', Book I, Chapter 11, discussing the intervention of Castor and Pollux at Lake Regillus in 498 BC also mentioned how two young men on white horses brought news of the battle of Pydna and the capture of the Macedonian King Perseus to Rome in 168 BC.

Plutarch in 'Aemilius Paulus', XXIV, states

> 'For it was only the fourth day after Perseus had been defeated at Pydna and at Rome the people were watching equestrian contests when suddenly a report sprang up at the entrance of theatre that Aemilius had conquered Perseus in a great battle and reduced all Macedonia.'

Dio Cassius in 'Roman History', Book 4, mentions how in 48 BC 'two young men' in Syria announced Caesar's defeat of Pompey at Pharsalia in Thessaly. Today we are naturally sceptical as to whether the news on these occasions was actually conveyed by Spacemen, however the importance surely lies in the fact that the Romans themselves believed that the Gods had brought remarkably prompt news of the victories, proving the Romans quite accepted the reality of Extraterrestrials and their occasional intervention in the affairs of Rome. Who are we two thousand years later to disagree?

167 BC 'Lanuvium. A burning torch was seen in the sky.' (Obsequens.)

166 BC 'In the territory of Veii wool grew from trees. (Note: was this substance 'Angel Hair', evidence of Spaceships?) Lanuvium, a Torch was seen in the sky, at Cassini the sun was seen for a few hours at night.' (Obsequens.)

163 BC 'At Capua the sun was seen by night. At Forini two suns were seen by day. The sky was afire. In Cephalonia a trumpet seemed to sound from the sky. There was a rain of earth. A windstorm demolished houses and laid crops flat in the fields. By night an apparent sun shone at Pisaurum.' (Obsequens.)

Similar phenomena in 203 BC and 82 BC may suggest the landing of a Spaceship.

154 BC 'At Compsa weapons appeared to fly through the sky.' (UFOs?) (Obsequens.)

in the sky. At Priverno grey wool covered the ground.' (Obsequens.)

A similar fall of wool in Central Italy in 49 BC is reported by Pliny.

Associated with UFO activity appears a gossamer-like substance known throughout history as 'Angel's Hair' or 'Threads of the Virgin', silvery filaments apparently synthesised in extremely high voltage discharges; these strands like nylon drape the ground, only to vanish when the temperature rises. 'Grey wool' following the 'appearance of a great fleet in the sky' suggest the manifestation of many Spaceships.

171 BC 'In the Roman Forum three suns were shining at the same time.' (Lycosthenes.)

170 BC The great fleet seen over Lanuvium in 173 BC was succeeded three years later by a celestial army massed over Jerusalem. According to the Second Book of Maccabees, Chapter V, v. 1-5

'About this time Antiochus prepared his second voyage into Egypt. And then it happened through all the city for the space of almost forty days, there were seen horsemen running in the air in cloth of gold, and armed with lances running like a band of soldiers. And troops of horsemen in array encountering and running one against another with shaking of shields and multitude of pikes, and drawing of swords, and casting of darts and glittering of golden ornaments and harness of all sorts.'

An army in the sky in 103 BC is reported by Julius Obsequens.

This intriguing spectacle dazzled the English in AD 1236. Matthew of Paris in 'Historia Anglorum' writes

'Also about this time in the month of May along the boundaries of England and Wales portents appeared in the sky of armed soldiers superbly although hostilely congregated. This is seen to be incredible to all who hear this unless the same thing is read 'in the beginning of Maccabees. The same thing was seen however assembled in Ireland, of which apparition we are taught by a certain close relative of the Duke of Gloucester.'

168 BC 'Rumours of the successful Roman victory in Macedonia swept Rome before the messengers arrived. The Magistrates were astonished. The news was proclaimed by Castor and Pollux.' (Livy, Book XLV, I.)

Latin literature apparently did not begin until five centuries after the founding of Rome, an astonishing illiteracy compared with the literary glories of Greece. The first important writer, Plautus (255-184 BC), wrote about a hundred and thirty plays of which only twenty survive; in 'Rudens' Arcturus descends from the skies to mingle among mortals, in 'Amphitryo' Jupiter and Mercury wing down to frolic in bawdy comedy showing that the Romans accepted celestial lovers more readily than we would today. The greatest contribution to culture made by Carthage are probably the six comedies of her famous son, Terence (195 – 159 BC) who taken as a slave to Rome then freed, penned elegant plays like Menander inspiring the early theatre, which later drew praise even from such a stylist as Cicero. Quintus Ennius (239-169 BC) modelled his thirty tragedies, all lost, on the works of Euripides, his 'Annals' in Homeric hexameters anticipated Virgil tracing the history of Rome from Aeneas to his own days, only fragments remain; about the same time Gnaeus Naevius banished for writing satirical plays criticising Rome's noble families turned his talents to a national epic on the First Punic War, nearly all lost. As far as can be determined from the few fragments left to us, these writers of the Third and Second Centuries BC expressed popular belief in the existence of the Gods and their occasional descent to Earth.

After defeating the Carthaginians at Zama in 202 BC the Romans turned their ambitions eastwards to the conquest of Greece and Syria, still torn by anarchy since the death of Alexander the Great in 323 BC. The three Macedonian Wars and the final destruction of Carthage in 146 BC probably attracted the attention of Spacemen more than the social and agrarian reforms perturbing Rome. A few references to celestial phenomena suggest surveilling Spaceships.

175 BC   'Three suns shone in the sky at the same time, several torches fell that night at Lanuvium.' (Obsequens.)
174 BC   'Three suns were seen.' (Pliny.)
173 BC   'At Lanuvium the appearance of a great fleet was beheld

152 BC 'In many places at Rome apparitions in togas were seen, on approaching they vanished from view.' (Obsequens.)

Apparitions had been seen about 260 BC, 218, 217 and 214 BC. The writers whom Julius Obsequens quoted evidently thought these spectres were Extraterrestrials, otherwise they would hardly have bothered to mention them.

146 BC 'After the death of Demetrius, King of Syria, who had for sons Demetrius and Antiochus, and shortly before the war with Achaia a comet shone big as the sun. It was at first dazzling enough to dispel the darkness of the night. Gradually its surface diminished and its brightness faded, finally it completely vanished.' (Seneca. 'Naturales Quaestiones.')

Was this a comet or a UFO? This year saw the complete destruction of Carthage by Scipio Aemilianus, younger son of Aemilius Paulus, victor of Pydna in Macedonia. The final ruin of this great city was probably watched by Spacemen, who had followed its century-long conflict with Rome.

140 BC 'At Praeneste and in Cephallonia it seemed that images had fallen from the sky.' (Obsequens.)

What were these 'signa'? Man-made metallic objects from some aerial ship?

137 BC 'At Praeneste a torch was seen burning in the sky.' (Obsequens.)
134 BC 'At Amiternum the sun was seen at night. Its light was seen for some time.' (Obsequens.)
127 BC 'At Fruosinne a burning torch was seen in the sky.' (Obsequens.)
122 BC 'In Gaul three suns and three moons were seen.' (Pliny.)
118 BC 'At Rome three suns were seen.' (Pliny, Book II XXXI.)

Pliny adds 'It is also reported that several suns were seen at midday at the Bosphorus and that these lasted from dawn to sunset.' Three suns were seen presumably at Rome in 174, 116, 44 and 42 BC also in AD 51.

116 BC 'In Latium three suns were seen this year.' (Lycosthenes.)
113 BC 'A light from the sky by night, the phenomenon usually called "night suns" was seen in the consulship of Gaius Caecilius and Gnaeus Papirius and often on other occasions causing apparent daylight in the night.' (Pliny, Book II, XXXIII.)

106 BC 'An uproar in the sky was heard and javelins seemed to fall from heaven. There was a rain of blood. At Rome a torch was seen.' (Obsequens.)

During the War with the Cimbri strange prodigies were seen. Plutarch in 'Gaius Marius' reports

103 BC 'Many signs also appeared, most of which were of the ordinary kind; but from Ameria and Tuda, cities of Italy, it was reported that at night there had been seen in the heavens flaming spears and sheilds, which at first moved in different directions, and then clashed together assuming the formations and movements of men in battle and finally some of them would give way, while others pressed on in pursuit and all streamed away to the westward.' (Reported also by Obsequens.)

103 BC 'The moon with a star appeared by day from the third to the seventh hour. At the third hour of the day an eclipse of the sun brought on darkness. On the voting-ground it rained milk. In Picenus three suns were seen.' (Obsequens.)

During the First Century BC the succession of Dictators, Marius, Sulla, Pompey, Caesar, ravaging the country and liquidating their enemies like gangsters in decades of Civil War finally exhausted the centuries-old Republic and made the people welcome the return of kingship under Augustus. Such tremendous conflict convulsing Rome would probably attract the Spacemen despairing at human folly.

100 BC 'In the consulship of Lucius Valerius and Gaius Marius a burning shield scattering sparks, ran across the sky at sunset from west to east.' (Pliny Book II, XXXIV.)

93 BC 'At Volsinii flame seemed to flash from the sky at dawn, after it had gathered together, the flame displayed a dark grey opening and the sky appeared to divide, in the gap tongues of flame appeared.' (Obsequens.)

91 BC 'At sunset a globe of fire in the northern region rushed across the sky emitting tremendous sound. In Spoletium a gold-coloured fireball rolled down to the ground and growing larger rose from the Earth towards the east becoming large enough to blot out the sun.' (Obsequens, confirmed by Orosius. L, v C18.)

88 BC 'In Stratopedon (Rhodes?) a great star was seen plunging from heaven. The apparition of Isis was seen attacking a "Harp" (a giant siege-engine) with a thunderbolt.' (Obsequens.)

This celestial attack recalls the 'Flying Shields' alleged to have dive-bombed Tyre during the siege by Alexander in 332 BC.

83 BC Sulla had assembled an army in Greece to invade Italy, on route to Patrae for the crossing to Brundusium the Romans found a strange humanoid at Apollonia near Dyrrachium in Illyria.

Plutarch in 'Sulla' reports

> 'Near by in Apollonia and in its vicinity is the Nymphaeum, a sacred precinct which sends forth in various places from its green dell and meadows streams of perpetual flaming fire. Here, they say, a Satyr was caught asleep, such as one as sculptors and painters represent and brought to Sulla, where he was asked through many interpreters who he was. And when at last he uttered nothing intelligible but with difficulty emitted a hoarse cry that was something between the neighing of a horse and the bleating of a goat, Sulla was horrified and ordered him out of his sight.'

The Satyr surprised by Sulla's soldiers recalls the God, Pan, worshipped by the Greeks, and even that strange boy, Kaspar Hauser, found at Nuremberg on 28 May 1828, who could hardly speak and appeared so alien to earthly environment like some person from another world. Satyrs haunting forests were depicted as elfin and green suiting their sylvan abodes. William de Newburgh in his 'Historia Anglicana', Vol. I, Cap. XXVII, 'De Viridibus Pueris' writes that during the reign of King Stephen at Alfpittes (Wolfpit) near Bury St. Edmunds, Suffolk, there emerged from a ditch in a field two children, boy and girl, green all over their bodies, clad in garments of unusual colour and unknown material '(emerserunt due puersi masculus et foemine, tota corpore virides et colores insoliti ex incognita materia veste operti'). The boy lived only a short time, his sister thrived, she later married and lived at Lynn. The pair said they came from St. Martin's Land, apparently a subterranean twilight world where the sun never shone. Was this Agharta, the civilisation said to flourish inside our 'Hollow Earth', miles beneath our feet?

The Etruscan God, Tages, sprang from a furrow in a field!

Such stories of a satyr by Plutarch and 'Green Children'

by William de Newburgh evoke those startling tales of humanoids from Spaceships haunting South America. To our bewilderment the reality of those little green men does seem confirmed by that extraordinary apparition at Luumaki, Finland, in 1965 testified by two very well-known people who, wishing to remain anonymous, are referred to as A and B in the following account from Vimana No. 2, 1967 published by the Finnish Interplanetary Society.

'On a lovely day in August A and B, together with some friends were picking whortleberries in a seldom frequented part of the forest. By about noon, A began to hear some sort of peculiar murmuring and "bubbling" sounds from the top of a nearby slope, though he could not detect anything unusual in the direction of the sound. After some time A again looked in the same direction and he now saw, at a distance of about 200 metres, a small manlike being standing on top of the slope, looking straight at him. This being and A stood staring at each other for some time, and then the little stranger started to walk towards A. The stranger was hardly a metre in height (about 3 feet), yet its head and shoulders appeared to be like those of a strong man. When this alien being started to move, it seemed to totter a bit at first, but soon regained its balance and walked with firm steps straight towards A, who like one paralysed stood looking at the approaching strange visitor whose face was carrot-red and whose body was covered by a skin-tight green apparel. The little man, however, soon changed direction and reached the edge of a small bog, where it just disappeared and was no longer to be seen.

B, who had also noticed the little man as well, said he had seen it later on when it came running quite close to A (and to me, the undersigned, who knew nothing of the event, but continued to pick whortle-berries, quite calmly about 10 metres from A). After a few strange movements the little man disappeared in a curious manner from the vision of B also.

A peculiar thing about this was that A was utterly incapable in any way of drawing my attention to the appearance of the little man, though we were quite close. Also, more than half a year passed before A could bring himself to talk about his strange experience and it was only then discovered that B had also seen the same "little green man."
Tapani Kiningas.'[178]

This experience evokes those leprechauns in Irish bogs; the induced amnesia recalls certain UFO 'Contacts' who only remembered their adventure during hypnosis as though the Spacemen had commanded their conscious mind to forget what had happened.

82 BC   'During the era of Sulla a great clash of standards and of arms with dreadful shouting was heard between Capua and Volturnum, so that two armies seemed to be locked in combat for several days. When men investigated this marvel more closely the tracks of horses and of men and the freshly trampled grass and shrubs seemed to foretell the burden of a great war.' (Obsequens.)[178]

The devastation near Capua in 82 BC parallels that sudden depression in an open meadow at Arpinum in 203 BC and the rain of earth in Cephalonia in 163 BC associated with intriguing omens in the skies. Such prodigies evoke 16 July 1963 when the people of Britain were astonished by an eight foot diameter crater, one foot deep in whose centre was a three feet deep hole, which had appeared overnight in a barley and potato field at Manor Farm, Charlton, in Wiltshire, radiating from the crater were four slits. Rumours of the landing of a spaceship from Uranus promptly goaded the Authorities to attribute the patch denuded of its potato crop to a meteorite which could not be found. Similar craters have appeared in many countries coincident with UFOs in the skies. It is believed that the gravitational field of the UFO exerts downward pressure causing a crater, on take-off the spacecraft's force field removes earth and crops which it jettisons elsewhere. The trampled ground near Capua in 82 BC seems evidence of a Spaceship.

73 BC   The Consul, Lucullus, led the Roman legions against Mithridates of Pontus, who was laying waste Asia Minor.

Mithridates, once boastful and pompous, had reorganised his forces in the Roman fashion, he disciplined the Barbarians into a well-drilled phalanx, replaced their rich trappings with armour and ships formerly decked with canopies and concubines now stored missiles and munitions of war. The King's immense array of 120,000 footmen, 16,000 horsemen and a hundred scythe-bearing four-horse chariots strained to hurl themselves upon the 35,000 infantry and 2,500 cavalry of Lucullus, eager to smash the invaders into the ground. Mithridates glanced proudly at his vast horde, the sun glinted on their armour, men yelled and brandished swords, horses neighed pawing the earth with impatience.

The King smiled; Rome itself was besieged by its own rebellious slaves under Spartacus, outnumbered four to one those silent legions awaited slaughter. He raised his hand to signal attack.

In the graphic words of Plutarch

'But presently as they were on the point of joining battle, with no apparent change of weather, but all on a sudden, the sky burst asunder, as a huge flame-like body was seen to fall between the two armies. In shape it was most like a wine-jar, and in colour like molten silver. Both sides were astonished at the sight and separated. This marvel, as they say, occurred in Phrygia, at a placed called Otryae.' (Near the Dardanelles, not far from Troy.)[177]

Astounded at this wonder from heaven, Mithridates avoided battle, his hordes fled north to besiege Cyzicus in the Sea of Marmos. Lucullus followed slowly cutting off all provisions, the King's vast army suffering from starvation disintegrated to rout; the Romans after a series of victories won immense booty. Mithridates in disgrace sought refuge in Armenia.

After masterly campaigns Lucullus restored Roman power in Asia Minor, then resigned the command to Pompey and returned to Rome in a spectacular triumph displaying mule-loads of precious stones, gold beakers, ingots of silver and more than two million pieces of silver coins. Lucullus poured forth his vast and splendid wealth in ostentation, even today 'lucullent' is a by-word for the most extravagant luxury. He introduced the cherry into Italy, his gardens were the wonder of Rome; near Naples he bred fish and built dwellings in the sea, erected observatories and poured forth money for paintings and statues. When not planning fabulous banquets he was establishing libraries and debating philosophy with his ardent friend, Cicero. Lucullus eventually lost his mind through taking drugs and died in 57 BC mourned by all Rome.

In 71 BC hundreds of gladiators, who had fought for freedom with Spartacus, were crucified by Licinus Crassus along the whole length of the Appian Way. Vae Victis!

'It was a beautiful, small craft, shaped more like a heavy glass bell than a saucer.... It was translucent and of exquisite colour.'[178]

This classic description by George Adamski of the Flying Saucer from Venus, which landed in the Californian Desert on 20 November 1952, has since been imitated by hundreds of witnesses describing the Spaceships astounding them; some soar to lyrical beauty, others delineate in aeronautical detail, all agree on the startling, breath-taking wonder transforming their lives.

More than a hundred years after that dramatic confrontation between Lucullus and Mithridates, Plutarch, whose writings inspired Shakespeare's plays, marvelled at the astounding apparition of this 'huge flame-like body like a wine-jar and in colour like molten silver' in eloquence worthy of the Bard himself. What prodigy from the heavens could possibly terrify proud Mithridates in the midst of his immense army ready to achieve his crowning ambition of driving the Romans into the sea? What miracle saved the legions from certain destruction? In 480 BC[179] that great light flamed over Salamis watching the Greeks smash the invasion-fleet of Xerxes; in 394 BC[180] the celestial 'beam' over Cnidus and the Spartans defeated at sea to lose the Empire of Greece; for a decade globes of fire followed Hannibal ravaging Italy looking down in 217 BC[181] on the Romans routed at Lake Trasimene, now in 73 BC Spacemen were studying this campaign of Lucullus in the East. The Spaceship burst down through the sky breaking the sound-barrier, its thunder and radiance paralysed the armies hushed at this Wonder between them. Even from some distance that unknown reporter was visibly thrilled, his account, alas, lost, impressed Plutarch a century later as it excites us today. The Celestials probably waited content to separate the contestants until the Barbarians ran terrified in retreat; local tradition probably told of other Spaceships landing in the past; a thousand years earlier the 'Gods' had materialised in this area amid the Trojan War. This Spaceship won the day for Rome; from that hour Mithridates toppled to destruction; more than eight hundred years later in AD 776 two Flying Shields would save those Knights of Charlemagne at Sigiburg.

While Lucullus was feasting his guests at those fabulous

banquets in his 'cups' did he sometimes recall that celestial 'wine jar', which once had stood between him and Mithridates? The Ship of the Gods?

66 BC 'In the Consulship of Gnaeus Octavius and Gaius Scribonius a spark was seen to fall from a star and increase in size as it approached the earth, and after becoming as large as the moon it diffused a sort of cloudy daylight, and then returning to the sky changed into a torch; this is the only record of this occurring. It was seen by the proconsul, Silenus, and his suite.' (Pliny, Book II, XXXV.)

Surely this seems one of the best sightings in all Antiquity, certainly Pliny thought so! Even our most cynical sceptics can hardly dismiss such a classic UFO as a meteor, fireball or the planet Venus. Today our Air Ministry would perhaps explain it away as some bomber making a mock attack, fortunately for their neighbours the Romans had no Air Force.

For several decades Rome was torn by rival Dictators, verging on civil war; the City's unrest would likely attract the interest of Spacemen. Plutarch commented 'Moreover even the Heavenly Powers seemed by earthquakes and thunderbolts and apparitions to foreshow what was coming to pass.[182]

63 BC 'A blazing beam from the west swept across the sky. All Spoletium was shaken by earthquakes.' (Obsequens, Manilius 1184.)

UFOs today are believed to pay particular attention to the Earth's fault zones, lights in the sky frequently coincide with earthquakes.

In troubled Rome nobles lorded in riotous extravagance, the poor lazed on public doles of bread and circuses; troops demobbed from the wars were shocked at their shameful neglect. During the consulship of Cicero an unscrupulous and profligate patrician, Catiline, played on the discontent of the mob and the grievances of the veterans and conspired to murder both Consuls then to set up his gangster rule. With surprising vigilance Cicero smashed the conspiracy and executed the ringleaders. Catiline died in forlorn battle the following year.

Crassus, who defeated Spartacus, was also noted for his multitude of slaves toiling to amass vast wealth which he prodigally squandered. In 60 BC with Pompey and Caesar Crassus shared in the triumvirate ruling Rome, then lured by the fabled riches of the East he invaded Parthia, modern Iran. After defeat at Carrhae, the head of Crassus was cut off and sent to Orodes, the Parthian King, who caused melted gold to be poured into the mouth of his fallen enemy saying 'Sate thyself now with that metal of which in life thou wast so greedy!'[183] Perhaps the main contribution of Crassus to posterity is that he is said to have started the first fire-brigade. He would rush to the scene of the conflagration but before extinguishing the flames would make the owner a bid for the building, the owner was only too pleased to sell, only then did Crassus get his water-pumps into action. A suggestion for poorly-paid fire-chiefs today![184]

The death of Crassus left Pompey and Caesar to their destined struggle for power. Gnaeus Pompeius, well-known as the Great, six years older than Caesar, a veteran of Sulla's civil wars, whose memories still rent Rome, had distinguished himself by brilliant campaigns in Africa, Syria, Jerusalem and Asia; in 52 BC he returned as sole Consul determined to pass laws aimed at his dangerous rival, Caius Julius Caesar born on 12th July 100 BC, is said to have been tall, fair and well-built with a rather broad face and keen dark-brown eyes; usually in sound health, like Napoleon he suffered from epilepsy. Adoring soldiers mocked their General's bald head but worshipped his military genius and brilliant audacity confounding his enemies; even in that licentious age Caesar was scoffed for his scandalous love-affairs; gossips swore he was every woman's husband and every man's wife. Foreseeing strife with Pompey Caesar sought army support; in nine years he bridged the Rhine and conquered the whole of Gaul. In 55 BC Caesar invaded Britain, lured it was believed by fresh-water pearls for which our island was famous. Caesar's varied talents were brilliantly displayed in his Commentary on the Gallic Wars, especially his colourful account of Ancient Britain.

On 1st January 49 BC the Senate dominated by Pompey

ordered Caesar to resign his command and return to Rome as a private citizen, where it was rumoured he would be tried in a court ringed with armed men, a sentence of death. Caesar followed his destiny; convinced he was the Son of Venus, inspired by the Gods, he rode with his battalions for Rome. At the River Rubicon, the frontier between Gaul and Italy, Caesar hesitated.

'As he stood in two minds, an apparition of superhuman size and beauty was seen sitting on the river bank playing a reed pipe. A party of shepherds gathered around to listen and, when some of Caesar's men broke ranks to do the same, the apparition snatched a trumpet from one of them, ran down to the river, blew a thunderous blast and crossed over. Caesar exclaimed, "Let us accept this as a sign from the Gods and follow where they beckon in vengeance on our double-dealing enemies. The die is cast".'[185]

Gaius Suetonius nearly two centuries later seemed impressed by this wondrous apparition, whose decisive encouragement to Caesar was to change the destiny of Rome; he probably accepted the Superman as Castor or Pollux who had intervened at Lake Regillus long before. 'The Twelve Caesars' glows with scandalous anecdotes about the Emperors, particularly Julius Caesar, the most fascinating personage in all Antiquity; the colourful account by Suetonius makes us mourn the loss of his 'Lives of Famous Whores' which would have titillated us today. Modern historians dismiss celestial interventions as superstitions but Suetonius, Secretary to Hadrian before dismissal for his notorious indiscretion with Sabina, the Emperor's wife, in one of the happiest periods in Roman times, had no doubts; Caesar believing himself descended from the Gods, was quite convinced. His exalted soul would surely long to question the apparition, he must have made determined efforts to find him. Caesar's awe would increase on learning the trumpeter had vanished.

Spacemen surveilling troubled Earth would concentrate their attention on Julius Caesar, this dynamic personality dominating Rome. Pliny's report of the rain of wool in Central Italy in 49 BC arouses our speculation as to whether it was actually 'Angel's Hair', white filaments, probably ionised particles usually associated with UFOs, possibly that 'manna from heaven' feeding the Israelites in the Wilderness and the 'heavenly ambrosia' beloved by the Greeks.

Surprised at Caesar's swift approach, Pompey fled to Greece where he massed a formidable force totalling 57,000 men. Caesar paused to crush opposition in Spain, then in 48 BC pursued Pompey in August to Pharsalus in Thessaly. Victory for Pompey mustering twice Caesar's strength seemed assured, his army spent the eve of battle feasting. This conflict possibly attracted the Spacemen. Plutarch comments

> 'Furthermore during the morning watch a great light shone out above the camp of Caesar, which was perfectly quiet and a flaming torch rose from it and darted down above the camp of Pompey. Caesar himself says he saw this as he was visiting the Watches.'[134]

When the sun rose Caesar breakfasted on corn-meal and cabbage then led his men to classic victory winning him mastery of the world and also the sumptuous dinner cooks had prepared for Pompey's celebration banquet. The celestial prodigies may have just been thunder and lightning not Spaceships, but Dio Cassius intrigues us by adding that the result of the battle was announced in Syria hundreds of miles away by 'two young men' who vanished. Shades of Castor and Pollux, who in 498 BC brought news of Lake Regillus to Rome, not forgetting that happy trumpeter by the Rubicon!

Pompey fled to Egypt where he was murdered by Theodotus of Chios on orders from King Ptolemy as he was stepping ashore to meet his wife, a great Roman weary for death. Caesar shed sincere tears on beholding Pompey's severed head; learning that Ptolemy was planning to murder him too, he promptly declared war on Egypt, although caught off his guard and without supplies his genius soon won. The first sweet fruit of victory was the King's exiled sister, Cleopatra, who was smuggled to him within a bedcover, the most glamorous smuggled goods in all history, this 'Serpent of Old Nile', a shrewd, seductive twenty, completely captivated that bald, old rake, aged fifty-three.

Alexandria rebelled, Caesar left his dalliance for an hour and set fire to his own fleet to prevent it falling into enemy hands; the flames spread to the famous Library founded by the first Ptolemy in 283 BC burning most of its 700,000 papyri, the few which survived were finally destroyed by the Caliph Omar in AD 651. The writing of these hundreds of thousands of scrolls by the greatest scholars of the Ancient World proves the vast erudition existing then, their almost total destruction means an immense chasm distorting our conception of Antiquity. After the birth of their son, Caesarion, Caesar left for Rome accompanied by Cleopatra, who somewhat snubbed by the Roman matrons soon returned to Egypt to await the love-lorn Antony. On the way home in 47 BC Caesar paused in Syria to defeat Pharnaces, son of the famous Mithridates of Pontus, in the great battle of Zela. With historic brevity Caesar announced his victory to Rome in three words. 'Veni! Vedi! Vici!' 'I came! I saw! I conquered!'

For decades Rome had been ravaged by Civil Wars. Dictators had bludgeoned their climb to bloody power only to be dragged down to death; invincible abroad, at home the Republic was rotten. Caesar shrewdly saw the only solution was return to the ancient Monarchy with himself, Son of the Gods, as King; neither the Senate nor the people, so servile to future Emperors, were ready. During the next two years sincere patriots and malcontents alike became alarmed at Caesar's growing arrogance and ambition; 'the lean and hungry' Cassius fomented a conspiracy of citizens with an open and deadly hatred of Caesar's pretensions to royal power, he seduced the support of the 'noble' Brutus, whom Caesar loved as a son. The conspirators decided to kill Caesar with daggers as he addressed the Senate on the Ides of March, 15 March 44 BC.

Spacemen following Caesar's career amid the stormy politics of Rome would possibly form some of the prodigies haunting this memorable year 44 BC. Plutarch in 'Caesar', LXIII, records

> 'But destiny it would seem, is not so much unexpected as it is unavoidable, since they say that amazing signs and apparitions were

seen. Now as for lights in the heavens, crashing sounds, all about by night, and birds of omen coming down into the Forum, it is perhaps not worth while to mention these precursors of so great an event, but Strabo, the philosopher, says that multitudes of men on fire were seen rushing up.'

Strabo then twenty years old probably spoke to eye-witnesses of these remarkable events; though known today for his famous work on Geography, he actually wrote a history in forty-three books, unfortunately lost; such erudition suggests a keen, analytical mind evaluating cogent facts. His reference to 'multitudes of men on fire' confounds scholars ignorant of UFO phenomena yet they do evoke that fiery Space Thing which scared Scoutmaster D. S. Desvergers[187] in 1952 at West Palm Beach, Florida, also those alarming 'little men' frightening peasants in South America. Livy mentions apparitions of men in shining garments seen in the Amiternum district in 218 BC. The description 'men on fire' approximates Biblical accounts of Angels glowing with light, who impressed the prophets.

The Brothers Grimm quote in 'Deutsche Mythologie', Volume I, an old story in the Brunswick dialect, 'Der feurige Mann' relating to AD 1129. Freely translated it tells

'In this year (AD 1125) a fiery man was haunting the mountains like an apparition. It was just on midnight. The man went from one birch-tree to another and set it ablaze. The Watchman said he was like a glowing fire. He did that for three nights then no more. George Miltenburger living in a so-called hop-field, Railbach, in the district of Freienstein, explained, "On the first appearance I saw a man burning all over with fire. One could count all the ribs on his stomach. He continued his way from one landmark to another until after midnight he suddenly vanished. Many people were struck by him with fear and terror because through his nose and mouth he belched forth fire and in dashing speed flew hither and thither in all directions." '

Was this fiery apparition an Extraterrestrial like those 'men on fire' haunting Rome?

On the last evening of his life Julius Caesar was dining with Marcus Lepidus when the conversation turned on the question of which death was best, before anyone else could answer Caesar cried out 'That which is unexpected!' That night Caesar dreamed he was soaring above the clouds and then shaking hands with Jupiter; his wife, Calpurnia, dreamed her husband's murdered body lay in her arms. Caesar awoke obsessed with fear and suspicion, when the seers warned him that all the omens were unfavourable, he yielded to the entreaties of his wife and resolved to send Mark Antony and dismiss the Senate. Finally Brutus, who was so treated by Caesar that he was named in his will as second heir, ridiculed the seers, told Calpurnia to have better dreams and led the hesitant Caesar to the Senate House. On his way Caesar was warned again by a seer to beware of those fatal Ides of March, someone handed him a note containing details of the plot on his life; he put it aside intending to read it later.[188] As soon as he took his seat the conspirators crowded around as if to pay their respects, then Casca struck the first blow in the neck, all the others backed him with their daggers like a wild beast, as Brutus stabbed him in the groin Caesar turned and reproached him in Greek 'You, too, my Son!' then sprawled in blood at the foot of Pompey's statue.

So died one of the greatest men in all history, murdered by his friends!

Within three years nearly all the assassins met violent deaths in shipwreck, battle or self-slain by the very daggers with which they had treacherously murdered Caeser.

The Senate voted Caesar divine honours, his heir was his 18 year old nephew, Caius Octavian, almost completely unknown. The disappointed Mark Antony gave the customary funeral oration, seeing the mob astounded by Caesar's generosity in bequeathing every Roman seventy-five drachmas, he displayed Caesar's bloody corpse rent with twenty-three dagger-wounds and in masterly denunciation demanded vengeance on his murderers. It was said that as Caesar's body lay on its ivory couch awaiting cremation two Divine Forms (Castor and Pollux) appeared and set fire to the couch with torches.[189]

After the funeral the mob hunted the murderers.

In 43 BC the uneasy triumvirate of Octavian, Antony and Lepidus massacred three hundred Senators indicted for the murder of Caesar and seized their possessions. Among those who perished was Cicero, probably the greatest writer in Latin Rome produced. A rival drama convulsed the skies. During all that year the sun grew pale, its light and heat diminished, fruits withered away in the chill atmosphere. Dio Cassius reports that at times the sunlight was even extinguished, a flash darted across the sky from east to west and a new star appeared; sometimes the sun manifested as three circles, one of which was surmounted by a fiery crown of sheaves, phenomena which may suggest UFOs. A great comet shone in splendour for seven nights. Ovid, who was born this year, later expressed popular belief that at Jupiter's command Venus had snatched up Caesar's soul from his murdered body and transformed it as a star, so that he could ever look down from his lofty throne upon the people of Rome.

The alleged appearance of Celestials at Caesar's funeral and his translation to the skies accord with the divine honours usually bestowed upon illustrious personages in Antiquity; such firm beliefs do suggest that the Romans clearly accepted the concept of the Gods, the Spacemen.

In 42 BC according to Pliny,[190] three suns were seen; if indeed they denoted Spacemen their attention would surely be attracted by the destiny of Brutus. After Caesar's murder Brutus and Cassius fled East in wanton rampage, sacking towns in Palestine and ravaging Asia Minor, then they returned to Macedonia for final confrontation with Octavian and Antony. In Asia Brutus captured Theodotus of Chios, murderer of Pompey, still revered by most Romans; in stern revenge he had him put to death with every conceivable torture, so as Plutarch comments,[191] Theodotus won more fame for his death than for his life. Brutus, an idealist, honoured even by his enemies, must have brooded on the retribution he meted out to the murderer of Pompey, remembering how he himself had murdered his own friend, Caesar. Conversant with those great tragedies of Greece Brutus knew the Gods decreed revenge.

The night before crossing the Hellespont with his army into Thrace Brutus lay in his dimly-lighted tent lost in meditation; he fancied he heard a noise at the door, looking towards the lamp almost extinguished, his eyes suddenly beheld a strange and monstrous apparition of a man, silent at his side. Terrified by this solemn visitant Brutus asked fearfully 'Who art thou, of Gods or men?' The phantom replied 'I am thy evil genius, Brutus, and thou shalt see me at Philippi.' Summoning courage Brutus replied 'I shall see thee.' Brutus unburdened his fears to Cassius, who following the Epicurean philosophy argued that men see only what they think they see; still brooding Brutus began to speculate on the ethics of suicide. On the plain of Philippi in Macedonia Brutus won his own fierce battle against Antony, Cassius lost his and bade his freedman behead him. Octavian stayed in bed with influenza. Again the phantom loomed before Brutus but departed without a word. Brutus understood. He lost the second battle and fell on his sword. A tyrannicide whom a kinder fate might have made King. Antony gave him an illustrious funeral.

The reality of this apparition is open to doubt, although Plutarch was sufficiently impressed to mention it in 'Caesar', LXXIX, also 'Brutus', XXXVI and XLVIII. Shakespeare's genius for melodrama promptly saw the phantom as the ghost of Caesar. Brutus was probably haunted by his guilty conscience, yet some remembering Faust and Mephistopheles, also those UFO, entities might view the apparition as a demon from infernal dimensions come for Brutus's soul.

Perhaps Philippi should be more famous for the first poetic protest against the futility of war. At Athens young Horace met Brutus, swayed by his republican ideals he accepted command of a legion. In the midst of the battle the poet saw war in all its horror, he flung away his shield and fled home. Later pardoned by Augustus, Horace secured the patronage of wealthy Maecenas, who gave him a private villa with a farm near the Sabine mountains; in these beautiful surroundings he wrote his lyrical Odes. Should Horace have stayed at Philippi and sought a hero's death, robbing posterity of a rare poet? Today dare any man answer?

Octavian and Antony now shared the world. Lepidus, who

took Africa, wisely withdrew from the inevitable conflict for supreme mastery. Antony sailed East in flamboyant triumph while Octavian ruthlessly consolidated the key-positions in the West. Like Alexander of old Antony sought new worlds to conquer; this 'international playboy' became irresistibly drawn towards Cleopatra queening the Nile. Accusing her of aid to Cassius Antony summoned Cleopatra to come to Tarsus. Lycosthenes reports that in 41 BC three suns merged into one, a similar prodigy occurred in the following year; this phenomenon might not have meant Spaceships but surely any Spaceman even from the furthest planet would have felt gloriously thrilled to watch this fateful meeting. Cleopatra 'sailed up the river Cydnus in a barge with gilded poop, its sails spread purple, its rowers urging it on with silver oars to the sound of the flute blended with pipes and lutes.' This wonderful description from Plutarch[192] was borrowed by Shakespeare in 'Antony and Cleopatra'[193] almost word for word. Their exotic amours interrupted by wars culminated in 31 BC with naval defeat by Octavius at Actium. Antony in theatrical climax stabbed himself. 'A Roman by a Roman valiantly vanquished.' Cleopatra cheated a Roman triumph by applying a poisonous asp to her breast; Octavian tried to frustrate her dramatic suicide and ordered snake-charmers to suck the poison from her wound. In vain! Cleopatra died as alluring as she had lived. The two lovers were buried together; playwrights have made them both immortal.

Octavian took the title 'Augustus Imperator' and for forty-one years gave Rome a Golden Age.

Literature in Augustan times bloomed as one of the fairest flowers in Antiquity, eclipsed only by those glorious plays of Periclean Athens. The poets of Rome deified the Emperor honouring the Gods; poems and plays approached Space-fiction. In his patriotic 'Aeneid' Virgil sang of Venus, Jupiter and Mars as if they existed in the skies ever ready to wing down to the aid of heroes. It is fascinating to study the superstitions which a thousand years later transformed Virgil into a mediaeval magician, almost as if we were now to make Shakespeare a Spaceman. An accretion of legends credited Virgil with a castle near Naples defended by an impenetrable barrier of air, mechanical horsemen on mechanical steeds, and a brazen head like some talking-computer which evaluated dangers and gave warning. 'He possessed a magic garden where no rain fell, protected by a wall of air, so that birds could not fly away; he boasted that he could make fruit-trees bear three times a year and his spirits fetched dishes for his banquets from the feasts of his foes.'[194] Mediaeval romances alleged that Virgil transported the daughter of the Sultan of Babylon to Naples on a bridge of air; his greatest feat of misplaced ingenuity was the invention of a marble hand which bit off the arm of any woman falsely swearing to her chastity; a poetic comparison with that marble statue of Don Gonzalo dragging the libertine, Don Juan, down to Hell. Such tales of enchantment do prove that people always believed in realms of magic, memories perhaps of Spacemen. The lovelorn Catullus had been too bewitched by his Clodia to bother about Gods but Ovid despite his 'Art of Love' which brought his banishment to the Black Sea, revelled in fables of Celestials and their love-affairs; he depicted the Gods like Film-Stars. Livy in his wonderful epic history presented all the peaks and chasms of tremendous events, he studiously recorded those prodigies in the skies convinced they influenced the destiny of Rome.

The widespread influence of astrologers and diviners amid the materialist Roman world seems strangely topical in our age of Science today, with popular interest in the Occult. Most Romans followed Zeno's stoic philosophy of duty and reason, fatalistic adherence to a divine plan obliging star-worship and obedience to the Gods; in reaction a few preferred the Epicurean concept of pleasure, free-will, convinced that the highest good for any Man is happiness. In a galaxy of stern Dictators, great Generals and brilliant Writers, who adorned that stormy first century before Christ the most intriguing personality to our modern Space Age is probably Lucretius, a mysterious figure of unknown origin believed to be born about 99 BC. It is strange that nothing is known of his birth or even his death, possibly about 52 BC; he was said to have been driven mad by a love-potion and to have perished by his own hand, somewhat surprising for a philosopher who wrote that 'sexual love ruins a man's health, wealth and reputation and makes him unhappy'. Living in Rome a wealthy Patrician during the period of civil war and bloodshed, Lucretius scorned the harsh code of duty and discipline and sought inspiration from the teachings of Epicurus born in 341 BC on the island of Samos like Pythagoras; he taught his followers to practise virtue because it leads to happiness and to cultivate peace of mind, the greatest of human treasures. In his lofty poem 'De Rerum Natura' – 'On the Nature of Things' – Lucretius set forth the philosophy of Epicurus in most profound verse which surprises us today with a universality of knowledge almost modern debating that there are many worlds in the universe; he says in Book 2, 1074-8, 'You are bound to admit that in other parts of the universe there are other worlds inhabited by different races of men and different species of wild beast.' More than sixteen hundred years later when Giordano Bruno said this in the same City of Rome, the Inquisition had him burned at the stake for heresy. Lucretius expounded the concept of Epicurus that 'Matter exists in the form of an infinite number of indivisible particles and atoms.' He wrote that 'atoms moving downwards through the void sometimes swerve a little from the straight course', a statement ridiculed for two thousand years until put forward a few years ago by the great Danish physicist, Niels Bohr, to initiate the fantastic discoveries of nuclear-physics. In curious anticipation of our own ultra-modern concept of Extraterrestrials, Lucretius located the homes of the Gods in the spaces between the worlds, apparently Etherians. Ovid in 'Amores' I, 15, 23-24, wrote 'The verses of sublime Lucretius are destined to perish only when a single day will consign the world to destruction.' Lucretius reminds us irresistibly of Count St. Germain, a Man of Mystery.

The Roman priests probably knew the secret of ever-burning lamps mentioned by the 'Lord' to Moses and found in Athens, Edessa and Antioch. The 12th century chronicler,

William of Malmesbury (ii. pp. 86-87) relates a marvellous discovery in AD 1046 of Pallas, the son of Evander, who had been slain by Turnus, described in the 'Iliad', Book X, the perpetual light in his sepulchre, a Latin epitaph, the corpse of a young giant, the enormous wound in his breast. ('pectus perofrat ingens, etc.'). A startling find, if true, since this famous duel occurred at nearly 1200 BC, so we are told!

In 1485 workmen in Rome searching for marble quarries discovered near the Appian Way an ancient Roman sarcophagus, on opening the lid they were startled to discover the body of a young woman in virgin bloom as if she had been interred that very day. The Florentine humanist, Bartolemeo Fonte, hastened to send a lyrical description to his friend, Francesco Sassetti, which fascinates us today. The brilliant writer, Mara Calabri, has translated Fonte's letter from Latin into Italian which we are privileged to interpret

'They discovered there a marble sarcophagus. On opening it they found a body on its back covered by a substance two inches thick, greasy and perfumed. The odorous crust was removed beginning at the head, there appeared to them a face of such limpid paleness it seemed as if the young lady were buried that day. Her long black hair still hung from her skull, parted and knotted to suit a young girl and fastened in a little net of silk and gold.

'Tiny ears, low forehead, black eyelashes, finally eyes of singular shape, under whose eyelids the cornea still appeared. Even the nostrils were still intact and so soft as to vibrate at the simple touch of a finger. Her red lips half-closed small and white teeth, her scarlet tongue near her palate. Her cheeks, tongue, neck, seemed to palpitate. Her arms hung down intact from her shoulders, so that had you wished you could have moved them. Her nails still adhered firmly to her splendid, long, outstretched hands, also if you had tried, you would not have succeeded in detaching them. Her breast, stomach and womb were on the contrary compressed at one side and after removal of the aromatic crust they decomposed. Her back, sides, and buttocks instead had conserved their contours and marvellous shapes, just like her thighs and legs which in life had presented even greater prizes than her face.

'In short, this must have concerned the most beautiful young woman of noble family during the period when Rome was at its greatest splendour. However the majestic monument under the crypt had been destroyed many centuries or so ago, without there remaining even an inscription. Also the sarcophagus did not bear any sign. We know neither the name of the young woman nor her origin nor her age.'[188]

Old Bartolemeo Ponte five hundred years ago in transparent delight paints a word-portrait of this young beauty which surely thrilled Leonardo da Vinci when he learned of this wonder. General belief attributed the body of Tullia, Cicero's daughter, who against the wish of her father married the ambiguous Cornelius Dolabella, and who died still young in 47 BC. The Romans were in close contact with Egypt; Cornelius Dolabella was with Julius Caesar at the Court of Cleopatra. Mara Calabri in touching words suggests that as a fine act of love the distraught husband might have found some Egyptian slave in Rome able to embalm his lovely wife's body. As for the lamp remaining lit for 1300 years Professor Zakharis Ghoneim, Cairo archaeologist, is quoted as saying that the pitch used for embalming was strangely radio-active, the lamp could have burnt radio-active dust which filled the room. Pope Innocent III is believed to have had the body buried again in secret to avoid troublesome problems for the Church. All that remains of Tullia is the careful drawing of the body in the Florentine's letter showing him to be not only a fine Writer but an excellent Artist.

Cicero translated the much-esteemed astronomical poem 'Phaenomena' by Aratus based on the works of Eudoxus, in the following century Seneca in 'Quaestiones Naturales' and Pliny the Elder in 'Historia Naturalis' wrote fascinating comments on the astronomical theories of the Greeks though they quoted little of Roman origin.

The Romans knew the magnifying properties of glass. Cicero tells that he had seen the entire 'Iliad' written on a skin of such miniature size that it could be rolled up inside a nut-shell; short-sighted Nero watched the gladiators in the Circus through a small ring containing a glass; mariners sometimes used an instrument called the 'nauscopita' to see distant shores. Like the Babylonians the Romans probably used telescopes for celestial observations; during many centuries the sky-watchers may have made fundamental discoveries recorded in works long since lost.

The Romans accepted the theorems of Euclid and teachings of Aristotle, untroubled by theories they concentrated on applied science evolved mainly from experience and commonsense, by trial and error they eventually built those beautiful villas, baths and aqueducts adorning their world. The priests toyed with electricity, craftsmen invented useful gadgets, many keen minds like Hiero of Alexandria in AD 100 must have played with steam kettles before James Watt but the absence of organised industry and the abundance of slave-labour discouraged the search for other sources of power. Sergius Crata, a contemporary of Caesar, is said to have invented central heating. Vitruvius dedicated to Augustus his famous ten volumes on architecture, plumbing, heating, canals and harbours. Celsus in AD 20 compiled an encyclopaedia on Science; only his treatise 'De Medicine' remains. In the reign of Tiberius an exile brought to Rome a cup 'which he dashed upon the marble pavement and it was not crushed or broken by the fall. Stained glass was found in a room at Pompeii; it seems not unlikely that some glass-maker practising his centuries-old craft might by chance have manufactured unbreakable glass, a process he could not repeat. Pliny confirms the use of asbestos, and among the 20,000 facts in his 'Historia Naturalis' details the pharmaceutical properties of hundreds of flowers and plants showing profound knowledge of botany accumulated by the Ancients through thousands of years. Plutarch and other writers narrating campaigns in the East make frequent reference to the inflammable nature of oil used for that fearsome weapon, the unextinguishable Greek fire like napalm.

The Romans were great engineers; victorious Generals owed much to their military technicians, who devised such deadly efficient catapults, siege-towers and engines of war, they soon learned from Carthage the vital lesson of sea-power and built swift, powerful galleys to master the Mediterranean. The Roman roads built for military use kept their Empire together, the speed with which the legions could be switched from Spain to Persia, the Thames to the

Danube, paralysed their enemies. Trade followed the Eagles, the Imperium became a 'Common Market' with uniform currency and law enabling merchants to bring their wares from the East and West for the people of Rome; in their wake wandered scholars spreading the classic culture of Antiquity. For more than a thousand years after the fall of Rome Latin was the universal language linking the intellectuals of Europe. Pottery found in India, coins in China, prove that Roman influence spanned the world; some coins unearthed in America and Romance words in Indian dialects are even alleged to prove that Roman ships apparently crossed the Atlantic, possibly blown there by storms. In the first century BC the Chinese Emperor Wu Ti despatched a certain Chang Ch'ier to the West hoping to form an alliance against the Huns; the Romans called China 'Serica' or 'The Land of Silk'; silk, peaches and apricots known as 'Chinese fruits' reached Italy and Greece via the long caravan-routes from the East, Augustus[196] sent ambassadors to China, memory of these may have inspired Marco Polo's epic travels from Venice to that fabulous Court of Kublai Khan. A popular Cambodian tradition concerns the Prince of Rama attributing to him the foundation of the great Buddhist temple at Anghor Wat; he is said to have come from the western end of the world, presumably from Rome.

The fascinating ruins of Pompeii destroyed by the eruption of Vesuvius in AD 79 reveal a pleasant panorama of everyday life showing both in the home and in the public squares the prosperous culture which the citizens of this sunny land leisurely enjoyed. In Rome the wealthy Patricians living on loot from the Empire and from the sweat of slaves squandered fortunes in fantastic extravagances; the poor subsided on doles, sex and circuses, an ominous parallel perhaps with our Britain today, which has also seen the decline and fall of this once great Empire.

Spacemen during the Augustan Age were apparently content with random surveillance. A 'torch' streaked across Roman skies from south to north making night seem as bright as day; a comet hovered over Rome for several days in 12 BC, then finally split into flashes resembling 'torches'. Such celestial phenomena may be recognised by astronomers as meteors, they could have been UFOs like those nine suns which in 9 BC appeared over Kyushu on 10th February throwing Japan into chaos. Spaceships visiting the Far East would probably visit the West and survey Rome.

Five years later in 4 BC a new 'star' is said to have shone in the Middle East. The sudden appearance of a Star suggests a Supernova, though its advent was not recorded by Hindu or Chinese astronomers, who kept ceaseless watch on the skies, nor by Pliny, Ptolemy, Josephus or Julius Obsequens, reliable chroniclers of this period. The 'star' was alleged to move and stop over Palestine; genuine stars seem fixed, the only wandering stars are the planets which move slowly in precise orbits. Astrologers suggest this apparent 'star' may have been a conjunction of the planets Mars, Jupiter and Venus, though these would not suddenly appear and move as one body.

It is profoundly significant that in this age of great writers and astronomers the only reference to the mysterious 'star' was made by an elderly Jew about eighty years later; he himself was probably not born when this 'star' allegedly appeared then later disappeared. Thirty years were to elapse before this particular year, 749 after the foundation of Rome, was to have such tremendous significance for him and the world.

Matthew wrote

'... and, lo, the star which they saw in the east went before them till it came and stood over where the young child was.'[19]

The only celestial object to appear suddenly close enough to the Earth to be visible within only a small radius, which moves guiding followers, then stands still, is an intelligently controlled Spaceship.

In a stable in Bethlehem Jesus was born!

Chapter Eleven
Space Gods of Scandinavia

The ancient North still broods in magic, its aura of enchantment allures explorers even today; those solitary wastes in silence fill men's souls with mystery shrouding that world of wonder lost long ago. Poets in Antiquity hailed the North as Hyperborea, Land of the Gods, its radiant skies illumined realms of fabulous splendour where Immortals basked in eternal Spring cut off from mankind by a barrier of ice; Apollo and other Celestials winged across the snows to revel there. The Greeks beside their warm Mediterranean marvelled at that mysterious region beyond Mount Olympus, abode of heroes, wizards, giants, dragons, waging fantastic wars in Earth and sky; from the North-East the Phoenicians brought those precious amulets of amber, elektron, alive with electricity. Dim race-memories echoed that titanic cataclysm which had shattered those fair lands of the North to desolation driving the Achaeans down to the Peloponnese; legends told how the sun changed its course, a comet shook the Earth itself to end a World Age; the climate cooled, the Gods fled from the chaos home to the stars leaving Man to build civilisation again. All the Ancients in East and West shared the same age-old story preserved in religion or epic romance; such sophistication distorted the past, the stark truth of that cosmic disaster is told in the myths of Scandinavia.

The wondrous realm in the North was completely swept away by the last Ice Age now dated by geologists as about 10,000 BC probably caused by that sudden cataclysm which submerged Atlantis; mammoths found trapped in ice prove the temperature fell quickly suggesting some cosmic catastrophe. Eskimos believe that thousands of years ago their ancestors were ferried by huge metallic birds from Central Asia, Ceylon and Mongolia to Greenland, arousing speculation as to why the Spacemen transported them to such inhospitable land when surely more pleasant spots would have welcomed them. Perhaps this exodus happened before the ice came?

The few survivors suffered shocking readjustment to their frozen world, legends distorted down the centuries remembered those rulers of the golden past as Gods; sometimes the Arctic ice would melt yielding most ancient treasures from the civilisation once gracing this wilderness. Men became nomadic hunters, millennia later as the glaciers receded their descendants slowly followed the reindeer northward to repeople the Scandinavian peninsula. Tools of bones and flints reveal exquisite excellence,[198] artistic rock-carvings show that these early Neolithic peoples shared the impressive intelligence characterising those splendid Cro-Magnons in France and Spain. Studies of pollen below deep bogs prove that luxuriant forests were felled to provide land for agriculture, the beginnings of civilisation. While Abraham was debating with the 'Lord' the destruction of Sodom and Gomorrah and those genial Celestials were honouring Prince Rama in Old India, more immigrants from the West invaded Denmark and Sweden. Central American traditions state that long ago the Quetzals with milk-white skins, blue eyes and light flaxen hair, sailed to a country in the East, to North-West Europe and became Norwegians. These Megalithic peoples built dolmens for their dead, collective graves with ornaments and jewellery for the after-life following the same lofty religion as the builders of those cyclopean Stone Age temples in Britain and France. Amber found in Denmark became greatly prized and was exported overland to the Mediterranean bringing culture and commerce from the sophisticated South.

The Danes were of Swedish origin, they claimed that Denmark was called after the hero, Dan, son of Yper, King of Uppsalir in Sweden, who conquered Zeeland then Jutland.[199] It is intriguing to speculate whether Dan really referred to the Danai, in ancient times they migrated from the North-West southwards to Mycenae, Homer mentions them as the Greeks besieging Troy; by coincidence Denmark and Greece are linked by their Royal Families today. Migrations across Europe fostered trade and the spread of ideas promoting a culture of impressive grandeur; beakers buried in Danish tombs resembled pottery from Scotland and Portugal, metal pins and pendants originated from the Danube brought over well-known trade-routes. About 1800 BC while Britons were building Stonehenge warriors wielding the double-headed axe of Minoan Crete overran Jutland, many Megalithic farmers fled to Norway and Sweden. During the Second Millennium BC Scandinavia basked in the Bronze Age culture of Knossos and Mycenae, that tremendous, restless civilisation dominating most of the known world. The golden treasures found in graves gleam with artistry and craftsmanship proving centuries-old skill, such costly votive offerings denoted a highly-organised society led by wealthy Princes and influenced by a powerful priesthood who taught resurrection and rebirth with devotion to the Sky Gods, those Wondrous Beings from Space surveilling the Earth. In our own cynical century we hesitate to leave a milk-bottle on our doorstep, four thousand years ago the bereaved reverently interred their dead with diadems and jewels for the life to come, profound religious beliefs prevented sacrilege; today would any millionaire risk burying a gold brick? Our growing knowledge of the Bronze Age increases our respect for the profundity of those ancient peoples, heirs to a wisdom rivalling our own. Some scholars identify Plato's Atlantis with Sweden contemporary with Knossos, its destruction is said to have been caused by the cataclysm which ravaged the West.

A classic description which may apply to Bronze Age Scandinavia has been given by Homer, who was probably inspired by tales of Mycenae. After the Fall of Troy about 1200 BC Ulysses was destined to wander for ten years before the Gods permitted him to return to his faithful wife, Penelope, on Ithaca. Scholars[200] generally place the wondrous adventures narrated in the 'Odyssey' as occurring in the Mediterranean, modern researches transfer the itinerary to the West European coast, construing details from Homer as corresponding to landmarks familiar today. This fascinating theory casts serious doubts on Ulysses's navigation, instead of sailing the few hundred miles from Troy near the Dardanelles to that small island of Ithaca off Western Greece, the hero is alleged to have been driven by a fierce storm along most of the Mediterranean through the Pillars of Hercules south to the Land of the Lotus-Eaters, the Canary Isles. Ulysses's crew longed to tarry on those sun-swept beaches now lyricised by our travel-agents, he urged them northwards to the shores of the savage Laestrygonians, ancient Lisbon. Escaping from the cannibals the Greeks crossed the Bay of Biscay to Aeaea, now Belle Isle, island of the sorceress, Circe, who turned his companions into swine. Months later Ulysses landed on Oygia, possibly Guernsey, where he languished in the toils of the nymph, Calypso, for seven seductive years; finally he tore himself from her charms. Keeping the Great Bear on his left the hero sailed up the North Sea until he was shipwrecked and cast ashore in the kingdom of Phaeacia, identified with modern Oslo. Naked and exhausted Ulysses was found by the young Princess Nausicaa who brought him rich attire and conducted him to her father, Alcinous. The tender sympathy between the old warrior and the unsophisticated Princess shines as one of the most exquisite episodes in classical literature, the dignity and courtesy displayed by the King and his Court to the castaway betoken a genial, noble society reminiscent of those Princes in contemporary India.

Homer in bejewelled verse[201] tells how the Goddess Athene appeared before Ulysses in the form of a fair maiden, she rendered the hero invisible and conducted him to the palace of Alcinous. Unseen by the populace Ulysses wandered among the cyclopean buildings characteristic of those Megalithic peoples, he who knew golden Mycenae and those topless towers of Ilium marvelled at the wonders of Phaeacia like that other traveller, Herodotus, touring mighty Babylon seven hundred years later. Massive walls shone with brass, doors on silver lintels gleamed with plates of gold, gorgeous carpets covered the polished floors under which ran pipes of water supplying baths and fountains. Spacious avenues embellished with statues led to the beautiful garden, where luxuriant vines and luscious fruits ripened in the balmy air. Ulysses resumed visibility and became honoured guest at the royal banquet attended by the Lords and Ladies of Phaeacia revelling in that genial civilisation centuries old. In those far-off days before television travellers, above all story-tellers, were most welcome. With magical eloquence Ulysses told how on that fateful night he leaped from the belly of the Wooden Horse to put sleeping Troy to fire and sword; he sighed at his storm-driven voyage to the Land of the Lotus-Eaters and blinded again the one-eyed giant, Polyphemus, from bewitching Circe he fled to languish with Calypso after adventures in the underworld surpassing our dull Science-Fiction. Such wonderful tales enthralled his listeners as for three thousand years they have enchanted all who read them. The King generously equipped Ulysses with a fine ship and encouraged the people to bestow on him lavish gifts, then the hero set sail at last homeward for Ithaca. Identification of Phaeacia with Norway may be open to doubt yet not impossible. About 1200 BC Scandinavia basked in temperate climate, people in cultured ease shared the graceful living of the South. The wily Ulysses would not spend ten years lost in the Mediterranean he knew so well, his travels must have taken him to those mysterious lands of the West.

The ancient literature of most countries agree that Spacemen apparently intervened in terrestrial affairs from the times of Abraham about 2000 BC to the Battle of Marathon, 490 BC, thereafter their visits were generally restricted to random surveillance. The Celestials landing in India and Greece would surely visit Scandinavia as Norse mythology somewhat gloomily recalls. Chronology is confused, study of pollen-samples suggests that probably about 500 BC the climate of Europe grew suddenly chill, due perhaps to changes in cosmic radiation, attenuation of the Earth's magnetic field or to some great cataclysm which would discourage visits by Spacemen. Much of Scandinavia became bleak and uninhabitable, mass-migrations abandoned the once populous North to the reindeer and arctic fox, whole tribes like the Lombardis, Burgundians, Teutons and Goths moved southwards to harass Rome. Only the most desperate catastrophe could have driven entire peoples from their ancestral home wandering and fighting like the Children of Israel for new lands in which to live. Such forced migrations in the harsh climate shattered the genial Bronze Age and marooned the Baltic in isolation from the civilised South. Bronze was succeeded by iron, in the Iron Age impoverished society warred for existence in the changed world, the arts and crafts of gracious living declined through grim necessity, sophisticated bronze-ware became displaced by simple tools of iron for peace or war. The growing pressure of the Celts dominating the West cut Scandinavia off from the culture of Greece and Rome, though Pliny and Tacitus speculated vaguely about those Suiones far beyond the Teuton forests who supplied Roman matrons with much-prized furs.

The Teutonic tribes torn with strife menaced the rich lands of the Mediterranean, in 390 BC Brennus and the Gauls crossed the Apennines and held Rome to ransom. Julius Caesar then Marcus Aurelius smashed the barbarians massing beyond the Rhine and Danube but the inevitable tide swept down from the Alps, weak Emperors lost battle after battle and paid tribute in land and gold, in vain for in AD 410 Alaric and his fierce Goths sacked the City bringing that once-great Roman Empire to an end. In the West the Anglo-Saxons began their invasion of Britain. For hundreds of years Scandinavia brooded in the Dark Ages, then suddenly in the eighth century its peoples surged forth from their fjords and islands in savage onslaughts to storm England, Ireland, France and Spain. Vikings invaded Russia and sailed down the Volga to form the famous Varangian Guard of Queen Irene of Byzantium. In the eleventh century Erik the Red braved the Atlantic to Vinland discovering America. The Vikings who in their sinister long-boats scourged all Christendom were inspired by heroic sagas of their Gods long ago.

Cyclopean temples and tombs all over the world show

that the Megalithic peoples of the Bronze Age shared the same worship of sun and stars, a cosmic religion taught by the Space Kings later deified as Sky Gods. Those wondrous tales of the Celestials told in the fascinating legends of India, Egypt, Babylon and Greece were surely sung by bards in Ancient Sweden, unfortunately if some Scandinavian poet did pen a 'Mahabharata' or an 'Iliad' no vestige of his verse enlightens posterity. The Linear scripts of Second Millennium BC Knossos and Mycenae probably encouraged writing in contemporary Scandinavia; the cataclysm depopulating the North about 500 BC completely destroyed the ancient culture, all literature was lost; the runes[202] or phonetic symbols found carved on rocks are believed to originate before the Christian era and evoke the writings of the Greeks or possibly the Celts. The catastrophic changes of climate and vast migrations brought a thousand years of barbarism, a chasm of dark confusion separated people from the past, yet down the centuries the ancient traditions were preserved by scalds not in the sophistication of the Sanskrit epics nor like the lusty Greek legends but in the Eddas, poems of brooding intensity perpetuating the Gods and heroes in Northern twilight, that darksome world of frost and ice.

In times without television which beguiles us today, entertainment during those long winter nights freezing the Northern world was left to the scalds, wandering minstrels welcomed at Court and camp-fire, who sang the ancient lays with wonderful imagery telling of the Heroic Age of the Gods, love and war in Heaven and Earth long ago. Christianity did not dominate Scandinavia until about AD 1000, the Church as in other lands tried to obliterate all pagan traditions, fanatical priests ruthlessly burned heathen records like the Christian Fathers destroyed so much of the literature of Greece and Rome, as centuries later the Jesuits smashed the ancient culture of Mexico. Only a few remnants of Teutonic literature remained, in England 'Beowulf', in Germany the 'Nibelungenlied', dramatised in the operas of Richard Wagner. A legendary history of the Danes, 'Gesta Danorum', source of Shakespeare's 'Hamlet', was compiled in about AD 1180 by Saxa Grammaticus, more enlightened than his fellow-priests, who recorded the old stories before they were lost.

The chief collection of the Norse myths are the 'Eddas', a word meaning 'great-grandmother' suggesting the 'old wives' tales. The 'Elder Edda' containing mythical and heroic poems by unknown authors is attributed to Saemund, an Icelandic nobleman about AD 1100. He had studied in France and Germany and wrote probably in Latin a 'History of the Kings of Norway', since lost. These ancient stories fascinated another Icelandic scholar, Snorri Sturlason,[203] a most picturesque character, a man of many talents, more worthy of the Italian Renaissance than that drab age. He married a wealthy heiress, wrote poetry and history, dabbled in Law and politics, his licentious way of life did not prevent him from becoming President of Iceland in AD 1215 when our own King John was reluctantly signing the Magna Carta, then he went on to Norway as Court Poet. In 1222 Snorri again became President, made a fortune from the fruits of high office and divorced his first wife to marry another probably younger heiress. Such scandalous conduct aggravated by political intrigue outraged Snorri's kinsmen, he was murdered in 1241 by his son-in-law encouraged by the King of Norway for whom Snorri had once written poetry, a warning to all Poets Laureate! This versatile libertine, loquacious with learning, was surely fitted to discourse on the Gods, he retold those old tales in delightful elegance and wit, his work being known as the 'Younger Edda'.

The most ancient records of Celestials visiting India, Egypt and Babylon date only from 1500 BC, Homer and Hesiod lyricised the Gods about 800 BC, the actual events probably occurred many centuries earlier; a further two thousand years were to elapse before the Eddas expounded the grim mythology of Scandinavia. For dark ages despite cataclysms, migrations, wars, which had devastated the Lands of the North, the old Sky Gods still loomed in race-memory dominating the living and the dead with a power Christianity has not eclipsed. Who were these tremendous

Cosmic personalities who across the chasms of the past could influence men to sacrifice, whose stern traditions inspired the Vikings to scourge Europe and a thousand years later in grandiose resurrection drove Hitler's Third Reich to crash in Götterdämmerung?

The mythologies of Greece and Rome confirm those chronicles all over the East telling similar Creation stories, glorying in wondrous Beings from the skies, who ruled the world in a Golden Age, mated with the Daughters of Men to sire Heroes, then warred against the Giants spanning the heavens in aerial cars, flashing death-rays, hurling super-bombs, slaying fiery dragons, finally as catastrophes convulsed the Earth the Celestials returned to the stars. Country after country relate these common traditions, the names of the Deities differ, in fact the Gods appear the same. Legends from Greece, Egypt and India agree that the Sun God worship originated from the North, Apollo associated with a swan probably symbolised an Extraterrestrial in a Spaceship. All peoples personified the Gods in terms of their own national idiom. The Indians extolled the Celestials as cultured, warm-blooded Space Kings, the Israelites as a stern, jealous Jehovah, the Greeks as lustful, genial Gods, images coloured by experience and climate. If the Eddas had not been written, if no Teutonic legends survived, we could fabricate the Norse myths merely by transporting the world-wide traditions of the Spacemen into that harsh, foreboding context of the North. Our theory finds empirical proof. When we 'scandinavianise' the ancient stories there crystallises the fateful, gloomy, ice-cold epic of the Northern Gods.

The Scandinavian Creation legends share the same cosmic wisdom of the Rig Veda, and Genesis suggesting some common source in far Antiquity from a remote civilisation or taught by Spacemen. The Voluspa[204] (Song of the Prophetess) mentions Ginnungap, a vast primordial gulf containing neither energy nor matter only latent potentiality, the Void postulated by our modern Science. The All-Father, the Absolute, brooding in Eternity summoned order from the Chaos creating Space and Time. In the North appeared

Nifelheim, a realm of freezing cold and darkness, in the South glowed the radiant Muspelheim, region of fire. Twelve frozen rivers flowed sluggishly southwards, the Almighty breathed a scorching wind which melted the ice to mists, from the vapours resolved Ymer, the Frost Giant, (male principle) and the gigantic cow, Audhumba, (female principle) symbol of generation in India and Egypt. From the androgyne, Ymer, sprang the race of Giants. The great cow yielded from its udder four streams of milk, cosmic energies, it licked huge icy boulders covered with a mineral salt from which appeared a noble Being of wondrous beauty, Bure, first of the Gods. Bure's son, Bor, married Bestla, daughter of a Giant, from them issued three brothers, Odin, Vili and Ve, suggesting the Sacred Trinity. The Hindus state that the first Brahman married Daintary, daughter of the depraved race of Giants,[205] Genesis recalls how the Sons of God mated with the Daughters of Men, the Greeks tell of the Gods lusting for mortal wenches, the Scandinavian legends surely stress the same familiar story of Spacemen winging down to marry Earth-women.

For ages before Earth was formed fierce war was waged between the Gods (Aesir) and the Giants (Vanir) echoing those Sanskrit tales of conflict between the Celestials and the Asuras, possibly inspiring the Tower of Babel story in Genesis and those world-wide legends of the Giants assaulting the Gods in the skies, suggestive of some ancient Space-war. Finally the Sons of Bor prevailed destroying Ymir, in a deluge of blood from his body the Earth was formed. Odin regulated the course of the sun, moon and stars and decided the climate,[206] such celestial disorder recalls those cataclysms mentioned in world-wide mythologies confirming some cosmic catastrophe convulsing the Earth long ago.

The Aesir built Asgard, a wonderful celestial city of golden and silver palaces, surrounded by a lofty wall with only one great gate entered by the bridge Bifrost (rainbow),[207] in the resplendent centre-hall, Valhalla, sat Odin on a golden throne, joining him in judgement on the nine worlds. To Valhalla the Valkyries translated Heroes slain in battle where they caroused and made love like the Faithful of Mohammed feasting with the Houris in Paradise. The Celestials in those erotic Sanskrit tales lived in wondrous realms in the sky like Zeus and his Court beyond Mount Olympus, they too gave judgement to men; most so-called Christians today imagine Heaven as a holiday-camp playing eternal bingo. The Tibetans described Sudarsoma, the City of thirty-three Gods in the skies; this wide-spread conception of a Celestial City peopled by Wondrous Beings who descended to Earth may have originally meant some advanced planet, some of the Spacemen. The Valkyries, Warrior Maidens, recall those seductive Apsaras, who winged down to their lovers in India seeking their battles in bed. Below Asgard lay Midgard, the Earth, peopled by the Sons of Bor, parallel to the Golden Age of the Gods in Greek legend. One day by the seashore Odin, Honir and Lodur beheld two trees, from the ash they shaped a man, Ask, from the alder, a fair woman, Embla; it is intriguing to note that the Popul Vuh states the human race was created out of a reed. Hesiod in 'Theogony' mentions that men were made from the ash-tree. In Midgard also dwelled a race of dwarf-smiths within the rocks, cunning workers of metal, evoking the Cyclops of classical mythology and perhaps those Subterraneans alleged to be living inside our Earth today. Beyond Midgard stretched icy Jotunheim, home of the Giants; below brooded Niefelheim, abode of the damned. All Creation was supported by the World-Tree, Ygdrasil, growing from the past through the present into the future, serpents gnawed its roots threatening to kill the Tree and destroy the universe.[208] This mundane Tree, symbol of eternal life, was known to the Tibetans as 'Kampun', to the Hindus as 'Aswatha' and was said in Egypt to have been symbolised by the Pyramid, link between Heaven and Earth.[209] The Babylonians, Greeks, Eskimos and American Indians believed in a World-Tree supporting the sky, origin of our English may-pole. Tree cults featured in ancient religions, this world-wide conception of a Tree or Tower from Earth to Sky leading to a Celestial World, garbled in our own fairy-tale of 'Jack and the Beanstalk', surely originated from some common source, those far-off days of communication between Earth and Heaven, the 'goings-up' and 'comings-down' mentioned in the Chinese 'Shoo-King', Part Four, Chapter 27, referring to Spacemen.

The twelve Norse Gods lacked the geniality of those twelve Olympians joyously disporting among the Greeks, all seemed obsessed with fate, defeat and death, conscious of inexorable doom; such Teutonic tragedy possibly originated from that cataclysm which once blasted the sunny Northern lands to twilight wilderness. Odin brooded in gloomy loneliness over the follies of men, his sombre thoughts were fed by two ravens perched on his shoulders, which flew down to the world to gather news. In his youth Odin surrendered an eye to drink from the Well of Wisdom; like the Egyptian God, Thor, he was deeply versed in magic lore and invented the ancient writing called runes, teaching civilisation to mankind. Odin travelled on the wind sometimes winging to Earth as a falcon, he often rode Sleipner a mare with eight legs, evoking the twelve-legged horse of Huschenk whom the peoples of the Caucasus regarded as a wondrous Teacher who built Babylon and Ispahan then flew northwards across the Arctic to a wonderful Continent. When Odin flashed through the heavens in his celestial car mountains crumbled and Earth blazed, he delighted in suddenly appearing in human form amid battles just as Castor and Pollux were believed to have aided the Romans at Lake Regillus in 498 BC and Athena the Greeks at Marathon, 490 BC; he led the Aesir to crush the Giants assaulting Valhalla driving them back in defeat to Jotunheim. Odin's wonderful spear resembled the staffs of power wielded by magicians. Odin's wife, Helda, was noted for racing her chairot through the sky. Odin was popularly visualised as a venerable figure with a long white beard and a broad-brimmed hat shading his face, symbolism for ancient wisdom; like Zeus he often descended to Earth in disguise bringing aid to men; when recognised he might change his shape or become invisible. The Swedes sacrificed prisoners-of-war to Odin; to prolong his own life King Aun of Upsala sacrificed his nine sons one after another;[210] such highly doubtful insurance probably shortened his life by well-deserved assassination. The Eddas venerate this All-Wise Father of the Gods with attributes given to Jehovah, Indra, Zeus and Jupiter, even Mercury, suggesting that all were actually the same Spacemen.

Odin's eldest son, Thor, was renowned as the strongest, most warlike of the Gods, hero of the Vikings. Around Thor's head was often depicted a circle of stars, which may have been symbolism for a Spaceman; his chariot had a pointed iron-pole and its spark-scattering wheels rolled over rumbling thunder-clouds[211] drawn by rams with silver bridles suggesting some primitive conception of a Spaceship motivated by atmospheric electricity, the lightning controlled by the ancient magicians, perhaps the same electrical forces propelling UFOs today. More than any other God Thor was identified with thunder and lightning. Thor's mighty hammer, which returned to his hand after each time he threw it, was manufactured by the Elves underground, as the wonder-weapons of Zeus were devised by the Cyclops. Before wielding his hammer or thunderbolt Thor was obliged to put on his iron gauntlets, he wore a magical belt which greatly increased his strength, suggesting the use of some mechanical device; like Hercules Thor used his weapon with maximum force when he fought high in the skies utilising more potent energies; his red beard symbolised lightning and strength. Thor gloried in continuous battles against the Giants; his most terrible conflict was waged fighting the World Serpent coiled around the Earth, a parallel to Indra, Zeus and Marduk who fought Sky Dragons suggesting War in the Heavens between Spacemen. This powerful God associated with war was also honoured for peaceful pursuits, he presided over agriculture, protected seamen, acted as a leech and gave his name to Thursday, the peasants' rest day. Thor's varied activities directing mankind may represent race-memories of the Space Kings.

Freyr, a Sky God, associated with light, had a wonderful ship built by the Elves, which could fly in any direction, this vessel large enough to hold all the Gods could be folded up and kept in a man's pouch;[212] like the Gods of Ancient India

Freyr was often depicted mounted on his car. In the very earliest ages the seven stars forming the Bear in the Northern Sky were thought of as a four-wheeled wagon, its pole being formed by the three stars that hang downwards;[213] this association, apart from the apparent likeness, may be due to ancient belief shared by Egyptians, Babylonians and Chinese that the Gods did appear to descend from the region of the North Star. Freyr was much loved by the Swedes, with his sister, Freyja, the pair resembled the twin Aswins of India, Castor and Pollux of Greece and Rome; they were always ready to descend to benefit mankind. Freyr was honoured as God of agriculture beneficence and plenty, he loved to carouse and feast with men.

Tyr, God of War, like Mars gave his name to 'Tuesday', the French 'mardi', his other title 'Tiwas' suggests derivation from 'Dyaus' or 'Zeus'. This Sky God was renowned for chaining the fearsome wolf, Fenrir, which bit off his right hand; sometimes he travelled in Thor's thunder-chariot. The evil genius of the Gods, Loki, wore shoes with wings bearing him swiftly through the air; often he appeared as a bird, symbolism for flight. Loki treacherously misused his magic powers to plot the downfall of the Gods, he caused the death of Baldur, the beloved Sun God, his heart pierced by a sprig of mistletoe, evoking the ritual slaying of Tammuz; in punishment Loki like Prometheus was chained to a rock, a serpent suspended there dripped venom on his head.

The beautiful Freyja, the Scandinavian Venus, is remembered in 'Friday', the French 'vendredi'; she was closely identified with the sky and drove in a chariot drawn by cats or in her 'featherschiff' bright and shimmering in the air like winged Athena. Freyja was worshipped as a fertility Goddess and feared for her occult feminine arts of prophecy and witchcraft. The Valkyries, winged maidens, who bore the souls of heroes to Valhalla, resemble the 'Angels' associated with the dead in Semitic theology and may be a race-memory of Space Beings; when they rode through the air their horses' manes shook the fruitful 'dew' down on the valleys below, perhaps the 'manna' or 'ambrosia' said to be produced by the radiation from Spaceships. Gna like Mercury and Iris was Messenger of the Gods flying down to Earth communicating with mortals suggesting a Space Being.

Inferior to the Gods were the Elves with wondrous powers. The 'Light Elves' like the Celestials of the Sanskrit epics were exceedingly fair, associated with the Sun; they wore delicate and transparent garments and lived beyond the clouds in Alfheim; these delightful folk resembled those Sylphs of the Middle Ages described in 'Le Comte de Gabalis';[214] today they recall Orthon from Venus[215] and the ravishing Aura Rhanes from Clarion,[216] Visitors from Space. In contrast the 'Night Elves', Trolls and Dwarfs like the Cyclops lived in solitude underground, ugly and ill-favoured they possessed subtle wisdom of the mysterious powers inherent in metals and fashioned wonderful weapons for the Gods and heroes. Female Elves, known to all peoples as Nymphs, Swan-Maidens or Dakinis, often had tragic romances with humans; tales of such fairy folk in all countries correspond with surprising similarity to Teutonic Märchen almost lending conviction to rumours that we share our Earth with a secret race hidden to men.

The Northern peoples believed that a time would come when the Gods, the Giants, the Dwarfs and all mankind would be destroyed. The Volüspa describes how this doom is foreshadowed by a three-year long winter with continuous snow, a severe frost, gales and watery sun accompanied by tremendous suffering, violence and warfare among men. Such discord shatters nature, earthquakes shake the world darkening the sun, seas engulf the land, multitudes of men and monsters roam the world. Teutonic mythology tells of a great earthquake which shook Creation, the whole universe was frozen in a long winter, probably a race-memory of some cataclysm suddenly changing the climate to destroy civilisation; bitter warfare raged among men. An inscription in runes carved on a Swedish memorial stone from Skarpalen is interpreted as 'Earth shall be torn asunder and high heaven'. Saxa Grammaticus in 'Gesta Danorum', vlll 262 possibly refers to this cataclysm in the stark words

'The sky seemed to fall suddenly on the earth, fields and woods, to sink to the ground, all things were confounded and old Chaos came again, heaven and earth mingling in one tempestuous turmoil and the world rushing to universal ruin.'[217]

The Eddas tell how the Earth basked in a Golden Age under the beneficent inspiration of the Gods; men dwelled in peace and lived long lives in innocence exactly as described in Hesiod's 'Theogony' concerning Ancient Greece. In this Northern Eden blessed by sunny fruitfulness Man rejoiced in civilisation taught by Wondrous Beings from the stars. Such perfection could not last, Man evolves by suffering. The Eddas hint that Odin in his wisdom knew that the world must end and men must die to be reborn to fresh glory, even the Gods must meet their doom, from death would spring new life. This vision of death and rebirth is the essence of all great religions. Odin brooding in Valhalla awaited Ragnarok, the dusk of the Gods. The proud Giants rebelled against the Gods and to assault Asgard rode over Bifrost, the rainbow-bridge which broke under their weight. The sea engulfed the land, the Giants launched Naglfor, a ship made from the nails of dead men. War was fought with titanic electrical blasts, dazzling light-beams and death-rays convulsing Earth and Sky burning the memories of men down generations unborn. The Elder Edda states that at World-End the Sun turns black, Earth sinks in the sea, the hot stars fall from the sky and fire peals high above Heaven itself. This vivid description recalls that marvellous account in the 'Drona Parva' 67 when the annihilating Agneya-weapon devastated Ancient India like celestial fire destroying civilisation at the end of a World Age. In this last great battle after heroic deeds Odin, Thor, Freyr and Tyr all were slain; the universe was consumed with fire, only the Sons of the Gods survived. A prophecy in the Edda states that the Almighty will create a new Heaven and a new Earth filled with abundance for the new race of men spiralling to new evolution.

A Lithuanian legend describes how the God,[218] Pramzimas, looked out of a window of his heavenly house like a Spaceman gazing down from his Flying Saucer; perceiving nothing but war among men he sent two Giants, Wandhui and Weyas upon the sinful Earth, who laid things waste for twenty nights and days. The Chinese Classic 'Shoo King'[219] (Part Four, Chapter 27) in almost similar words mentions that the Lord Chang-ti troubled by the wickedness of men commanded Tchang and Lhy to cut away every communication between Heaven and Earth, there were no more 'goings up' or 'comings down'. From Lithuania to China the Ancients told the same story of conflict between the Gods and men. Surely this world-wide tradition is true.

The forests and lakes of Finland brooding in all their wild beauty were haunted by Spirits who influenced men's lives by subtle spells not with the harsh aggression of those Gods dominating Scandinavia. Ukko, Lord of Heaven, delegated authority to Ahto, God of the Sea, and his wife, Vellamo; Tapio, God of the Forests, and his wife, Mielikki, Tuoni, God of Hades, Phuri, God of the North Wind, Etelätär, Goddess of the South Wind, Terhenstar, Goddess of the Clouds, and lesser Deities governing homes and handicrafts. Divine beneficence was menaced by Hiisi, the Evil One, bedevilling mankind. Celestials vaguely suggesting Spacemen included Panu and Päiväter, Son and Daughter of the Sun and Kuutar, Daughter of the Moon; reverence was paid to Otava, Constellation of the Great Bear, source of those 'Shining Ones' venerated by the Egyptians. In this land of trees Tammater, Goddess of the Oak, and Hongatar, Goddess of the Fir, were attended by Katajater, Nymph of the Juniper, Pohlajatar, Nymph of the Mountain Ash, and Sinetar, Nymph of Blue Flowers. The primeval Giant, Antero Vipunen, and Iku Thurso, the Water Giant, represented the race of Giants, Dwarfs, Demons and Monsters, all posed ever-present perils propitiated by powerful spells of sorcerers working their magic under the stars.

For centuries the rune-singers sang the legendary songs, episodes from the 'Kalevala',[220] meaning 'The Land of Heroes'. The 'Iliad' symbolises the soul of Greece, the 'Ramayana' enchants India, but no national epic is so deeply enhallowed in the heart of a nation as the 'Kalevala';

the humanity of its men and women beset by perils in this wild, enchanted land, the haunting sylvan scenery, the magic imagery, the secret spell of waters and woodlands, inspired Sibelius to enshrine in his great music the soul of Suomi, ancient Finland.

> Ilmeter, Virgin of the Air, descends into the sea and becomes fertilised by the winds and waves, from the egg of an eagle – or duck – are fashioned Heaven and Earth. After thirty years in her womb she gives birth to Väinämöinen, a divine minstrel, who flies on an eagle to the castle of Pohjola in Lapland, where the witch, Louhi, promises him her beautiful daughter, if he will forge the mysterious Sampo, eventually cast by his brother, Ilmarinen. Lemminkainen, a cheerful adventurer, carries off the fair Kylliki, and marries her, he is killed seeking to shoot the swan of Tuonela then restored to life. Väinämöinen goes to Tuonela, Hades, for the three magic words enabling him to finish a boat. Väinämöinen makes a kantele or harp and charms all Nature with his song and heals people from the plague sent by the Witch-Queen; amid great frost his music draws the Sun and Moon down to Earth, the Witch-Queen hides them in a cave and steals all the people's fire. Väinämöinen conquers Pohjola, Louhi returns the Sun and Moon to the sky. Väinämöinen bequeathes his songs and music to the people of Kalevala and sails off in a copper boat to loftier regions to a land between Earth and Heaven.[291]

This heroic poem compiled from oral traditions by Elias Lönnrot in 1849 with its 22,795 lines of wonderful poetry inspired Longfellow's 'Hiawatha'.

Above all the lands of the North Lapland was celebrated for its magic singers and soothsayers, wizards, who controlled the elements. The 'Kalevala' abounds in scenes of magic, conjuration, spells over animals and men and all the forces of Nature, the Laps still cherish secret stones, 'sajda', talismans of sorcery. The Finno-Ugric animism in the North from Finland to Siberia peoples the Universe with spirits or genii, all objects have an elemental force dominated by a greater force. Surely these magicians inherited a most ancient science from that wondrous civilisation of the Gods or Spacemen, still symbolised by the Shamans of the North in their cult of the Bear.

The Finnish 'Kalevala' like the Estonian 'Kalevipoeg' sharing the world-wide concept of the Cosmic Egg anticipates our own scientists who state the Universe exploded from a single atom born from spatial energy; biologists believe that life evolved from the sea.

The capture of the Sun and Moon by the Witch-Queen plunging Finland into freezing darkness associated with plagues and wide-spread misery probably refers to that same cataclysm bewailed in legends all over the world; fire falling from Heaven into a lake suggests some cosmic body crashing to Earth. In his very fine translation W. F. Kirby sixty years ago commented that the catastrophe may concern an early period.

'... when as Old Persian books tell us, the climate of some parts of Asia (?) was changed from nine months summer and three months winter to nine months winter and three months summer....'[222]

The ancient Finns attributed pestilence to the anger of the Gods and Demons, primitive superstitions world-wide.

Väinämöinen's ascension in a copper-boat to a land in the skies parallels the translation to the stars of that other culture-hero, Quetzalcoatl. Can Finland and Mexico be linked by the same memory of Spacemen?

The 'Kalevala' ranks with the 'Gilgamesh Epic' the 'Ramayana', 'Kret of Ugarit' and the 'Odyssey', all tell in simple, moving words the stories of men and women befriended by Immortals long ago. The poetry, the passion, the drama of noble deeds, the hopes and desires of questing humanity meeting their destiny watched by the Gods, transcend the long centuries to enthrall us today. Surely those people in far Antiquity, whose mind could create such wonderful literature so full of sublime wisdom, so exquisitely expressed, were heirs to a great and profound culture inspired perhaps by Celestials from the stars.

The Icelandic tale 'Eireks Saga Vidforla' recounts Eirek's travels to the mythological Deathless Land; written in the fourteenth century it is believed to have originated as an ancient heathen myth later somewhat christianised, Paradise being substituted for the pagan Glaeswellin. In 'Curious Myths of the Middle Ages' Sabina Baring-Gould[223] describes how Eirek, a son of Thrond, King of Drautheim, with a Danish friend of the same name went to Constantinople, crossed Syria and India and came to a strait crossed by a stone bridge guarded by a dragon. The Norseman stood sword in hand, walked into the maw of the Dragon and to his delight was instantly transported to Paradise. These 'Dragons' of Antiquity now appear to us to have been primitive conceptions of Spaceships; entering a Dragon's mouth was probably the ancient equivalent of travelling in a Flying Saucer like Adamski, Lobsang Rampa and other 'Contacts'. Eirek claimed to have been translated to another world. The Saga vividly related that

'... The land was most beautiful and the grass as gorgeous as purple, it was studded with flowers and was traversed by honey rills. The land was extensive and level so that there was not to be seen mountain or hill, and the sun shone cloudless without night and darkness, the calm of the air was great and there was but a feeble minimum of wind and that which there was breathed redolent with the odour of blossoms.... After a short walk Eirek observed what certainly must have been a remarkable object, *namely a tower or steeple self-suspended in the air without any support whatever*, though access might be had to it by means of a slender ladder. By this Eirek ascended into a loft of the tower and found there an excellent cold colation prepared for him. After having partaken of this, he went to sleep and in vision beheld and conversed with his Guardian Angel who promised to conduct him back to his fatherland but to come for him again and fetch him away from it for ever at the expiration of the tenth year after his return to Drautheim.'

Eirek returned to India and after a tedious journey of seven years reached his native land where he related his adventure to the confusion of the heathens and to the delight and edification of the Faithful.

'... And in the tenth year and at break of day as Eirek went to prayer God's spirit caught him away and he was never seen again in this world, so here ends all we have to say of him.'

Nennius in 'Historia Brittorum' written in the ninth century records that in ancient times a Spanish fleet brought people to Ireland when a 'tower of glass' appeared, the summit of which was crowded with men. The ships attacked the 'tower' which destroyed them. Elijah too spoke with 'Angels' and was translated to the skies never to be seen again. Today Eirek's story seems strangely credible, there is now reason to believe that throughout history chosen individuals in many countries have been transported to other worlds by Spacemen.

A plaintive Icelandic story tells how Helge Thoreson like Eirek also visited the Land of the Glittering Plains and married Ingeborg, fairest of Gudmund's twelve daughters; he came home with much treasure. During a great storm on Yule Night two strange men suddenly appeared and took Helge away. A year later all three materialised before King Olav Trygeveson at his feast and gave the King two great drinking-horns, as the Bishop blessed the gift the hall was plunged into darkness, in the confusion Helge and his companions vanished. The following Yuletide the two men again returned with Helge now stricken with blindness. Helge complained that he had been forced to return home because of all the prayers offered for him; his 'spirit-bride' with whom he had lived so happily had made him blind to prevent him casting amorous eyes on Earth-women. This poignant tale is strangely reminiscent of those haunting romances of Old India and the Middle Ages telling of tragic love between mortals and maidens from other realms.

The Germans knew Odin as Woden, identified with Mercury, he gave his name to 'Wednesday', the French 'mercredi', his fateful influence loomed over Teutonic destinies from the Dark Ages to Nazi Germany's Third Reich. In the twelfth-century an unknown poet compiled sagas of the Northern heroes into 'Das Nibelungenlied', which has inspired the Germanic peoples like the 'Iliad' did Ancient Greece. The story of Sigurd and Brynhild told in the Eddic poems and the Volsung Saga was transferred to the romantic Rhine with Siegfried and Brünnhilde.

The Nibelungenlied[224] greatly inspired Richard Wagner who infused the old tale with the original Norse mythology in his own libretto of 'The Ring' in four dramatic operas, 'Das Rheingold', 'Die Walküre', 'Siegfried' and 'Die Götterdämmerung', he transformed the epic into an allegory whose real hero is Wotan. Wagner's social ideals were vividly expressed by wonderful characterisation in music which revolutionised the forms of the classical composers and ushered in those strange orchestrations still startling today. Leit-motivs introduce the great roles and dramatic music evokes the episodes with novel harmonies shocking the Victorians who first heard them; the Valhalla theme, the Ride of the Valkyries, the Siegfried Idyll and the Trauermarsch remain unsurpassed in melodic inspiration. While the revolutionary Wagner was not consciously writing 'Space Opera', his 'Ring' with Wotan and the Gods, Valkyries, Heroes, Giants, Dwarfs, Dragons, Magic Ring, Enchanted Sword, Fiery Mountain, all characterised in music, surely suggest those wonders associated with Spacemen.

Wagner offered several explanations for 'The Ring', all different, then vaguely agreed with Schopenhauer that his works showed 'the sublime tragedy, the negation of Will.' Bernard Shaw in his provocative essay 'The Perfect Wagnerite'[225] swore with characteristic immodesty that he knew exactly what Wagner was really striving to say; much of 'The Ring' represents 'the portraiture of our capitalist industrial system from the socialist's point of view in the slavery of the Nibelungs and the tyranny of Alberic.' He alleged that Wotan is the Divine Establishment entangled in its own laws and longing for the 'Ideal Man' to extricate the Cosmic Will for new evolution. Siegfried, a young anarchist beyond fear and conscience, destroys the Old Order to make way for the New. In exasperation Shaw deplores that the allegory collapses and Siegfried fails. Nazi Germany was to see the failure of its own Siegfried!

With studied diffidence we advance the suggestion that Wagner, well-versed in mythology, was perhaps unknowingly dramatising the retreat of the Space Kings from domination of Earth the Götterdämmerung may represent the end of a World-Age. Wagner might be surprised at this interpretation; Shaw most eloquent on subjects he knew least would sardonically disagree. Whatever its true meaning 'The Ring' tells the titanic tragedy of the Gods confirmed in mythologies all over the world. Will operas written a century hence sing of Martians consorting with Earthwomen?

Can all those Wagnerites at Bayreuth be listening to Spacemen?

Woden has been confused with Votan, Culture-Hero of the Quiches whose myths declare he came from the East; Votan was said to have aided Solomon in the building of his wonderful Temple. The most ancient 'Oera Linda Boek' states Woden was a Frisian Chief, who sailed from North-West Europe across the Atlantic to Yucatan, where he and his descendants founded a great empire.

In Teutonic mythology Wotan was depicted as a one-eyed Giant wearing a sky-dome hat and a sky-cloak flecked by clouds, sometimes he drove a star-chariot or the stars themselves; in folk-lore he was feared as the Wild Huntsman, the Headless Rider or the Erl König, dreaded in old England as Herne the Hunter. The German soul is steeped in mysticism brooding over the Dark Forces of Nature, Night and Death; for many centuries the Church pursued fanatical pogroms against witches, popular Märchen abounded in tales of goblins living in forests or caves, in the eighteenth century romantic writers and composers were fascinated by the Supernatural. After 'Faust' evoking phenomena suggestive of Spacemen, Goethe's most popular poem is probably 'Erl-könig' which describes a father riding late through the dark and wind with his son in his arms. The child pleads that the phantom Erl-könig threatens to carry him off to a beautiful land, the terrified father hastens on, when reaching the farm his son is dead.

The Wild Huntsman wore a curious hat with a broad brim and was followed by an infernal pack of fiery misshapen dogs and wolves rushing through the air with a terrifying sound; any venturesome onlooker would be whirled up in the air and his neck broken. Associated with the Wild Huntsman was the Schimmelreiter or Headless Rider mounted on a white horse, who wore a strange, broad-brimmed hat, the hat shape, pack of celestial hounds, aerial speeding through the night resemble present-day descriptions of UFOs.[226]

The belief in alien astronauts persisted in Teutonic minds since the days of Charlemagne when laws were passed against aerial demons. None in his 'Anzeigen', Vol. 4, p. 304, wrote

'A violent thunderstorm lasted so long that a huntsman on the highway loaded his gun with a consecrated bullet and shot it off into the blackest cloud; out of it (as out of the sky) a naked female fell dead to the ground and the storm blew over in a moment.'

We know now what to do the next time it rains!

A similar bizarre incident is mentioned by Montanus in 'Deutsche Volksfeste', p. 37, concerned with wizards flying through the clouds who were shot down. In Carinthia[227] the people shot at storm-clouds to scare away 'evil spirits' that held counsel in them, a custom popular among the Tibetans and even by the early Irish who feared the malevolent entities confined in the inner spaces of the air. Today our UFO literature abounds with alleged hostilities from Spacemen.

More than a hundred years ago the great German mythologist, Jacob Grimm, in 'Deutsche Mythologie' made a detailed comparison between the German and the Greek Gods, completely unaware of our present conception of Spacemen. He was profoundly impressed by the similarity of the Norse and Classical Deities descending from the skies to mingle among men, and quoted scores of descriptions from the Eddas and Northern Märchen, which agree with the 'Iliad', 'Odyssey' and other Classics with an exactness beyond chance coincidence. He concluded

'I think that on all these lines of research, which could be extended to many other parts as well, I have brought forward a series of undeniable resemblances between the Teutonic mythology and the Greek. Here, as in relation between the Greek and Teutonic languages, there is no question of borrowing or choice, nothing but unconscious affinity, allowing room (and that inevitably) for considerable divergence. But who can fail to recognise or who invalidate the surprising similarity of opinions on the immortality of the Gods, their divine food, their growing up overnight, their journeyings and transformation, their epithets, their anger and their mirth, their suddenness in appearing and recognition on parting, their use of carriages and horses, their performance of all natural functions, their illnesses, their language, their servants and messengers, offices and dwellings?'[228]

Today the learned Grimm would recognise that the astonishing verisimilitude between the Teutonic and Greek

Gods is due to the obvious fact that they were all the same Celestials from Space.

The North has not always been barren and cold, the Yogis teach that the First Race of Mankind dwelled there, coal mined in Spitzbergen proves the former existence of tropical forests, ancient cities discovered under the ice support the old Germanic legend of Thule, a vanished civilisation peopled by magicians. The UFOs approach through the polar-vents in the Van Allen radiation-belts; as agreed by the Ancients it was likely that Celestials would first land in the North. A century ago H. Sachs in his 'Schwank der Lappenhäuser' related how the Lapps made a ship of feathers and straw then carried it upon a hill with a view of launching out in it when the wind should fall. Did these Northern wizards still remember their old Space Kings?

The belief in Nordic Supermen still haunts imagination to torture men's souls. Hitler's mad dreams conjured the pagan Gods from Valhalla to conquer Europe, only to drag his Third Reich down to Götterdämmerung.

In the summer of 1946 our modern age of UFOs was heralded by ghost-rockets and luminous bombs speeding through the skies of Sweden to announce the return of the Spacemen.

The silent desolation of the North conceals most ancient mystery. The secret may be found among those Space Gods of Scandinavia.

Chapter Twelve
The Cross

The Star of Bethlehem presaging the Birth of Jesus was followed by wonders in the heavens inspiring the early Christians culminating in AD 312 in that famous Cross seen by Constantine which promoted the establishment of Christianity as the official religion of Rome.

Dio Cassius writing about AD 200 in Book LVI states

AD 9   'The Temple of Mars in the field of the same name was struck by lightning and many locusts flew into the city and were devoured by swallows, the peaks of the Alps seemed to collapse upon one another and to send up three columns of fire, the sky in many places seemed ablaze and numerous comets appeared at one and the same time, spears seemed to dart from the north and to fall in the direction of the Roman Camp.'

AD 14   'Thus the sun suffered a total eclipse and most of the sky seemed to be on fire, glowing embers appeared to be falling from it and blood-red comets were seen.'

Admiral Pliny whose scientific curiosity led to untimely death in AD 79 amid the burning lava burying Pompeii and Herculaneum, wrote in 'Historia Naturales', Book XI-XXIV

AD 17   'There are also meteoric lights that are only seen when falling, for instance one that ran across the sky at midday in full view of the public when Germanicus was giving a gladiatorial show, of these are two kinds, one sort are called 'lampades' which means 'torches', the other 'bolides', 'missiles', that is the sort that appeared at the time of the disaster at Modena (when Decimus Brutus was besieged there by Antony in 44 BC). The difference between them is that 'torches' make long tracks with their front part glowing, whereas a 'boles' glows throughout its length and traces a longer path.'

Ovid who died in AD 18 related 'In the middle of the night I saw the Sun truly a glittering white.'

In the fourteenth century, Dechany monastery at Kosovskaya Metchia, southern Yugoslavia, are found numerous frescoes which seem actually to depict Angels flying in Spaceships like our astronauts. The Yugoslav magazine 'Svet' in 1964 published a fascinating article with photographs entitled 'Spaceships on the Dechany Crucifix. Sputniks in our frescoes. Could ancient icon-painters have depicted Spaceships in Dechany?' In the leading ship a man without an angel's halo holds an unseen control-column and is looking back at another ship carrying a similar astronaut, both craft seem stream-lined with clearly visible jets. Angels below cover their eyes and ears with their hands dreading the glow and noise, others show startled surprise. The control-figure represents the crucified Christ. The fresco depicting the Resurrection of Christ shows the Messiah apparently in a Space-rocket with a two-wing stabiliser. Another Resurrection painting on an icon in the Moscow Theological Academy dating back to the seventeenth century appears to show Christ in a stream-lined capsule emitting smoke which vaguely represents a Spaceship.[229]

On the domed ceiling of the Alexander Nevsky Memorial Church in Sofia, Bulgaria, the renowned Japanese expert, Yusuke J. Matsumura, was thrilled to behold a Golden Flying Saucer. In Roumania at the Princeley Church in Tirgaste, north-west of Bucharest, he saw a wall-painting of Christ apparently about to board a Spaceship accompanied by persons wearing spherical helmets; at Varna on the Bulgarian shore of the Black Sea the cathedral was full of frescoes representing Saints with a reddish rocket-shaped machine taking-off.[230]

AD 36 The conversion of Paul on the Road to Damascus by that blinding light from heaven with an admonitory voice reproaching him is attributed to sudden psychic illumination; theologians insist that the future St. Paul had an inner vision. Those dogmatic priests should read the great Seneca who lived in Rome at the time and possibly met Paul, though he did not say so.

One night shortly before his death in AD 37 shortly after that light on the Damascus road, the Emperor Tiberius was aroused by the alarming news that Ostia was in flames, the fire could be seen from the hills of Rome. Tiberius promptly despatched the Roman fire-brigade who galloped to the sea-side resort post-haste with their pumps to be confounded by the obvious fact that there was no fire. High in the sky loomed a mysterious object in the form of a fiery beam, diffusing its sombre light like that of a flame mingled with smoke filling the sky of the city with its sinister rays. The phenomenon which caused the glow continued for a great part of the night and then disappeared taking with it the mystery of that extraordinary apparition. Seneca probably saw it.

In AD 43 when the Roman legions led by Aulus Plautus invaded Britain a UFO like shining light is said to have streaked across the sky from East to West.

AD 51 'Three suns were seen during the consulship of the future Emperor Claudius when Cornelius Ofitus was his colleague. (Pliny.)[231]'

AD 54 'During the reign of Claudius a Comet coming from the North rose towards the zenith to be carried then towards the East becoming less and less brilliant. (Seneca.)[232]'

AD 60 'Indeed we have been able to contemplate for six months that Comet which appeared in the happy reign of Nero. (Seneca.)'

During this so-called 'happy reign' of Nero about AD 64 Peter and Paul were martyred, the Christians were savagely persecuted.

In AD 65 the Jews in Jerusalem suffering Roman oppression were cheered somewhat irrationally by signs in the skies which some prophets read as portents of happiness instead of omens of misfortune.

Josephus in 'Wars of the Jews', Book VI, Chap. V – 3, says

'Thus there was a star resembling a sword, which stood over the city, and a comet that continued a whole year. Thus also before the Jews' rebellion and before those commotions which preceded the war, when the people were come in great crowds to the feast of unleavened bread, on the eighth day of the month Xanthicus (Nisan) and at the ninth hour of the night, so great a light shone round the altar and the holy house, that it appeared to be bright day-time, which light lasted for half-an-hour.'

At the Feast of the Passover the eastern gate of the inner court of the Temple, which was of brass and vastly heavy requiring twenty men to shut it with difficulty, though securely bolted, opened of its own accord about the sixth hour of the night.

> 'Besides these a few days after that feast, on the one and twentieth day of the month Artemiscus (Ivar) a certain prodigious and incredible phenomenon appeared. I suppose the account of it would seem to be a fable, were it not related by those that saw it, and were not the events that followed it of so considerable a nature to deserve such signals, for before sunset chariots and troops of soldiers in their armour were seen running about among the clouds and surrounding of cities.'[233]

More than two hundred years earlier in 170 BC just before the rebellion of Judas Maccabeus against Antiochus IV similar apparitions of galloping horses in golden armour and companies of spearmen were seen in the skies of Jerusalem for forty days.[234]

In AD 66 the Jews goaded to revolt massacred the Roman garrison and soon controlled the whole country. Nero appointed Vespasian, distinguished during the conquest of Britain, to quell the insurgence; in the following year with his son, Titus, he routed the Jewish patriots in Galilee and among the thousands of prisoners captured their General, Joseph, who retired from warfare to become better known as the historian, Flavius Josephus. Nero in 68 committed his much-applauded suicide; his successors, Galba, Otho and Vitellius in quick succession ruled only eighteen months before the Imperial throne passed to Vespasian who promptly ordered Titus to suppress renewed rebellion in Jerusalem.

Josephus tells of Ananus, a husbandman, who for four years before the war began went around Jerusalem crying day and night of the dire tribulations to come. Albinus, the procurator, had him whipped till his bones were laid bare yet he continued to lament 'Woe is Jerusalem!' until the siege started.

> 'And just as he added at the last "Woe, woe to myself also," there came a stone out of one of the engines and smote him, and killed him immediately; and as he was uttering the very same presages, he gave up the ghost.'

Josephus vividly describes the terrible siege, the dreadful famine, the catapults pounding the Temple walls until only the smoke-blackened Wailing Wall was left forlorn for future Jews to mourn their tragic past. Thousands of Jews were killed, thousands more taken prisoners.

During the next two centuries the various Christian sects contended with the pagans and quarrelled with each other.

Edward Gibbon critical of those confused times states

> 'The ancient Christians were animated by a contempt for their present existence, and by a just confidence of immortality of which doubtful and imperfect faith of modern ages cannot give us any adequate notion.... It was universally believed that the end of the world, and the kingdom of heaven, were at hand. The near approach of this wonderful event had been predicted by the apostles, the tradition of it was preserved by their earliest disciples, and those who understood in their literal sense the discourses of Christ himself, were obliged to expect the second and glorious coming of the Son of Man in the clouds before that generation was totally extinguished which had beheld his humble condition upon earth and might still be witness of the calamities of the Jews under Vespasian or Hadrian.'[238]

Most Christians believed that at any moment Christ with a triumphant band of Saints would descend from heaven in glory to reign for a thousand years in the New Jerusalem, a wondrous city of gold and precious stones in a Garden of Eden. This fervent expectation led people to scan the skies with an eagerness transcending even our own UFO watchers so hopeful today.

Very few records of those troubled centuries now remain; the following sightings must be typical of many since lost to us.

Celestials apparently continued to haunt the skies.

AD 71 'Moreover in the East and West two suns were seen at the same time, of which one was faint and pallid, the other powerful and clear.' (Lycosthenes.)

Pliny, in 'Historia Naturalis', Book II, CXXII, states

AD 76 'There are also stars that suddenly come to birth in the heaven itself.... "Javelin-stars" quiver like a dart, these are a very terrible portent. To this class belongs the comet about which Titus Imperator Caesar in his consulship wrote about in his famous poem, that being its latest appearance down to the present day. The same stars when shorter and sloping to a point have been called "Daggers". These are the palest of all in colour and have a gleam like the flash of a sword and no rays....'

Today such stars that suddenly come to birth and look like 'Javelins' would be considered UFOs, possibly Spaceships.

AD 98 'At Tarquinia, an old town in Campania, Italy, a burning torch was seen all about the sky. It suddenly fell down. At sunset a burning shield passed over the sky at Rome. It came sparkling from the west and passed to the east.' (Lycosthenes.)

That philosopher-Emperor, Marcus Aurelius, like Lucullus against Mithridates two centuries earlier, had cause to thank the heavens. Dio Cassius in his 'Roman History', Vol. LXXII states

AD 174 'During a great battle against the Quadri, Marcus Aurelius feared for his whole army, a whole legion of Christians prayed to their God, who immediately gave ear and smote the enemy with a thunderbolt and comforted the Romans with a shower of rain. Marcus was greatly astonished at this, and not only honoured the Christians by an official decree but also named their legion the "Thundering" Legion.... Numerous thunderbolts fell into the ranks of the foe, water and fire descending simultaneously consumed the barbarians. The rain like oil made the fires spread.'

The brilliant Peter Kolosimo[236] quoting his erudite friends, Renato Gatti and Roberto Pinotti states

AD 192 'During the reign of Commodius a particularly bright object crossed the sky; the historian, Elio Lampridio, hints at it; he is one of the "scriptores historiae augustae" and is in his "Life of Commodus". Herodian, too, in his "History of the Empire after Marcus Aurelius" supports this with "There were many marvels in those days ... stars were seen in mid-air and in broad daylight." (Book 1)....'

AD 193 'Emperor Pertinax during the three months of his brief reign, had some coins minted not with the imprint of some star or other (a common motif when it was a question of immortalising events considered to be supernatural) but with a real sphere complete with strange antennae like those of our own artificial satellites.'

The same money shows a woman raising her hands to what appears to be an unidentified flying-globe.

The successor to Pertinax, Didius Julianus, reigned only

sixty-one days and was beheaded like a common criminal. Dio Cassius commenting on the conspiracy states

AD 193 'Three men attempted to secure control of affairs. Severus, Niger and Albinus.... These were the three men portended by the three stars that suddenly came to view surrounding the sun when Julianus in our presence was offering the sacrifices of Entrance in front of the Senate House. These stars were so very distinct that the soldiers kept continually looking at them and pointing them out to one another, declaring that some dreadful fate would befall the Emperor.' (Book LXXXIV.)

AD 217 'A great fire filled the entire interior of the temple of Serapis at Alexandria but did no damage beyond destroying the sword with which Antoninus had slain his brother. In Rome moreover a spirit having the appearance of a man led an ass to the palace seeking its master as he claimed and stating that Antoninus was dead and Jupiter was now Emperor. Upon being arrested for this and sent by Matermianus to Antoninus, he said "I go as you bid, but I shall face not this Emperor but another." And when he reached Capua he vanished.' (Dio Cassius. Vol. XI. Book LXXIX.)

Three years later the Celestials aided the Japanese Empress Jingo to invade Korea.

AD 230 'Armies of footmen and horses were seen in the air over London and other places in England. They were fighting. This was in the time of the Roman Emperor Alexander Severus.'

AD 249 'When Decius ascended the throne of the Roman Empire it rained blood in Britain, and a terrible bloody sword was seen in the air for three nights, soon after sunset.'

Harold Wilkins quotes these two intriguing sightings from a little-known 'History of England' written long ago by John Sellers.[237]

AD 268 Amid the barren deserts of Arabia a few cultivated spots rise like islands out of the sandy ocean. Palmyra, a fine city of white marble with a magnificent temple of Baal, was an opulent centre on the caravan-routes between the Persian Gulf and the Mediterranean bringing the rich commodities of India to the West; its beauteous Queen, Zenobia, became a living legend, esteemed the most lovely of her sex. Edward Gibbon marvelled that Zenobia 'equalled in beauty her ancestor, Cleopatra, and far surpassed that princess in chastity and valour. She was of dark complexion, her teeth were of a pearly whiteness and her large black eyes sparkled with uncommon fire, tempered by the most attractive sweetness. Her voice was strong and harmonious. Her manly understanding was strengthened and adorned by study.'[238]

An exotic Queen boasting fabulous beauty tutored by the philosopher, Longinus, ruling a wonderful desert city seventeen hundred years ago! Did this alluring siren attract the Spacemen?

The Italian scholar, Alberto Fenoglio, tells a fascinating tale, which we translate with pleasure, if not conviction.

'On a day not determined, to the astounded and terrified eyes of the people of Palmyra and of the merchants, always numerous, since the caravans which traded between Egypt and Persia thus linking Africa and Asia, had to pause in the City of Palms, there appeared two great fiery spheres which rotated one near to the other and then suddenly separated while long flashes criss-crossed. One of the spheres, as if feeling itself in danger, came down passing at lightning-speed over the city, so that the temperature suddenly increased and many palm-trees withered. The duel continued for some time with pursuits and flashing discharges, until one of the globes was transformed into an enormous cloud and from it fell stones or bits of the disintegrated object which sank into the sand, while the other globe disappeared high in the sky.'[239]

Four years later the legions of Aurelian stormed Palmyra. Zenobia fled on her fleetest dromedary but was overtaken by Roman cavalry and later displayed in Aurelian's spectacular triumph at Rome. 'The beauteous figure of Zenobia was confined by fetters of gold, a slave supported the gold chain which encircled her neck and she almost fainted under the intolerable weight of jewels.' Aurelian presented Zenobia with an elegant villa at Tivoli where according to Gibbon she insensibly sank into a Roman matron.

AD 312. Constantine, surnamed the Great, Master of the West fought with Emperor Maxentius for possession of Italy and marched on Rome. Still a pagan he sought support from the Christians. In the graphic words of his biographer, Eusebius, Bishop of Caesarea

'He called upon this God therefore in his prayers entreating and beseeching him that whatever he was, he would manifest himself to him and reach out his right hand (to his assistance) in his present affairs. Whilst the Emperor was putting up these prayers and earnest supplication, a most wonderful Sign from God appeared, which (Sign) had any other person given a Relation of it, would not easily have been received as true. But since the Victorious Emperor himself told it to us who write this history, a long while after, namely at such time as we were vouchsafed his knowledge and converse and confirmed his relation with an oath, who will hereafter doubt of giving credit to his Narrative? Especially when the succeeding times gave an evident attestation to this Relation. About the Meridian hours of the Sun, when day was declining, he said he saw with his own eyes the Trophy of the Cross in the heavens, placed over the Sun made up of light and an inscription annexed to it containing the words BY THIS I CONQUER and that at the sight thereof an amazement seized both him and all his Military Forces which followed him as he was making a Journey some whither and were spectators of the Miracle.'[340]

Edward Gibbon, somewhat sceptical, grumbles because the credulous Eusebius forgot to question witnesses, yet he grudgingly admits

'This amazing object in the sky astonished the whole army as well as the Emperor himself, who was yet undetermined in the choice of a religion, but his astonishment was converted into faith by the vision on the ensuing night. Christ appeared before his eyes, and displaying the same celestial sign of the cross, he directed Constantine to frame a similar standard and to march with an assurance of victory against Maxentius and all his enemies.'[341]

The Fiery Cross was seen by Constantine and his army on their march towards Rome across the Alps, possibly at Autun in Gaul or near Andernach on the Rhine or even near Verona. Constantine welcomed this omen, he allied with the Christians, defeated and killed Maxentius at the Battle of the Milvain Bridge; now Emperor he established Christianity as the State religion nearly three hundred years after the death of Christ. Without aid from the Christians convinced by that shining Cross in the skies Constantine might have met defeat, when paganism would have triumphed and Christianity possibly extinguished.

Eusebius states that Christ appeared to Constantine as he slept. Could this Vision have been a Spaceman?

Gibbon in sardonic disdain quotes the celebrated orator, Nazarius, who 'laboured to exalt the glory of Constantine.'

'Nine years after the Roman victory, Nazarius describes an army of divine warriors, who seemed to fall from the sky, he marks their beauty, their spirit, their gigantic forms, the streams of light which beamed from their celestial armour, their patience in suffering themselves to be heard, as well as seen by mortals, and their declaration that they were sent, that they flew, to the assistance of the great Constantine.'

Lycosthenes dredged from contemporary records several celestial phenomena which lend credence to the Cross seen by Constantine. In AD 384 a terrible sign shaped like a pillar shone in the sky during the reign of Theodosius; in 393 strange lights were seen, then a bright globe at midnight which absorbed many small stars. At Antioch in 394 the night skies were haunted by an immense apparition, oddly described as a 'woman' moving erratically over the city emitting sudden bursts of sound which appalled the people below. This terrifying prodigy may suggest some Spaceship?

Prehistoric peoples world-wide carved stone crosses. Did they symbolise Spaceships?

William of Newbury in 'Historia Anglicana' mentioned that in 1189 'The Emblem of Our Lord with a dazzling milk-white whiteness and the conjoined form of a man crucified' hung in the sky at noon above the village of Dunstable near London. In 1227 Matthew of Paris in 'Historia Anglorum' reported a crucifix in the air beheld by crowds in Germany.[242]

Flying Saucers and Extraterrestrials still haunt Italy studied by researchers who watch the skies like those old Etruscans long ago. Sightings and reported landings during our twentieth century are summarised by the brilliant Gruppo Clipeologico Fiorentino in their fascinating work UFO in Italia, which records that amazing Cross in the heavens seen by Dr. Alberto Perego, the distinguished author and diplomat, on 6th November 1954 at Rome.

'As he himself relates that day about 11 o'clock, he found himself in the Tusculan Quarter, in the neighbourhood of a mineral-water factory, when he noticed in the sky a formation of UFOs very high like little white dots. Fascinated by the spectacle he ascended to the terrace of the factory to see better. Other UFOs continued to arrive, so many that after half an hour Perego calculated that at least fifty must have been present over Rome. But the crucial moment of the sighting occurred towards midday, two perfect V-formations of twenty dots steering one to the other from opposite directions. After a few seconds they met joining at the apexes of the Vs and forming thus a perfect "Greek Cross". According to the estimation of Perego the Cross was formed over Vatican City.'[243]

Celestial crosses 312 and 1954! Do Spacemen still inspire Christianity?

The Ancients themselves in their religions, philosophies, even in their daily lives, fervently believed that somewhere in the stars lived 'Gods' who sometimes descended to people on Earth.

We too may have much to learn from those Spacemen in Greece and Rome.

Bibliography

The Author wishes to express his gratitude and sincere acknowledgements to the Authors and Publishers of the literary works enumerated below and to all Authorities inadvertently omitted.

1. Hesiod, *Theogony*, Loeb Classics, Heinemann, London.
2. Aeschylus, 'Prometheus Bound' (Trans. Lewis Campbell), *World's Classics*, Oxford University Press.
3. Ovid, *Metamorphoses* (Trans. Mary Innes), Penguin Classics, London.
4. Hamilton, Edith, 'Mythology', *Mentor*, New American Library, New York.
5. MacDonnell, Arthur A., *A History of Sanskrit Literature*, Heinemann, London, 1900.
6. Kramer, Samuel Noah, *Mythologies of the Ancient World*, Anchor, New York.
7. Diodorus Siculus, *Biblioteca Historica*, O.U.P., Oxford, 1956.
8. Apollodorus, Loeb Classics, Heinemann.
9. Plutarch, *Theseus*, Loeb Classics, Heinemann.
10. Plutarch, 'Themistocles', XV. Loeb Classics, Heinemann.
11. Drake, W. Raymond, *Spacemen in the Ancient East*, Neville Spearman Ltd., London, 1968.
12. Rose, H. J., *A Handbook of Greek Mythology*, Methuen, London, 1958.
13. Guerber, H. A., *The Myths of Greece and Rome*, Harrap, London, 1965.
14. Kramer, Samuel Noah, *Mythologies of the Ancient World*, Anchor, New York, 1961.
15. Genesis 1-3.
16. Genesis 1-26.
17. Bullfinch, *Mythology*, Spring Books, London, 1953.
18. Graves, Robert, *Greek Myths*, Cassell, London, 1958.
19. Pfister, Frederick, *Greek Gods and Heroes* (Trans. H. Sorel), McGibbon & Kee Ltd., London, 1961.
20. Pausanias, X, 24-3.
21. Hamilton, Edith, 'Mythology', *Mentor*, New American Library, New York.
22. Shklovsky, J., 'La Vie et la Raison dans l'univers', *Planète*, No. 17, J/A, 1961.
23. Agrest, M., 'Des Cosmonautes dans l'Antiquité', *Planète*, No. 7, N/D, 1962.
24. Kitto, W. D. C., *The Greeks*, Penguin.

25. Rose, H. K., *A Handbook of Greek Mythology*, Methuen & Co. Ltd., London, 1958.
26. Williamson, George Hunt, *Road in the Sky*, Neville Spearman Ltd., London, 1959.
27. Nilson, Martin P., *A History of Greek Religion* (Trans. F. C. Fieler), Oxford University Press.
28. Servier, Jean, 'Je ne crois pas au progrès', *Planète*, 18, S/O 1964.
29. Kraspedon, Dino, *My Contact with Flying Saucers*, Neville Spearman Ltd., London, 1958.
30. Plato, *Symposium* (Trans. Sir. W. Livingstone), Oxford University Press.
31. King, Dr. George, *The Nine Freedoms*, The Aetherius Society, Los Angeles.
32. Williamson, Dr. George Hunt, *The Saucers Speak*, Neville Spearman Ltd., London, 1963.
33. Varro, *De Lingua Latina*.
34. Cory, I. P., *Ancient Fragments*, W. Pickering, London, 1828.
35. Adamski, George, *Inside the Spaceships*, Neville Spearman Ltd., 1966.
36. Menger, Howard, *From Outer Space to You*, Souvenir Books, Clarkesburg, W. V. a. USA.
37. Williamson, George Hunt, *Other Tongues, Other Flesh*, Ray Palmer, Amherst Press, Wisconsin, USA.
38. Herodotus, *History*, Book 1, 180-3 (Trans. Enoch Powell), Oxford University Press, 1949.
39. Exodus, XXV.
40. Williamson, George Hunt, *The Saucers Speak*, Neville Spearman Ltd., London, 1963.
41. Wilson, H. H., *Rig Veda Sanhitae*, Vol. II, W. H. Allen, London, 1854.
42. Encyclopaedia Britannica.
43. Werner, E. T. C., *Myths and Legends of China*, Harrap & Co. Ltd., London, 1956.
44. Aston, W. G., *Nihongi, or Chronicles of Japan*, G. Allen & Unwin, Ltd., London.
45. Cory, I. P., *Ancient Fragments*, W. Pickering, London, 1828.
46. Saggs, H. W. P., *The Greatness that was Babylon*, Sidgwick & Jackson, London, 1946.
47. Pritchard, J. B., *Ancient Near Eastern Texts*, Princeton University Press, USA.
48. Gordon, Cyrus H., 'The Greeks and the Hebrews', *Scientific American*, Feb. 1965.
49. Drake, W. Raymond, *Gods and Spacemen in the Ancient West*, Sphere, London, 1974.
50. Plato, *Timaeus*.
51. Plato, *Phaedrus* (Trans. R. W. Livingstone), World Classics, Oxford University Press.

52. Kolosimo, Peter, *Odissea Stellare*, Sugar Editore, Milano.
53. Clypeus, 29., *Anno VII*, No. 3, P.O. Box 604, Torino.
54. Farish, Lucius, *Controversial Bulletin*, *Omega*, Route One, Plumerville, Arkansas, 72127.
55. Lissner, Ivar, *The Living Past*, Penguin, London, 1967.
56. Stobard, J. C., *The Glory that was Greece*, Four Square Books, London, 1962.
57. Plato, *Critias*.
58. Seneca, *Medea*, (Trans. T. R. Suedemann), Bantam Books, New York, 1966.
59. Victor, Paul Emile & Pelton, Arlette, 'L'enigme Piri Reis', *Planète*, 29 J/A 1966, Paris.
60. Pelton, Arlette, 'Civilisations avancées avant la dernier glaciation', *Planète*, 30, S/O 1966, Paris.
61. De Grazia, Alfred D., *The Velikovsky Affair*, Sidgwick & Jackson, London, 1966.
62. Hawkes, Jacquetta & Woolley, Sir Leonard, *Prehistory and the Beginnings of Civilisation*, Allen & Unwin, 1962.
63. Thucydides, *History* (Trans. Foster Smith), Wm. Heinemann, London.
64. Taylor, Anne, 'Dig goes on before the Flood', *The Observer*, London, 10 Sept., 1967.
65. Velikovsky, Immanuel, *Oedipus and Akhnaton*, Sidgwick & Jackson Ltd., London, 1960.
66. Oxford Classical Dictionary, Oxford University Press, 1948.
67. Ovid, *Metamorphoses*, (Trans. Mary Innes), Penguin Classics.
68. Shepherd, Walter, *Outline History of Science*, Ward, Lock & Co., Ltd., London.
69. Deuil, Leo, *The Treasury of Time*, Pan Books, London, 1960.
70. Cottrell, Leonard, *The Bull of Minos*, Pan Books, London, 1956.
71. Ceram, C. W., *Gods, Graves and Scholars*, Gollancz, 1952.
72. Planète, M/A 1968, 42 Rue de Berri, Paris, 8.
73. Plato, *Laws*, 664 (Trans. R. W. Livingstone), Oxford University Press, Oxford.
74. Drake, W. Raymond, *Gods and Spacemen in Ancient Israel*, Sphere, London, 1976.
75. Iliad, Book 10.
76. Iliad, Book 20.
77. Iliad, Book 5.
78. Aeneid, Book 1.
79. Ovid, *Metamorphoses*, Book X.
80. Odyssey, Book 10.
81. Odyssey, Book 13.
82. Odyssey, Book 16.
83. Plautus, *The Rope and other plays* (Trans. E. F. Watling), Penguin, London.
84. Hebrews, XIII-2.

85. Schuré, Edward, *Great Initiates*, Rider & Co., London.
86. Bethurum, Truman, *Aboard a Flying Saucer*, De Vorss, Los Angeles, 1953.
87. Kolosimo, Peter, *Odissea Stellare*, Sugar Editore, Milano.
88. Gordon, Cyrus H., *Before the Bible*, Collins, London, 1962.
89. Marlowe, Christopher, *Dr. Faustus*.
90. Goethe, Johann Wolfgang von, *Faust*.
91. Iliad, Book III.
92. Pollock, John, *Helen of Troy*, Robert Hale, London, 1965.
93. Plutarch, *Aegis and Cleomanes* (Trans. B. Perrin), Loeb Classics, Heinemann.
94. Hus, Alain, *Greek and Roman Religion*, Burns & Oates, London, 1962.
95. Plato, *Selected Passages* (Trans. R. W. Livingstone), Oxford University Press, Oxford.
96. Villars, Montfaucon de, *Le Comte de Gabalis*, A. C. Nizat, Paris, 1963.
97. Lane, Meade, *The Flying Saucer Mystery*, Borderland Research Assn., Vista, California.
98. Lorenzon, Coral, 'UFO Occupants in United States Report', *The Humanoids*, Neville Spearman Ltd., 1969.
99. Aston, W. G., *Nihongi or Chronicles of Japan*, G. Allen & Unwin Ltd.
100. Herodotus, *History* (Trans. Enoch Powell), Dent, Everyman, London.
101. Plutarch, *Sulla* (Trans. Bernadette Perrin), Loeb Classics, Heinemann.
102. Plutarch, *Themistocles XV* (Trans. B. Perrin), Loeb Classics, Heinemann.
103. Aeschylus, *Plays* (Trans. Lewis Campbell), Oxford University Press.
104. Sophocles, *Plays* (Trans. Sir George Young), Dent, Everyman, London.
105. Lucian, *Works* (Trans. A. M. Harmon), Loeb Classics, Heinemann.
106. Euripides, *Plays*, Dent, Everyman, London.
107. Drake, W. Raymond, *Gods or Spacemen?* Amherst Press, Amherst, Wisconsin, 1964.
108. Aristotle, 'Meteorology', Loeb Classics, Heinemann.
109. Pliny, 'Historia Naturalis', Loeb Classics, Heinemann.
110. Plutarch, 'Lysander' (Trans. B. Perrin), Loeb Classics, Heinemann.
111. Diodorus Siculus, *Biblioteca Historia*, Oxford University Press, Oxford.
112. Seneca, 'Naturales Quaestiones', Loeb Classics, Heinemann.
113. Blavatsky, Mdm. H. P., *Isis Unveiled*, Theosophical University Press, Pasadena.

114. Michael, Aimé, 'Une Nouvelle Evidence de Piri Reis dans la Grèce antique', *Planète*, M/J, 1967.
115. Trench, Brinsley le Poer, *Men among Mankind*, Neville Spearman Ltd., London.
116. Aratus, *Phaenoma*, John Lamb, London, 1848.
117. Blavatsky, Mdm. H. P., *Isis Unveiled*, Theosophical University Press, Pasadena.
118. Sputnik, December 1967, 2 Pushkin Square, Moscow.
119. Edwards, Frank, *Stranger than Science*, Pan Books, London.
120. Fenoglio, Alberto, 'Cronistoria su Oggetti Volanti nel Passato', *Clypeus*, Anno III, No. 2, 1967, Torino.
121. Annales Laurissenses, Migne's 'Patrologiae', Tom. CIV, Saeculum IX, Anno, 840.
122. Lucian, *A True Story* (Trans. A. M. Harmon), Loeb Classics, Heinemann.
123. Lucian, 'Icaramenippus' ('The Sky Men') (Trans. A. M. Harmon), Loeb Classics, Heinemann.
124. Farish, Lucian, *Controversial Bulletin*, Omega, Route One, Plumberville, Arkansas, 72127.
125. *INFO Journal*, Vol. 1, No. 2 International Fortean Organisation, 801 North Daniel St., Arlington, Virginia.
126. Jessup, Dr. M. K., *The Expanding Case for UFO*, Arco, London, 1950.
127. Lumley, Henry de, 'A Paleolithic Camp at Nice', *Scientific American*, May, 1969.
128. Anati, Emmanuel, *Camenica Valley*, Jonathan Cape, London, 1964.
129. *INFO Journal*, Vol. 1, No. 4, International Fortean Organisation, 801 North Daniel St., Arlington, Virginia.
130. Beaumont, Comyns, *The Riddle of Prehistoric Britain*, Rider & Co., London.
131. Geoffrey of Monmouth, *History of the Kings of Britain*.
132. Vaughan, Agnes Carr, *Those Mysterious Etruscans*, R. Hale, London.
133. Huergon, Jacques, *The Daily Life of the Etruscans*, Weidenfeld & Nicolson, London.
134. Settimo, Gianni V., *Clypeus*, III, No. 2, 1966, P.O. Box 604, 10100, Torino.
135. Kolosimo, Peter, *Non è Terrestre*, Sugar Editore, Milano.
136. Vallée, Jacques, 'A Description of the Entities associated with the Type 1 Sightings', F.S.R., J/F 1964.
137. Barbadoro, Giancarlo, 'Un Enigma al British Museum', *Laforghiana*, Anno III, No. 10, Ott. 1969, Torino.
138. Cecarelli, Silviano, 'Mario Zuccala's Strange Encounter', *Flying Saucer Review*, J/F 1962.
139. *Flying Saucer Review*, P.O. Box 25, Barnet, Herts, EN5 2NR.
140. Pliny, 'Historia Naturalis', Loeb Classics, Heinemann, London.

141. Athenaeus, *Deipnosophistae* or *Banquet of the Learned*, Book III, 515 (Trans. G. B. Sellick), Heinemann.
142. Polybius, *History*, Loeb Classics, Heinemann, London.
143. Cicero, *De Natura Deorum*, Loeb Classics, Heinemann.
144. Cicero, *De Divinatione*, Loeb Classics, Heinemann.
145. Dio Cassius, *History*, Loeb Classics, Heinemann.
146. Plutarch, *Romulus* (Trans. B. Perrin), Loeb Classics, Heinemann.
147. Livy, *History of Rome*, Book 1, CXVI, 6/8, Loeb Classics, Heinemann.
148. Apollodorus, *History*, Loeb Classics, Heinemann.
149. Fuller, John, *The Interrupted Journey*, Dial Press, Inc., New York.
150. Steiger, Brad & Whitenour, Jane, *Flying Saucers are hostile*, Tandem, New York.
151. Creighton, Gordon, *The Humanoids*, Neville Spearman Ltd., London.
152. St. Luke XXIV–4.
153. Flavius Philostratus, *The Life of Apollonius of Tyana*, Loeb Classics, Heinemann.
154. Plutarch, *Numa Pompilius* (Trans. B. Perrin), Loeb Classics, Heinemann.
155. Dionysius of Halicarnassus, *Roman Antiquities*, Loeb Classics, Heinemann.
156. Pliny, *Historia Naturalis*, Loeb Classics, Heinemann.
157. Plutarch, *Sulla* (Trans. B. Perrin), Loeb Classics, Heinemann.
158. Bloch, Raymond, *The Origins of Rome*, Thames & Hudson, Ltd., London.
159. Dionysius of Halicarnasseus, *Roman Antiquities*, Loeb Classics, Heinemann.
160. Plato, *The Republic*, 487 (Trans. A. D. Lindsay), Dent, Everyman, London.
161. Macaulay, Lord T. B., *Lays of Ancient Rome*.
162. Steiger, Brad and Whitenour, Jane, *Flying Saucers are hostile*, Tandem, New York.
163. Lorenzen, Coral, 'The Great Flying Saucer Hoax', *APRO*, Wm. Frederick Press, New York.
164. Plutarch, *Aemulius Paulinus'* XXV, (Trans. B. Perrin), Loeb Classics, Heinemann.
165. Chionetti, Marta Luchino, *Corrado Licostene*, University of Turin, 1960.
166. Cramp, Leonard G., *Pieces for a Jig-saw*, Somerton Press, Cowes, I.O.W.
167. Lycosthenes-Obsequens, *Prodigiorum Libellus*, Julius Samuel Luchmanns, Lugduni, Batavorum, 1770.
168. Plutarch, *Timoleon* (Trans. B. Perrin), Loeb Classics, Heinemann.

169. Chionetti, Marta Lucchino, *Corrado Licostene*, University of Turin, 1960.
170. Dio Cassius, *Roman History*, Loeb Classics, Heinemann.
171. Pliny, *Historia Naturalis*, Loeb Classics, Heinemann.
172. Lycosthenes-Obsequens, 'Prodigiorum Libellus', Julius Samuel Luchmanns, Lugduni, Batavorum, 1770.
173. Appian, *Roman History*, Book VII, Loeb Classics, Heinemann.
174. Livy, *History of Rome*, Book XXX, Loeb Classics, Heinemann.
175. *Space Link*, Vol. 5, No. 1, Dec. 1967, 15 Freshwater Court, Crawford Street, London, W.1.
176. Cramp, Leonard, *Pieces for a Jigsaw*, Somerton Press, Cowes, I.O.W.
177. Plutarch, *Lucullus* (Trans. B. Perrin), Loeb Classics, Heinemann.
178. Leslie, D. & Adamski, G., *Flying Saucers have landed*, Neville Spearman Ltd., London.
179. Plutarch, *Themistocles XV* (Trans. B. Perrin), Loeb Classics, Heinemann.
180. Pliny, *Historia Naturalis* VI, XXXI, Loeb Classics, Heinemann.
181. Livy, *History of Rome*, Book XXII-1, Loeb Classics, Heinemann.
182. Plutarch, *Cicero*, XIV (Trans. B. Perrin), Loeb Classics, Heinemann.
183. Blakeney, C. H., *A Smaller Classical Dictionary*, Everyman, Dent, London.
184. Montanelli, Indro, *Rome, the First Thousand Years* (Trans. A. Oliver), Collins, London.
185. Suetonius, *The Twelve Caesars* (Trans. Robert Graves), Penguin.
186. Plutarch, *Caesar* XI & *Pompey* LXVIII (Trans. B. Perrin), Loeb Classics, Heinemann.
187. Lorenzen, Coral, 'The Great Flying Saucer Hoax', *APRO*, Wm. Frederick Press, New York, 1962.
188. Plutarch, *Caesar* (Trans. B. Perrin), Loeb Classics, Heinemann.
189. Suetonius, *The Twelve Caesars* (Trans. Rogert Graves), Penguin, London.
190. Pliny, *Historia Naturalis*, Book II-XXX, Loeb Classics, Heinemann.
191. Plutarch, *Brutus*, XXXIII (Trans. B. Perrin), Loeb Classics, Heinemann.
192. Plutarch, *Antony*, XXVI (Trans. B. Perrin), Loeb Classics, Heinemann.
193. Shakespeare, William, *Antony and Cleopatra*, Act II, Scene 2.
194. Butler, E. M., *Myth of the Magus*, Cambridge University Press.
195. Calabri, Mara, 'La Fanciulla e La Lampada', *Il giornale dei Misteri*, No. 7, ott. 1971, Corrado Tedeschi Editore, Firenze.
196. Lissner, Ivar, *The Living Past*, Penguin, London, 1957.
197. St. Matthew, 11-9.
198. Davison, Dorothy, *The Story of a Prehistoric Civilisation*, Watts & Co., London, 1951.

199. Turville-Petre, O., *The Heroic Age of Scandinavia*, Hutchinson University Library, London.
200. Phillipe, Robert, 'Ulysse, est-il allé en Bretagne?', *Planète*, M/J 1965.
201. Odyssey, Book VII.
202. Turville-Petre, O., *The Heroic Age of Scandinavia*, Hutchinson University Library, London.
203. Mackenzie, Donald A., *Teutonic Myth and Legend*, Gresham, London.
204. Ellis-Davidson, H. R., *Gods and Myths of Northern Europe*, Pelican, 1964.
205. Blavatsky, Mdm. H. P., *Isis Unveiled*, Theosophical Publishing Co., Pasadena.
206. Bullfinch, *Mythology*, Spring Books, London, 1963.
207. Mackenzie, Donald A., *Teutonic Myth and Legend*, Gresham, London.
208. Hamilton, Edith, 'Mythology', *Mentor*, New American Library, New York.
209. Blavatsky, Mdm. H. P., *Isis Unveiled*, Theosophical Publishing Co., Pasadena.
210. Spence, Lewis, *The Outlines of Mythology*, Premier, Fawcett, World Library, New York.
211. Blavatsky, Mdm. H. P., *Isis Unveiled*, Theosophical Publishing Co., Pasadena.
212. Ellis-Davidson, H. R., *Gods and Myths of Northern Europe*, Pelican, 1964.
213. Grimm, Jacob, *Deutsche Mythologie* (Trans. J. S. Stollybrass), Edinbrugh University Press.
214. Villars, Montfaucon de, *Le Comte de Gabalis*, A. C. Nizat, Paris, 1964.
215. Leslie, Desmond & Adamski George, *Flying Saucers have landed*, Neville Spearman Ltd., London.
216. Bethurum, Truman, *Aboard a Flying Saucer*, De Vorss, Los Angeles, 1953.
217. Ellis-Davidson, H. R., *Gods and Myths of Northern Europe*, Pelican, 1964.
218. Grim, Jacob, *Deutsche Mythologie* (Trans. J. S. Stollybrass), Edinburgh University Press.
219. Blavatsky, Mdm. H. P., *The Secret Doctrine*, Theosophical Publishing Co., Pasadena.
220. Kirby, W. F., *Kalevala, The Land of Heroes*, Everyman, Dent, 1951.
221. Ibid.
222. Ibid.
223. Baring-Gould, Rev. D., *Curious Myths of the Middle Ages*, Rivington, London, 1861.

224. Mackenzie, Donald A., *Teutonic Myths and Legends*, Gresham, London.
225. Shaw, Bernard, *Major Critical Essays*, Constable & Co., London.
226. Ledger, Joseph R., 'Saucers or Ghosts', *Flying Saucer Review*, S/O 1962.
227. Grimm, Jacob, *Deutsche Mythologie* (Trans. J. S. Stollybrass), Edinburgh University Press.
228. Ibid.
229. Zaitsev, Vyacheslav, *Visitors from Space*, Sputnik 1, Moscow.
230. Matsumura, Yusuke J., 'Golden Flying Saucer unveiled on Cathedral Domes' Mural Paintings', *UFO News*, Winter 1973, C. B. A. Yokohama.
231. Pliny, *Historia Naturalis*, Loeb Classics, Heinemann.
232. Seneca, *Naturales Quaestiones*, Loeb Classics, Heinemann.
233. Josephus, *Wars of the Jews*, Book VI, Chap. V-3.
234. II Maccabees V v 1-5.
235. Gibbon, Edward, *The Decline and Fall of the Roman Empire*, Vol. 1, Ch. XV, Everyman, Dent, London.
236. Kolosimo, Peter, 'Non è Terrestre', Sugar Editore, Milano.
237. Wilkins, Harold T., *Flying Saucers on the Attack*, Ace Books Inc., New York.
238. Gibbon, Edward, *The Decline and Fall of the Roman Empire*, Vol. 2, Ch. XI. Everyman, Dent, London.
239. Fenoglio, Alberto, 'Cronistoria su Oggetti Volanti Del Passato', *Clypeus*, Anno IV. No. 2, 1966.
240. Eusebius, *Life of Constantine*, Book 1, Chap. XXVIII, Valuzius, Cambridge, 1692.
241. Gibbon, Edward, *The Decline and Fall of the Roman Empire*, Vol. 2, Ch. XX. Everyman, Dent, London.
242. Drake, W. Raymond, *Gods and Spacemen Throughout History*, Neville Spearman Ltd., London, 1975.
243. Boncompagni, Solas, etc., *UFO in Italia*, Corrado Tedeschi Editore, Firenze.

www.ingramcontent.com/pod-product-compliance
Lightning Source LLC
Chambersburg PA
CBHW081914170426
43200CB00014B/2726